Unfastened

Unfastened

Globality and Asian North American Narratives

Eleanor Ty

University of Minnesota Press
Minneapolis
London

The University of Minnesota Press gratefully acknowledges financial assistance provided by Wilfrid Laurier University Research Office for the publication of this book.

Chapter 1 was first published as "Abjection, Masculinity, and Violence in Brian Roley's *American Son* and Han Ong's *Fixer Chao*," *MELUS: Journal of the Society for the Study of the MultiEthnic Literature of the United States* 29, no. 1 (Spring 2004): 119–36, and was subsequently reprinted in *Transnational Asian American Literature: Sites and Transits*, ed. Shirley Geok-lin Lim, John Blair Gamber, Stephen Hong Sohn, and Gina Valentino (Philadelphia: Temple University Press, 2006), 142–58; reprinted with permission from *MELUS*. A version of the Coda was published as "Rethinking the Hyphen: Asian North American and European Ethnic Texts as Global Narratives," *Canadian Review of American Studies* 32, no. 3 (2002): 239–52, http://www.utpjournals.com; reprinted with permission of the Canadian Association for American Studies.

Copyright 2010 by the Regents of the University of Minnesota

All rights reserved. No part of this publication may be reproduced, stored in a retrieval system, or transmitted, in any form or by any means, electronic, mechanical, photocopying, recording, or otherwise, without the prior written permission of the publisher.

Published by the University of Minnesota Press
111 Third Avenue South, Suite 290
Minneapolis, MN 55401-2520
http://www.upress.umn.edu

Library of Congress Cataloging-in-Publication Data

Ty, Eleanor Rose, 1958–
  Unfastened : globality and Asian North American narratives / Eleanor Ty.
    p. cm.
  Includes bibliographical references and index.
  ISBN 978-0-8166-6507-5 (hc : alk. paper) — ISBN 978-0-8166-6508-2 (pb : alk. paper)
  1. American literature—Asian American authors—History and criticism.
2. Canadian literature—Asian authors—History and criticism. 3. Asian Americans—Intellectual life. 4. Asians—Canada—Intellectual life.
5. Asian Americans in the motion picture industry. I. Title.
  PS153.A84T9   2010
  810.9'895—dc22   2009012627

Printed in the United States of America on acid-free paper

The University of Minnesota is an equal-opportunity educator and employer.

17 16 15 14 13 12 11 10   10 9 8 7 6 5 4 3 2 1

Contents

Acknowledgments	vii
Introduction: Reading Globality	ix

I. Doing Global Dirty Work

1. The 1.5 Generation: Filipino Youth, Transmigrancy, and Masculinity	3
2. Recuperating Wretched Lives: Asian Sex Workers and the Underside of Nation Building	20

II. Performing and Negotiating Transcultural Identities

3. "All of Us Are the Same": Negotiating Loss, Witnessing Disability	43
4. Feminist Subversions: Comedy and the Carnivalesque	63

III. Future Perfect: Feminist Resistance to Global Homogeneity

5. Shape-shifters and Disciplined Bodies: Feminist Tactics, Science Fiction, and Fantasy	89
6. Scripting Fertility: Desire and Regeneration in Japanese North American Literature	108
Coda: Rethinking the Hyphen	129

Notes	143
Works Cited	151
Filmography	167
Index	169

Acknowledgments

I thank my colleagues in the Department of English and Film Studies at Wilfrid Laurier University for providing a collegial and intellectually stimulating teaching and working environment that enables me to pursue my research interests. I am grateful to the dean of arts, the research office, and the academic vice president for their encouragement of my research by giving me a course release and financial support. The project was initially funded by a Social Sciences and Humanities Research Grant. My very able graduate student assistant, Jenny Hei Jun Wills, helped enormously with her careful reading and comments.

For lively and thought-provoking conversations about reading and teaching Asian American and Asian Canadian literature, I thank Patricia Chu, Rocío Davis, Monica Chiu, Glenn Deer, Roy Miki, and Shirley Geok-lin Lim. I am fortunate to have the warmth, laughter, music, and energy at home from my husband, David Hunter; my children, Jason, Jeremy, and Miranda; and the abiding presence of my mother, Vicenta.

Introduction
Reading Globality

> For several years now, "globalization" has been the mantra for the expansion of international trade and foreign investment and the integration of markets. But we are now beginning to see a reality beyond globalization—the world of "globality." This is not so much a process as a condition, a world economy in which traditional and familiar boundaries are being surmounted or made irrelevant.
>
> —Daniel Yergin, "The Age of 'Globality'"

In an article in *Newsweek* ten years ago, Daniel Yergin made observations about globality based largely on the merger of big, big companies from different countries, such as car manufacturers Daimler-Benz and Chrysler,[1] pharmaceutical makers Hoechst (Germany) and Marion Merrill Dow (United States), and consumer electronics king Sony (Japan) and Columbia Pictures (United States). He noted that "the world is entering into a new type of capitalism." Governments are "retreating from control of the commanding heights of their economies: they are privatizing and deregulating. Barriers to trade and investment are coming down rapidly. Ever-cheaper communications and ever-faster computers, along with the Internet, are facilitating the flow of goods and services, as well as knowledge and information. Increasingly, companies are integrating their global strategies with global capital markets." Globality, as Yergin and others have noted, has come about because of improved technology and enhanced modes of transportation. According to Yergin:

> Companies and investors operate in a twenty-four-hour world. Currency traders see the same information at the same time, and can act on it simultaneously, whether they are in Singapore, London or New York (assuming only that they are all awake at the same time). Billions of dollars move at the push of a button. Global branding is the great game. Work is networked among North America, Europe and Asia via computer. And even the very idea of a corporate headquarters is beginning to become a metaphysical concept; increasingly, the corridors in which managers run into each other are not physical but electronic."

Globality has changed our world enormously: not only the way we work, but our values, our way of production and consumption, even our sense of space and time. Martin Shaw notes, "In its simplest meaning, globality is the condition or state in which things are global" (*Theory of the Global State*, 17). He argues that globality is a condition that has not been forced on us but that we have embraced, or in some cases accepted: "Globality is not the result of a global teleology" but "the outcome of the conscious and intentional actions of many individual and collective human actors" (17).

Globality and the Domestic: A Personal Anecdote

At about the time of the big mergers that Yergin wrote about (around 2000), I was raising two young children: one was almost three and the other almost one then. Playing with them at the park near my home in suburban Mississauga[2] one morning, I met a young Filipina with a little blond boy. Immediately I knew that she was a nanny in Canada's live-in caregiver program.[3] My children were on the swings nearby; both had brown hair and their father's Scottish-Canadian coloring. After a friendly visual acknowledgment and the recognition that we were "kababayan" (folks from the same town/country), we exchanged the usual hellos and introductions. Daisy, who had just turned 20, told me that she was working in her first domestic position. She had been in Canada for only about eight months. "Oh," I told her, with a smile, "I've been here for over twenty years now." She gave me a look of disbelief, mixed with scorn, and said, "What? You've been here over twenty years, and you are still a nanny?" I had to explain somewhat embarrassingly that the two children I was watching were my own and that I was not a nanny but a "teacher" at a university. We were both diasporic Asians, but our situations then were not similar.

I've told this story to a few friends, and we have laughed at Daisy's mistaking me for a nanny and especially at her assumption that I was so lazy or hopeless that I was stuck in that position for such a long time. Yet the encounter is revealing of how aspects of globalization have now permeated our domestic sphere and even our psyches. It is no longer unusual to find strangers in our familial space mothering our children or taking care of our geriatric parents. An estimated five million women from the Philippines work in domestic service in more than 130 countries of the world. They provide elder care, child care, and/or housecleaning and cooking in private homes in countries such as the United States, Canada, Spain, Italy, Singapore, Hong Kong, England, Saudi Arabia, and other countries around the world.[4] Feminist scholars have called them "servants of globalization" (Parreñas, *Servants of Globalization*), and their work is viewed as an example of the "flexibilization of labour" that "has cheapened women's work ... and has created a slave-like situation as they are forced to work for measly wages under poor working conditions" (Citizenshift, "Feminization of Migration"). Globality has resulted in our association today of certain racialized bodies as those suited to particular kinds of migrant labor: Filipina nannies, Indonesian housekeepers, Sri Lankan cooks, and so on.[5] In the instance I have mentioned, the association was why Daisy did not recognize me as the natural mother of the children I was watching.

At the same time, this scene illustrates the incredible opportunities afforded by the movement of people across the globe. Within a single generation, immigrants to North America have established themselves as professionals in corporations, in institutions of higher learning, in law, in health and medicine, and even in sports. This mobility can be seen as an example of the triumph of our systems of immigration and multiculturalism, but it has also created many disjunctions and tensions within the group.[6] Daisy's comments indicated that she believed she would work herself out of her position as a domestic. In her mind, this job was a way to achieve permanent resident status in Canada. She saw herself not as a permanent "servant of globalization" but as someone with agency. I have juxtaposed these two accounts—one a very public story of big mergers and the other an inconsequential, perhaps humorous one of misidentification at the private level—because they illustrate the importance of everyday stories. The condition of what we call globality cannot be understood by simply looking at statistics, corporate mergers, and business practices. We need the narratives of those who are profoundly affected by displacements to see how they are dealing with the changes brought about by the increase in mobility and the unfastening of identities from their national affiliations. These everyday narratives illustrate the ways people negotiate, cope with, and surmount the complexities brought about by the breaking down of boundaries and barriers, be they regional, national, or sectarian, relating to gender, class, or religious affiliation.

Globalization, Globality, and Mobility

Although some critics argue that globalization had already begun by the end of the nineteenth century, the term has only recently been used widely to refer to the accelerated pace of marketization, use of technology, and transnational movement of people and things seen in the last decade. I use the term *globalization*, as a number of scholars do, to refer to "new corporate strategies" (Ong, *Flexible Citizenship*, 4), to the "new international division of labor," and to "challenges to the nation-state as the basic organizational unit of society" (Dirlik, *Global Modernity*, 163). In the late nineteenth century and the first part of the twentieth, worldwide transcontinental connections were already present, but these links were relatively weak. Martin Shaw defines today's globality as "the breaking down of spatial limits. It is defined, in some accounts, as the tendency of social relations to achieve global reach or scope, together with the intensification of such global interconnections due to the compression of relations of time and space [...]. These tendencies are also connected to the increased understanding of the world as a common human environment. Ecological globalists represent human life as part of the planetary system of our globular Earth ("War and Globality"). For Shaw, globalization and the global order fully came into being only in the early 1990s after the end of the cold war, which opened the former communist world to world markets and communications.[7] Before the destruction of the Berlin Wall in 1989, when there was a perceived threat from communist Russia, "American public opinion toward

China was on a virtually war-level footing" (Teles, "Public Opinion and Interest Groups," 44). While Pakistan allied itself with the Southeast Asia Treaty Organization, the Central Treaty Organization, and the United States, India "was the Soviet Union's most valued Third World ally" (Bhutto, "Pakistan's Foreign Policy," 148). Today, however, in the new post–cold war world order, the three countries to which the United States and Canada have outsourced the most jobs are China, India, and Mexico (Myers, "US Underestimates Jobs Lost to Outsourcing").

I use the term *globality* rather than *globalization* because it is less charged with economic and corporate connotations. Issues of globality include concern for the earth and our environment, heath and the spread of disease across national borders, the globalization of markets, and the production of goods. Manfred Steger distinguishes between globalization and globality by defining *globality* as a "social condition characterized by the existence of global economic, political, cultural, and environmental interconnections and flows that make many of the currently existing borders and boundaries irrelevant" (*Globalization*, 7), *globalization* as "a set of social processes that are thought to transform our present social condition into one of globality" (8).

My book deals with the way recent novels, plays, and films by Asian North Americans engage critically with globalization and what Shaw calls "globality." In particular, many Asian North American authors manifest an attitude of "critical globality," a term Alys Weinbaum and Brent Edwards define as "thinking about structures of domination as confluent across national borders, and at the same time unevenly felt within them, [...] paying attention to the relationship of historical reciprocity between class and race in the context of western imperialism and overdevelopment, again, both within nations and among them, [...] being suspicious and questioning of the term 'globality' itself" ("On Critical Globality," 270). These authors use their novels, plays, and/or films to interrogate, critique, and sometimes even playfully engage with the effects of globalized conditions. Their works reveal their acute awareness of the inequalities that have resulted from the globalization of markets, the overuse and misuse of the environment and natural resources, and the consequences of the breakdown of national geographical or spatial limits.

As a number of scholars have noted, globalization has not brought about the kind of freedom and amelioration of the standard of living of people in all parts of the world that some once thought it would. Masao

Miyoshi has noted that in postcolonial countries many once-colonized nations in the Third World are still struggling with the management of an independent state and also with the effects of globalization: "Once absorbed into the 'chronopolitics' of the secular West, colonized space cannot reclaim autonomy and seclusion; once dragged out of their precolonial state, the indigenes of the peripheries have to deal with the knowledge of the outside world, irrespective of their own wishes and inclinations" ("A Borderless World?" 6). In place of nation-states, Miyoshi warns that transnational corporations, some of whose net assets exceed the gross domestic products of more than half of the countries of the world (15), "will increasingly require from all workers loyalty to the corporate identity rather than to their own national identities" (17). "The nation-state no longer works, [...] it is thoroughly appropriated by transnational corporations" that are indifferent to the regions of poverty they create or to the rights of workers (20).[8] Other consequences include the loss of indigenous culture, the development of a certain homogeneity among the members of the transnational class, who become "variants of one 'universal'—as in a giant theme park or shopping mall" (23); increased migration into "huge urban slums without the protection of a traditional rural mutual dependence system" (24); and environmental destruction as a result of industry.

Similarly, Arif Dirlik has argued that global capitalism has brought about certain universalizing phenomena since the 1980s: "global motions of people (and, therefore, cultures), the weakening of boundaries (among societies, as well as among social categories), the replications in societies internally of inequalities and discrepancies once associated with colonial differences, simultaneous homogenization and fragmentation within and across societies, the interpenetration of the global and the local, and the disorganization of a world conceived in terms of 'three worlds' or nation-states" (*The Postcolonial Aura*, 72). He notes that although global capitalism admits different cultures into the realm of capital, it is only "to break them down and to remake them in accordance with the requirements of production and consumption, and even to reconstitute subjectivities across national boundaries to create producers and consumers more responsive to the operations of capital" (72).

Among creative writers, Asian American and Asian Canadian authors have been at the forefront of the discussion about the social dimension of globalization. They have manifested particular interest in critical globality because globalization has reshaped the lives of those peoples in the south more profoundly than it has people in the north. Cultural critic Shaobo Xie warns that "the West still poses or imposes itself as the centre of the world" ("Is the World Decentered?" 55) and that "global capitalism feeds on difference to create sameness at the other end" (66). Other issues that these authors explore in their works are similar to those that have been raised by a number of economists and labor analysts. Bernhard Gunter and Rolph Van der Hoeven note that some of these include the effects of the shift in manufacturing, which has moved from industrialized countries to developing countries, and the way this shift has caused some worrying effects, including the fact that "a large number of developing countries, where 30% of the world's population lives, have become progressively marginal to the global economy and employment and labour standards have been declining in these countries" ("The Social Dimension of Globalization," 12); the way "globalization has increased income inequality within a country as well as across countries" (13); the fact that women and children have become more integrated into formal employment because of globalization, yet discrimination against women continues; and the reality that the participation rate of children has been detrimental to them (16). In addition, migration patterns have greatly changed: "Traditional migration channels, particularly from Europe, have dried up, while many new ones are being created, notably in South-East Asia; [...] today's migrants increasingly come from poor countries" (18). Thus, along with globalization, Asian Americans and Asian Canadians have experienced increased geographical mobility in recent years.

In her groundbreaking study *Reading Asian American Literature*, published over a decade ago, Sau-ling Wong argued that "America is founded on myths of mobility," of a nation built on expanse, wilderness, and freedom (118). She noted that American writers from the nineteenth century onward have been "drawn to images of motion expressing a range of now overlapping, now contradictory meanings—adventure, exploration, escape, home-seeking, quest, aimless meandering" (119). Similarly, Asian American literature has also been a "literature of movement, of motion" (120).[9] However, the crucial difference between the two groups, according to Wong, is that one group experiences mobility as "Extravagance" while the other experiences it as "Necessity." Whereas mainstream America experiences mobility as the "horizontal movement across the North American continent," with connotations of "independence, freedom, an opportunity for individual actualization and/or societal renewal—in short, Extravagance," Asian Americans associate mobility with "subjugation, coercion, impossibility of fulfillment for self or community—in short, Necessity" (121). Wong wrote, "In Asian American literature, [...] there has from the beginning been a keen collective awareness of immobility as a historical given" (123). Some examples of this paradox of mobility/immobility include the exclusion laws prohibiting Chinese from entering the country and owning land before the Second World War, the coerced movement or internment of Japanese Americans during World War II, the detainment of immigrants on Angel Island,[10] and the endless movement of early Filipino migrant farmworkers (123–27). Asian American mobility was particularly fraught with economic, social, and political implications during the first part of the twentieth century.

In the last ten years or so, Asian American and Asian Canadian mobility has shifted from the kind of experience based on Necessity that Sau-ling Wong has insightfully described and from the kind of migration experienced by Asian indentured workers of the nineteenth century that Lily Cho urges us to remember (in "The Turn to Diaspora") to a more liberatory kind of practice of mobility. Mobility can still be fraught for Asian North Americans, for example, for illegal workers or refugees, but on the whole, I would argue that the boundary between what Wong described as "Extravagance" and "Necessity" has broken down considerably. Popular travel writer Pico Iyer notes: "For more and more people, then, the world is coming to resemble a diaspora, filled with new kinds of beings—Gastarbeiters and boat people and *marielitos*—as well as new kinds of realities: Rwandans in Auckland and Moroccans in Iceland. One reason why Melbourne looks ever more like Houston is that both of them are filling up with Vietnamese *pho* cafes; and computer technology further encourages us to believe that the remotest point is just a click away" (*The Global Soul*, 10–11). Mobility for Asians in North America, as for many other peoples, is no longer mainly the politics of immobility. Statistics about immigration patterns from both the United States and Canada show that countries in East, Southeast, and South Asia are among the top four countries sending people to North America.

For the fiscal year 2003, the top countries sending legal immigrants to the United States were Mexico, India, the Philippines, and China, and since the 1990s the top countries sending immigrants to Canada have been China, India, the Philippines, Hong Kong, and Sri Lanka, replacing the British Isles, Italy, Germany, the Netherlands, and the United States, which were the top sending countries in the 1950s (Migration Policy Institute, "Legal Immigration to US Still Declining," 2; Statistics Canada, "100 Years of Immigration to Canada"). In the last decade, an unprecedented number of Asians have moved to North America, shifting the makeup of the visible minority population in cities like Los Angeles, New York, Toronto, and Vancouver. In the United States, the majority of these immigrants, about 63 percent, tend to move to and live in six states: California, New York, Texas, Florida, New Jersey, and Illinois (Migration Policy Institute, "Legal Immigration to US Still Declining," 2). In Canada, half of all visible minorities are expected to be either Chinese or South Asian by 2017, with the Chinese living in Vancouver and South Asians predominantly residing in Toronto (Statistics Canada, "Study"). This increase in the Asian American and Asian Canadian population, along with advances in media technology, communication, and travel, mean that the traditional divide between East and West has become less discernible. Himadeep Muppidi reminds us that "the globality that we inhabit allows us no pure non-European or non-western positions" (*The Politics of the Global*, 19). The consequence of global mobility and the increase in transnational links between ethnic communities within North America and also with their countries of origin are manifold. The subjectivities and sociocultural activities of this group of Asian North Americans are and will be very different from those of the earlier generation of immigrants from China and South Asia, who came primarily as laborers and did not enjoy the same kind of real and virtual diasporic communities.

One important question that interests me and is discussed in this book is the way Asian North American identities have been constructed in the past and the ways we are and ought to be representing ourselves and reconceptualizing our collective identity. In their introduction to *Transnational Asian American Literature: Sites and Transits*, Shirley Lim,

John Gamber, Stephen Sohn, and Gina Valentino contend that "Asian American literary criticism may be said to fall into distinct, although not wholly partitioned, periods and thematic categories: critical work produced prior to 1982, between 1982 and 1995, and from 1995 to the present" (5). They maintain that in the first period, introductions to anthologies "defined Asian American literature through the inclusion or exclusion of certain Asian American national groups" (6). In the second period, Asian American literary critics, such as King-Kok Cheung, Elaine Kim, Shirley Lim, Amy Ling, Stephen Sumida, and Sau-ling Wong "pushed the debate on what should constitute Asian American identity and broadened the notion of an Asian American canon" (6–7). In the last period, "contemporary Asian American criticism is traversed by theories associated with postmodernism, poststructuralism, psychoanalysis, and discourses on globalization, diaspora, transnationalism, and postcolonialism" (8). As I see it, these divisions are less distinct in literary and cultural productions. The main change occurred around the 1990s, when creative works shifted from those that were mainly autoethnographic to those that are no longer tied to ethnic and national identities. There is a growing body of works with more experimental forms, structures, and content: narratives with protagonists who are either less identifiably Asian or whose plots are not primarily concerned with the struggle between the traditions of the Old and New worlds. These Asian American works mirror the changes that are taking place in the larger political, social, and global arena. In Canada, Asian Canadian literary criticism has had a more "protracted birth," as Donald Goellnicht has observed ("A Long Labour"). Asian Canadian literature was read before the 1990s mainly as postcolonial literature, ethnic literature, or part of Canadian multicultural literature (see Goellnicht, "A Long Labour," and Ty and Verduyn, introduction to *Asian Canadian Writing*). Only in the last decade or so has the term *Asian Canadian* been more widely used to refer to a field of study and as a category of people.

With the recent shift in demographics in both Canada and the United States, it is useful for scholars and critics to be aware of the implications of what Himani Bannerji calls the "passion of naming" ("The Passion of Naming," 17), of the way we as critics participate in the articulation, creation, and constitution of a collective psyche or subjectivity. Bannerji argues that "the questioning and reconstructing of identities have to take place in the context of this hegemonic history—and involves situating them within their particular social, cultural and ideological relations and forms. It is also important to remember that the task is always more than one of simple negation" (28). For the same reason, Kandice Chuh calls for "conceiving Asian American studies as a *subjectless discourse*" in order to "create the conceptual space to prioritize difference by foregrounding the discursive constructedness of subjectivity" (*Imagine Otherwise*, 9). Both scholars ask that we pay attention to the way we name and characterize ourselves as a group. We need to continue to theorize ways of representation and the construction of Asian North American subjectivity that take into account the varying psychosocial, cultural, and historical experiences of this increasingly large and diverse group. In the past, coalitions have been made based on a shared history of discrimination and the experience of racism against Asian Americans and Asian Canadians. And although it is still important to remember this history and to speak of this experience, I question the efficacy of maintaining a group identity based primarily on a perpetuation of the sense of otherness and nonbelonging. Lisa Lowe has argued for the need for a practice of identity politics within Asian American discourse. She reminds us that "Asian American is not a natural or static category; it is a socially constructed unity, a situationally specific position that we assume for political reasons" ("Heterogeneity, Hybridity, Multiplicity," 39).

Diversity among Asian North Americans

I use the term *Asian North American* here as I did in my previous book, *The Politics of the Visible in Asian North American Narratives*, to indicate and highlight the general similarities in historical treatment, experiences, cultural categorization, and social perception of subjects we call Asian Americans and Asian Canadians.[11] For many literary critics and scholars, the term *Asian American* already implies or encompasses Asian North American rather than just the United States. For example, King-Kok Cheung defined Asian American literature "as works by people of Asian descent who were either born in or who have migrated to North America" in her useful volume *An Interethnic Companion to Asian American Literature*, published over a decade ago. The works of Asian Canadian writers and filmmakers such as the Eaton sisters, Joy Kogawa, Richard Fung, and Shani Mootoo are often simply studied under the rubric of Asian American or South Asian American literature (see Wong, *Reading Asian American Literature*; Eng and Hom, *Q & A*; and Srikanth, *The World Next Door*). Several Asian North American authors have affiliations with both the United States and Canada: Bharati Mukherjee has lived in both countries; Larissa Lai was born in California but now lives in Vancouver; Ruth Ozeki, (half) Japanese American, now resides in Vancouver. Cheung notes that "Asian American literature" itself has evolved from an initial focus on writings by people of "Chinese, Filipino, and Japanese descent" to include writings by Americans of Bangladeshi, Burmese, Cambodian, Chinese, Filipino, Japanese, Korean, Indian, Indonesian, Laotian, Nepali, Pakistani, Sri Lankan, Thai, and Vietnamese descent" (2, 3). In the introduction to her study of South Asian American literature published in 2004, Rajini Srikanth defines "South Asian American" as a "category that encompasses those individuals in the United States and Canada whose ancestral origins lie in one or more of these seven countries ... Bangladesh, Bhutan, India, the Maldives, Nepal, Pakistan, and Sri Lanka" (1). With the heightened awareness of the Middle East after 9/11, there have also been a number of attempts to include West Asia under the rubric of Asian America, for instance, at sessions in conferences, such as those of the Association for Asian American Studies. Under "Asian Canadians" in Wikipedia, in addition to the already mentioned groups, Armenian, Arab, Lebanese, Iranian, Iraqi, Assyrian, Syrian, and Afghan Canadians are included among the various ethnic groups ("List of Canadians of Asian Ancestry"). The inclusion of West Asia under Asian North American is still not a common practice, for some scholars of the Middle Eastern diaspora prefer to be in the category "Arab and Arab American studies" (see Abdulhadi, Naber, and Alsultany, Introduction to *Gender, Nation, and Belonging*).

For the works that I am examining, the term *Asian North American*, encompassing East, Southeast, and South Asian American and Canadian literature and film, is the most suitable for the present. The term *Asian North American* overtly signals the examination of works from Canada and the United States.[12] A number of other terms, such as "transnational" (see Sau-Ling Wong, "Denationalization Reconsidered"), "Asian diasporas in the Americas," or "hemispheric" (see Erika Lee, "Hemispheric Orientalism"), have been suggested to compare the situations of Asian Canadians and Asian Americans in Canada and the United States and to look at historical events that occurred in both countries. Iyko Day points out that each of these terms has particular resonances and issues in her essay, "Lost in Translation: Uncovering Asian Canada." Day notes, "An Asian North American critical framework is both old and new. The rubric has been in use since at least the 1970s, and until recently the primary focus of this framework has been directed at empirically-based analyses of material parallels between Canada and the U.S." (78). Donald Goellnicht ("A Long Labour") and other Canadian scholars, such as Henry Yu (*Pacific Canada*) and Marie Lo ("Passing Recognition"), caution against essentializing "Asianness" and remind us that there have been some historical instances in which Asian Americans have been treated differently from Asian Canadians. For example, in her nuanced discussion of the reception of *Obasan*, Marie Lo points out that "how 'Japanese' is coded and racialized in Canada is very different from how 'Japanese' is coded and racialized in the United States" ("Passing Recognition," 313). Thus, I use the term *Asian North American*, and also the terms *Asian American* and *Asian Canadian*, as the situation calls for. In 2000, Goellnicht urged Asian American studies to place "greater emphasis...on Asian diasporas rather than on 'claiming America'" in order to build coalitions, and to "gain greater recognition from governments, cultural institutions and reading audiences at home" ("A Long Labour," 21–22). Though I have employed the term *diaspora* in this study, I am also hesitant to apply it as an umbrella term, given that not all Asian North Americans feel that they belong to a "diaspora," and not all of them have experienced the same sense of dispossession that diaspora scholars such as Safran and Cho emphasize in their definitions of the term.[13]

The impulse for this book and much of my work in recent years has come from the desire to respond to the calls for a "strategic alliance" (Goellnicht, "A Long Labour," 22) between Asian Americans and Asian Canadians, a realization of the power and political necessity of solidarity or "strategic essentialism" within Asian ethnic groups (Lowe, *Immigrant Acts*, 82). At the same time, identities have become "unfastened" by the recent changes brought about by globality. I use the term *unfastened* both to refer to subjectivities that have "not been fastened" to specific nations, languages, or religions and to refer to borders—geopolitical, psychic, class, cultural, community, and social—that have "been loosened, opened, or detached" (Brown, *The New* Shorter Oxford *English Dictionary*). Today, in the United States and Canada, the politics and the binaries of dominant and minor, here and there, oppressor and oppressed have become more complicated. The question for scholars in the field is how to approach this panethnic group composed of Chinese, Indian, Filipino, Vietnamese, Korean, Japanese, Pakistani, Sri Lankan, Tamil, Thai, Cambodian, Taiwanese, Hmong, and Laotian people, all with their varying histories, classes, categories of immigration, and economic and religious backgrounds. The paradigms used to analyze and discuss the Russian, Irish, German, Italian, Polish, and other European immigrants of the first half of the twentieth century—such as immigration, settlement, acculturation, and gradual assimilation to the dominant society—are not necessarily suitable. For one thing, Asian immigrants, like blacks viewed as "people of color" or categorized as "visible minorities," will not as easily follow the path of Irish and eastern European ethnics, who, though initially seen as "not quite white" in the mid–nineteenth century, slowly became regarded as white over the course of the twentieth century (Roediger, "Whiteness and Ethnicity," 329).[14] At the same time, other groups, such as Asian Indians and Mexicans, though partially identified as white became nonwhite in the United States (326). As critics of white studies note, whiteness, in part, was made possible only by the distinction made between Europeans and blacks and, to a lesser extent, Asians, who were figured as other and therefore nonwhite (see Koshy, "Morphing Race into Ethnicity," 156, 165, 185–86). We are the "others" who make white identity possible.

Another problem within the field of Asian American and Asian Canadian studies that did not occur in the case of European immigrants is the rapid shift of demographics in the post-1970s group of immigrants. The accelerated pace of new immigrants from countries such as China and India in recent years means that there is less chance that a stable body of Asians can settle in and become absorbed by the existing communities around them. What Douglas Massey notes as the difference in the pattern of earlier European immigrants and those of Asian and Latin American immigrants in the United States is applicable also to the situation in Canada. Massey notes that for European immigrants, there was a hiatus in their immigration between 1931 and 1970, "which allowed the slow social processes that aid assimilation to take effect," as well as a period of economic expansion which made economic and social mobility easier. These conditions do not exist for Asian and Latin American immigrants (quoted by Koshy in "Morphing

Race into Ethnicity," 189). In the United States, the Asian American population experienced the fastest growth rate from 1980 to 1990, as well as from 1990 to 2000. Latinos and Hispanics had the second-fastest growth rate, while the growth rate for whites was the lowest (Le, "Population Statistics and Demographics"). In Canada, there was similarly a decrease of immigrants from European countries after the 1980s and a corresponding increase of immigrants from Asian countries. New waves of Asian immigrants encourage the maintenance of healthy ethnic and diasporic Asian communities. In addition, the advances in telecommunications and travel mean that transnational networks between immigrants and their homelands can be maintained, so that there is less need for the kind of assimilation into WASP culture that European immigrants experienced. Today, roughly 50 percent of Asian Canadians are born outside of Canada, compared to less than 20 percent of ethnic Europeans. In 2000, 68.9 percent of Asian Americans were born in foreign countries, compared to 11.1 percent of the total U.S. population that was foreign-born (Lai and Arguelles, *The New Face of Asian Pacific America*, 30). These differences will have a great impact on the formation of the ethnic identity of Asian Americans and Asian Canadians, who are less bound by physicality, by geography, and by national affiliations than the European immigrants.

One notable difference between the United States and Canada is the "official" attitude toward people of Asian origins. Although Asian Americans are positioned in a bipolar place between "black" and "white" in the United States (see Okihiro, "Is Yellow Black or White?" 75), Asian Canadians are placed in the category of "visible minorities" in Canada's official governmental discourse. This category, which racializes Asian Canadians, is a legislated classification that groups all non-Caucasians, including Chinese, Japanese, Filipinos, South Asians, Nigerians, Jamaicans, and Ethiopians, as other.[15] In the United States, although Asian Americans, who are favorably compared to blacks and Latinos but stereotyped in the process, deal with the consequences of the "model minority" myth, in Canada other issues, such as the efficacy of the official Multiculturalism Act, have been the subjects of lively debates in discussions about race. Some criticize Canada's policy of official multiculturalism because they see its function as the management of differences. For example, Kogila Moodley argues that Canadian multiculturalism promotes a "festive aura of imagined consensus" (as quoted by

Eva Mackey in *The House of Difference*, 66). C. Mullard points out that the model highlights the "three S's: saris, samosas, and steel bands" in order to diffuse the "three R's: resistance, rebellion, and rejection" (as quoted by Mackey, 66).[16]

In addition to rapidly changing demographics, the widely different economic, social, and religious backgrounds of immigrants of the last twenty years have also rendered it more difficult to talk about Asian Americans and Asian Canadians as a group. In the last twenty years, with the rise of transnational corporations and the dynamic economic growth of countries such as Hong Kong, Taiwan, Singapore, South Korea, and Malaysia, it is no longer possible to speak of Third World countries and people with the implication of poverty and backwardness (see Ien Ang, *On Not Speaking Chinese*, 6). As Ien Ang notes, Asia "is touted as the model for an affluent, hypermodern future, not the residue of a traditional and backward past, as classic Orientalism would have it" (6). Susan Koshy points out the need to look more closely at differences in class positions within national communities in Asian America:

> The increase and mobility of Asian capital across national boundaries, and the entry of Asians into the technical-managerial class has created a situation where Asian America is a site of both resistance and exploitation. This is particularly problematic because the exploitation of Asian sweatshop workers, restaurant workers, and migrant workers by small and large Asian capital often deploys the discourse of ethnic and family loyalty to enforce discipline and extract compliance. In addition, the postindustrial forms of historic abuses such as slavery have assumed gigantic dimensions in the transnational era and flourish within closed national and diasporic networks that are difficult to penetrate. ("Morphing Race into Ethnicity," 163)

As Kandice Chuh notes, "'Oppression,' 'marginalization,' and 'resistance,' keywords in dominant narratives of Asian American studies, are terms that each require redefinition within this globalized context, as 'by whom' and 'against what' are questions that are increasingly difficult to answer with certitude" (*Imagine Otherwise*, 7).

New Spaces for Asian North Americans

Other scholars have a more positive view of the effects of globalization and mobility on diasporic communities. Patrick Imbert believes that instead of fighting over territories, which are finite geographical spaces linked to roots, we should conceive of spaces as "locations," which are knowledge-based, "geo-symbolic displacements" (*Converging Disensus*, 17). According to his definition, location "has more to do with 'taking place' than with 'having a place'" and is "produced out of interaction, exchange, and by confronting alterity" (17–18). New wealth is created from polycultural and transcultural connections, from being able to negotiate in different languages and with a number of global and local communities. Imbert welcomes what he calls "economic liberalism" and expansion, describing the affirmative effects of a future based on "location" instead of territorialization: "location becomes a site of contacts in progress where there is room for surprise, difference, productivity, and the capacity to be efficient in different environments" (34).

Robin Cohen is similarly encouraging about globalization. He outlines five aspects of globalization that have "opened up new opportunities for diasporas to emerge, to survive and thrive." These include

> a world economy with quicker and denser transactions between its subsectors due to better communications, cheaper transport, a new international division of labour, the activities of transnational corporations and the effects of liberal trade and capital-flow policies; forms of international migration that emphasize contractual relationships, family visits, intermittent stays abroad and sojourning, as opposed to permanent settlement and the exclusive adoption of the citizenship of a destination country; the development of "global cities" in response to the intensification of transactions and interactions between the different segments of the world economy and their concentration in certain cities whose significance resides more in their global, rather than in their national, roles; the creation of cosmopolitan and local cultures promoting or reacting to globalization; and a deterritorialization of social identity challenging the hegemonizing nation-states' claim to make an exclusive citizenship a defining focus of allegiance and fidelity in favour of overlapping, permeable and multiple forms of identification. (*Global Diasporas*, 157)

Unlike Dirlik and Miyoshi, Imbert and Cohen are optimistic about many of the changes brought about by globalization. For example, Cohen believes that "by being attached to a strong and tightly integrated diaspora, family- and kin-based economic transactions are made easier and safer" (160). In terms of space, he notes that "members of diasporas are almost by definition more mobile than people who are rooted in national spaces. They are certainly more prone to international mobility and change their places of work and residence more frequently" (168–69).

Instead of seeing all post-1965 Asian immigrants to America and Canada as victims of oppression, as "exiles" (Campomanes) or those caught "between worlds" (Ling, *Between Worlds*), I aim to locate them somewhere between the conditions proposed by Miyoshi and those proposed by Cohen. I would like to conceive of them as "unfastened," mobile subjects in a global age. Anthropologist Aihwa Ong has suggested the term "flexible citizenship" as a way of describing Chinese businessmen who are able to develop a "flexible notion of citizenship and sovereignty as strategies to accumulate capital and power" (*Flexible Citizenship*, 6). Regarding them, Ong notes: "In their quest to accumulate capital and social prestige in the global arena, subjects emphasize, and are regulated by, practices favoring flexibility, mobility, and repositioning in relation to markets, governments, and cultural regimes" (6). As useful as Ong's theories are for discussing capitalist entrepreneurs, the paradigm does not describe the experience of large numbers of Filipinos who move across the globe as migrant workers, domestics, and health care and hospitality workers (see Parreñas, *Servants of Globalization*, 18).[17] Barbara Ehrenreich and Arlie Hochschild note that not only has globalization been responsible for the "female executives" jetting "about the world" that we see in TV commercials; the process of globalization has also caused a "far more prodigious flow of female labor and energy: the increasing migration of millions of women from poor countries to rich ones, where they serve as nannies, maids, and sometimes sex workers" (*Global Woman*, 2). Ong's notion of flexible citizenship also has limited application to the many South Asians who come to America and Canada with skills and training that they are unable to use and end up working at low-paying jobs. James Clifford observes that "travels and contacts are crucial sites for an unfinished modernity" and that human location is "constituted by displacement as much as by stasis" (*Routes*, 2). Terms such as *dislocation* and *displacement* usually have a negative connotation, suggesting refugees, exiles, temporary workers, and other unsettled immigrants. I would like to use them in more encompassing ways, not just having to do with moving from one's originary culture but also with traveling out of one's usual place of habitation, as Clifford does. Though many Asian North Americans are displaced, in the negative sense, and work at marginal jobs, there are also increasing numbers of professionals and entrepreneurs who attain comfortable economic and social status in Canada and the United States.

Although a number of narratives by Asian Americans and Asian Canadians depict feelings or a state of restlessness or unbelonging, not everyone experiences dislocation or displacement the same way. I would like to use and recuperate the terms *mobility* and *displacement* without misrepresenting the place of Asian North Americans as a whole by situating them in a position of always not at home and marginal. Displacement as perpetual exile and unbelonging goes against the strategy of "claiming America" by and for Asian Americans,[18] while displacement as movement, that is, taking the place of something else, suggests agency and subjectivity. Asian North Americans are not always put in situations not of their own volition.

The novels, plays, and films I have chosen to examine in this study depict protagonists who experience much movement between cultures, social classes, communities, nations, and continents. Not only do raw materials, goods, and products move much more today because of globalization; people, cultural practices, and ideological beliefs do, too. Extending the work of recent literary and cultural scholars who have looked at contemporary cross-cultural and minority works using discourses of the transnational, diasporic, postcolonial, and cosmopolitanism (see Lim, *Transnational Asian American Literature*; Kamboureli, *Scandalous Bodies*; Miki, "Altered States"; and Rajan and Sharma, *New Cosmopolitanisms*), my project focuses on texts and films that overtly thematize globality, global movements, and their effects on the everyday. Although many of these works reveal the inequality brought about by globalization, not all of the movements or displacements are negative. One useful way of approaching these texts is through James Clifford's notion of travel as a "complex range of experiences: practices of crossing and interaction that troubled the localism of many common assumptions about culture" (*Routes*, 3). Instead of viewing travel simply as a supplement to social existence, Clifford suggests that we see "practices of displacement" as "*constitutive* of cultural meanings rather than as their simple transfer or extension [...]. Cultural centres, discrete regions and territories, do not exist prior to contacts, but are sustained through them, appropriating and disciplining the restless movements of people and things" (3). Clifford's notion of travel encompasses "the worldly historical routes which both constrain and empower movements across borders and between cultures" (6). He notes that since 1900 practices of crossing "have been powerfully inflected by three connected global forces: the continuing legacies of empire, the effects of unprecedented world wars, and the global consequences of industrial capitalism's disruptive, restructuring activity" (6–7).

Using Clifford's paradigm to look at the mobility of Asian North Americans has the advantage of allowing us to see what Viet Nguyen, in another context, calls the "flexible strategies" of Asian American authors. In *Race and Resistance* Nguyen argues that by focusing mainly on resistance and accommodation, Asian American intellectuals have ignored the "flexible strategies that concern struggle, survival, and possible assimilation" shown in Asian American literature (5). Similarly, what I would like to stress in my study are the different ways of reading, interpreting, and understanding globality and the global movement of Asian North Americans in the twentieth century. Instead of seeing Asian North Americans simply as fatalities of globalization, I want to look at how globalization and travel have pushed them to seek new spaces, both geographically and psychically; to renegotiate identities; and to search for alliances with other marginal ethnic, racial, or gendered subjects. Globalization has both constrained and empowered Asian North Americans, as Clifford has noted. Yet what has not been studied or theorized enough is the way Asian North Americans have also been travelers, explorers, and the subject of quest narratives. Clifford writes that "in the dominant discourses of travel, a nonwhite person cannot figure as a heroic explorer, aesthetic interpreter, or scientific authority [...]. Victorian bourgeois travelers, men and women, were usually accompanied by servants, many of whom were people of color. These individuals never achieved the status of 'travelers'" (*Routes*, 33). Even in the twentieth century, Asians who travel across the globe are represented as migrant laborers, sojourners, refugees, or, at best, immigrants. Yet their travels— whether they be for work, to join families, for study, or for leisure— have reshaped the face of metropolitan cities across North and South America, the Caribbean, and Europe, and even within Asia.

Even as I use the term *mobility*, I am aware that travel and displacement can mean very different things to different people depending on their economic and political capital. Pheng Cheah cautions, for instance, against too strong a celebration of mobility and points out that "Clifford endows cosmopolitan mobility with a normative dimension, claiming for it an important role in cultural and political transformation

[...]. Cosmopolitan movements are presented as exemplary instances of active resistance to localism and cultural homogenization under global capitalism" (*Inhuman Conditions*, 87). One objection Cheah has to critics, such as Clifford and Homi Bhabha (*The Location of Culture*), who highlight the powers of hybridity and mobility, is that hybridity, enabled partly by mobility, is a "theory of resistance that reduces the complex givenness of material reality to its symbolic dimensions and underplays the material institution of capitalist oppression at a global systemic level" (Cheah, *Inhuman Conditions*, 94). I agree with Cheah's reservation against relying too much on the symbolic power of hybridity and with his point that cultural hybridity does not automatically lead to a realm of "flux and freedom" (89). Yet, over the last twenty or thirty years we have seen many significant and energizing changes that have resulted from the kind of cultural resistance described by Clifford and Bhabha and from what Arjun Appadurai calls "the work of imagination" (*Modernity at Large*, 5–7). Discussing the effects of migration, Appadurai points out that "diasporas bring the force of the imagination, as both memory and desire, into the lives of many ordinary people, into mythographies different from the disciplines of myth and ritual of the classic sort [...]. These new mythographies are charters for new social projects, and not just a counterpoint to the certainties of daily life" (6). What many Asian North American narratives thematize is the fluidity of contemporary transcultural identities and the layering of subject positions within that identity. The mobility suggested here is not necessarily a physical one but can also be one of movement through social, cultural, or psychic scapes.

These recent narratives, in the form of plays or films, whether realist, postmodern, or science fiction, tell stories that are no longer simply about the tensions between the older generation and Westernized youths, about Asian American identity and assimilation, but encompass a wide range of subjects and forms. They depict relations not only between Asian Americans and dominant white culture but also between Asian Americans, Asian Canadians, and members of other ethnicities, and they often use postmodernist techniques—of parody, exaggeration, irony, and/or a decentered narrator—rather than primarily realist narratives. The narratives produced in the last decade by Asian Americans and Asian Canadians question, play with, and disrupt the genre, themes, and trajectory of the ethnic autobiography and at the same time expand our notions of what constitutes being Asian in North America. In provocative and playful ways, these authors treat their Chinese, Japanese, Filipino, or Indian culture not as an intrinsically inherited cultural identity but as something that is learned, reiterated, and "performed," in Butler's sense of the term (*Bodies That Matter*, 95). They show how the subjectivities of Asian people in America and Canada are constituted by what Ien Ang calls "a discursive construct" of Asianness that "operates in practice, in different historical, geographical, political and cultural contexts" (*On Not Speaking Chinese*, 40). "Asian American" or "Asian Canadian" are terms of identification; each is a choice, albeit somewhat constrained, rather than a pre-given identity. Often in North America, Asianness is represented simply as one aspect of the character's life and is not stereotyped or exoticized. At the same time, many Asian North American authors are concerned with issues that have emerged as a result of the recent phenomenon of globalization. Many of their narratives explicitly or implicitly critique such problems as global capitalism, corporatization, and the transnational exploitation of labor.

I limit my discussion in this project to works that consciously explore the impact of globalization on Asian North Americans, as well as their condition of globality. Although a number of these works, such as those by Kwa, Keller, and Kuruvilla, are set in time periods that predate the last twenty years of intense globalization, they nevertheless manifest the attitude of "critical globality." All the authors convey how globalization and travel have changed the particularities of the world we live in by depicting local and quotidian practices, by giving details of the joys, pains, disappointments, and pleasures of the everyday. Through the sights, smells, tastes, and tactility of the everyday world, these authors and filmmakers express the ways Asian North Americans have handled, negotiated with, manipulated, and even enjoyed their mobility in the globalized world. Michel de Certeau has argued that "many everyday practices (talking, reading, moving about, shopping, cooking, etc.) are tactical in character" (*The Practice of Everyday Life*, xix). De Certeau distinguishes between a "strategy," which requires a subject's "will and power (a proprietor, an enterprise, a city, a scientific institution)" versus a "tactic," which "cannot count on a 'proper' (a spatial or institutional localization), nor thus on a border-line distinguishing the other as a visible totality. The place of a tactic belongs to the other" (xix).

My concern with looking at the tactics deployed in Asian North American works and my focus on the everyday have also been inspired by feminists who seek heroism not in great epic battles but in the ordinary. For example, feminist philosopher Kelly Oliver, influenced by Julia Kristeva, discusses the importance of recognizing female geniuses. She explains that in *Female Genius* Kristeva suggests "that genius and geniuses are necessary for psychic life: we need geniuses to validate the exceptional within our own lives, which is as true for women as it is for men" (*The Colonization of Psychic Space*, 159). Oliver points out, however, that the possibility of creativity and sublimation, which she describes as the transfer of bodily affects into signification—poetry, prose, philosophy, music, physics, and so on—is "missing from the lives of girls and women and other marginalized people insofar as they are circumscribed by values, meanings, and images that foreclose their agency as meaning makers" (161). In order to rectify this problem and to decolonize our psychic space, she suggests that we look for the excesses and singularity of the everyday. Oliver writes, "The flavors and textures of everyday life can give meaning and joy if they are valued and have meaning within culture. Food, clothes, home, garden, beautiful and functional domestic spaces can be valued and even display female genius, the extraordinary within the ordinary" (164). Applying Oliver's notion of singularity to Asian North American cultural productions, we see how Asian North Americans are able to find ways to use and reinscribe available meanings and to transform local, social spaces within an increasingly globalized culture.

My approach to these texts is indebted to insights and energies developed by these and other feminist, cultural, critical race, gender, socio–anthropological, diasporic, postcolonial, and Asian North American studies of the last two decades. The areas of these studies provide oppositional practices and theoretical paradigms that are useful to the examination of the powerful effects of globalization in contemporary culture. They tend to link the everyday and the small with the global and the large. In the 1980s, for example, even before the discourse of "global/local," feminists proclaimed their belief that "the personal is the political." This attitude, linking local practices and beliefs to public, national, continental, and global ones, is still a cornerstone of many groups of cultural workers and is one of the reasons I focus on everyday lives and everyday practices in this study. In globalization studies, Rob Wilson and Wimal Dissanayake observe, "If local struggles figure as allegories of larger, more systemic alteration, then part and whole will have to be rethought and reimagined as figuring the contemporary world-system of global capital in all its concreteness" (*Global/Local*, 7). At the same time, I take heed of Arif Dirlik's caution that "the local is valuable as a site for resistance to the global, but only to the extent that it also serves as the site of negotiation to abolish inequality and oppression inherited from the past, which is a condition of any promise it may have for the future" ("The Global in the Local," 38). *Unfastened* examines novels, plays, and films by Asian Americans and Asian Canadians that speak to some of the most urgent questions raised by local/global developments in multicultural North American society.

Critical Readings

The texts I have chosen to study here are those narratives published in the last decade that highlight issues brought about by global mobility and transcultural exchanges. These are some of the most exciting literary, dramatic, and cinematic texts currently being produced, not just within the field of Asian North American but in contemporary culture. The book engages with existing discussions of Asian North American or global literature and theories of globalization. I have deliberately avoided earlier canonical texts of Asian American and Asian Canadian literature, such as those by Bulosan, Kingston, Kogawa, Chin, and Hagedorn, because those authors belong to a different generation of autoethnographers and have been much discussed by critics already (see, for example, Sau-Ling Wong, *Reading Asian American Literature*; Rachel Lee, *The Americas of Asian American Literature*; David Li, *Imagining the Nation*; and others). In this project I am interested in bringing more attention to less-known contemporary authors who have produced fascinating and critically absorbing works. Many of them are women who seek alternatives to the telling of the story as well as to the postmodern narrative of progress; they wish to find other options besides lifestyles based on capitalism and consumption. Most of them are critical of the effects of global migration; some, however, represent the creative and fruitful potential of globality and movement.

In Part I, "Doing Global Dirty Work," the four novels I discuss reveal the detrimental effects of movements across continents or between countries. The protagonists in Brian Roley's *American Son* and Han Ong's *Fixer Chao* move from the south to the north because of their desire to ameliorate their economic conditions, to escape the poverty of the Philippines. In both these novels the young male protagonists resort to cheating, theft, and violence in order to cope with their lives in America, which have been changed by transnational migration. The young adults in the novels see themselves as failures because their everyday lives do not match up to their high expectations of the American dream. Their only sense of empowerment comes from the criminal lives they lead. As Inderpal Grewal notes, "Imaginaries of 'America' were divergent and various, and this conjunction of consumer cultures and democratic rights cultures traveled to many regions outside of the United States" (*Transnational America*, 9). Although these boys do not achieve economic or social success in America, they nevertheless are able to negotiate power within the limited sociocultural sphere in which they live. In Lydia Kwa's *This Place Called Absence*, the Asian Canadian protagonist looks back in history to the late nineteenth and early twentieth centuries, a time when hundreds of Chinese girls were lured from their villages in rural China and brought to Singapore to work as prostitutes, or *ah ku*, to service the large population of male coolie workers there.[19] Through the protagonist's imagination, Kwa commemorates the lives of these girls from a hundred years ago, who became virtual slaves in their brothels. Kwa's novel draws parallels between the present-day narrator's sense of dislocation and the two *ah ku*, whose names the author finds in a historical document. She links her protagonists through the use of objects and repetition, through their lesbian desires, depicting the prostitutes as heroines with lives and interests rather than as simply victims. Her novel acts as a kind of witnessing or testimonial to the thousands whose travels and travails have been forgotten and whose lives were not properly documented.

As Clifford notes, war has been one of the primary reasons for travel and dislocation (*Routes*, 6–7). American involvement in Korea during the Korean War (1950–53) and the continued presence of U.S. troops on the Korean peninsula caused the movement and relocation of numerous Korean women who were enticed into working as prostitutes on American military bases in South Korea. In Nora Okja Keller's *Fox Girl*, these women and their children, often born of American fathers, live in Korea's America Town, one of a number of camptowns where foreigners and foreign habits dominate. The camptown existence can be seen as a quintessential example of what Mary Louise Pratt calls "contact zones, social spaces where disparate cultures meet, clash, and grapple with each other, often in highly asymmetrical relations of domination and subordination—like colonialism, slavery, or their aftermaths as they are lived out across the globe today" (*Imperial Eyes*, 4). The camptown is a hybridized space of America and Korea where American soldiers temporarily make their homes and where Korean women live a precarious existence based mainly on their sexuality. In *Fox Girl* Keller shows the degradation of these Korean women, who are treated like animals and whose work is sanctioned by the local authorities as well as the American military. For them a globalized way of life has only highlighted the unequal power structures of this not-quite-America, not-quite-Korea contact zone. At the end of the novel, the protagonist escapes and travels to Hawaii. It is there that she is able to break free of the predictable pattern of life of the camptown woman.

In Part II, "Performing and Negotiating Transcultural Identities," I look at four different texts that explore ways of navigating between Asian and North American traditions and values. What is different about these works is that the first two, Betty Quan's *Mother Tongue* and Sunil Kuruvilla's *Rice Boy*, add the dimension of disability to familiar ethnic issues of acculturation, immigration, and transcontinental movement. The teenage boy in Quan's play, who is deaf and mute and speaks in American Sign Language, highlights the social, psychological, and other barriers faced by those who cannot "speak" and easily communicate in the language of the dominant culture. In the play, travel is not only from the Old World, China, to the New World, Canada, but also across North America. The boy with deafness is faced with the frightening prospect of loss and of being left behind because of his sister's desire to travel. In Kuruvilla's play, mobility is signaled by having a stage with simultaneous settings in India and Canada. A girl in India, intelligent but with a disability, with limited mobility and prospects, is juxtaposed against minoritized figures in Canada whose lives are also circumscribed by their religious affiliations, race, or ethnicity. Both plays depict stories of growing up in a globalized world where ethnic identities do not follow pre-given scripts but must be constantly negotiated and performed.

The other two works discussed in this part of the book signal a more playful interaction of cultures in contemporary society. Nina Aquino and Nadine Villasin's play *Miss Orient(ed)* and Deepa Mehta's film *Bollywood/Hollywood*, both set in Toronto, demonstrate the energetic potential of transnational connections and hybrid globalized cultures. These two works reveal the ways in which travel and cultural encounters can produce vigorous new subjectivities. In both works the authors use humor, song, and dance to reflect the ways Asian Canadians influence, and at the same time are shaped by, local diasporic communities and the dominant Western culture. The theatrical production *Miss Orient(ed)*, for example, set in the world of the "Miss Pearl of the Orient" beauty pageant, reveals the ways in which contemporary Filipinas, who have been stereotyped, socialized, misconceptualized, and misoriented, still are able to contest the ways their bodies have been used in the diaspora. Although the bodies of these Filipinas, as beauty queens, are viewed nostalgically as the embodiment of the lost motherland, their revamping of Filipino dances, customs, and beliefs demonstrates a comic questioning of these traditions. The contestants' staging of their racialized and gendered bodies demonstrates the performativity of these identities. The setting of the beauty pageant is significant, because it is a site where the diasporic community gathers to collectively celebrate and reflect on their imagined homeland. It also has much potential for mobility, because it brings together diasporic peoples of various socioeconomic classes. A beautiful and talented woman not necessarily from an upper class can be "crowned" and elevated to the position of queen. At least within the beauty pageant community for that year, the beauty queen reigns supreme.

Deepa Mehta also looks at some of these questions in her parodic film *Bollywood/Hollywood*. With its Bollywood and Hollywood musical style that includes dancing, singing, and colorful sets, the film creates a carnivalesque atmosphere where a politics of transgression becomes possible within a popular genre. With this film Mehta brings the popular Hindi genre of the Bollywood musical into the North American mainstream cinema and video industry, equating Bollywood movies with Hollywood romantic blockbusters such as *Pretty Woman*. The film critiques in a playful way various stereotypes about diasporic South Asians at the same time that it highlights the ways a diasporic community sustains itself through ritualistic performances of Indianness. Instead of depicting the lives of a struggling immigrant family, Mehta focuses on a wealthy Indian Canadian family and their romantic aspirations, reconfiguring the typical immigrant story into a fairy tale. This family takes advantage of some of the new spaces and transnational networks created by global cities, as described by Robin Cohen and Patrick Imbert.

In Part III of the book, "Future Perfect: Feminist Resistance to Global Homogeneity," I look at four books that do not use realism as a primary mode of narration to represent or critique our globalized world. In both Asian American Chitra Divakaruni's *The Mistress of Spices* and Asian Canadian Larissa Lai's *Salt Fish Girl*, which use fantasy and magic realism, the female protagonists, a spice vendor and a rebellious young woman with a disability, are marginal figures who use "tactics" rather than strategies to subvert the existing global capitalist order. Both novels feature female protagonists who are shape shifters, endowed with the ability to transcend geographical as well as temporal boundaries. Divakaruni and Lai use familiar cityscapes, such as Oakland, California, and Vancouver, British Columbia, respectively, but they defamiliarize the locations; in Lai's case, the city becomes a futuristic dystopia. They use myths and stories from their cultures, transporting them into these contemporary or futuristic settings, thwarting readers' expectations of the genres of European, Chinese, and Indian myths and legends as well as our preconceptions of how females in these stories are supposed to act. Both protagonists employ what de Certeau calls "tactics" to subvert their conquerors' or masters' laws from within, "not by rejecting them or by transforming them, [...] but by many different ways of using them in the service of rules, customs or convictions foreign to the colonization which they could not escape" (*The Practice of Everyday Life*, 32).

Similarly, Hiromi Goto's *The Kappa Child* and Ruth Ozeki's *All Over Creation* subvert global capitalism and notions of productivity and consumption at the same time that they critique our misuse of the environment by their employment of myths, science fiction, and/or science. Both novels challenge stereotypes of the model minority Asian American, especially Japanese North American docility, through their creation of barely functional but rebellious heroines. And both novels evaluate the influence of the traditional nuclear family by questioning the authority of patriarchs and their parallels in the business world, corporate managers or presidents of companies. These works at once reveal the powerful influence of technology and capitalist enterprise in our daily lives and show means of resistance for those who seem to be disenfranchised.

I conclude the book with a coda ("Rethinking the Hyphen") that opens up the possibility of Asian global literature. As more Asians in the diaspora inhabit transnational spaces, they affiliate themselves—psychically, socially, if not legally—with more than one country or community. Using examples from a number of "cosmopolitan" Asian authors, such as Michael Ondaatje, Salman Rushdie, and Ang Lee, I speculate whether such hyphenated terms as Asian Canadian and Asian American are still the only or best terms to use in describing Asian writers in the diaspora. Globalization, migration, and the media have changed much of the way we conceive of belonging, locations, and identities, and the categories we use to classify or sell books and to study authors in courses and scholarly works will ultimately need some more rethinking, shifting, and displacement. My book contributes to the lively and important discussions of these and other crucial issues already in progress.

I
Doing Global Dirty Work

1
The 1.5 Generation: Filipino Youth, Transmigrancy, and Masculinity

> Globalism is not an abstraction but a concrete activity whose mode of being has its effect on the local body.
>
> —Dana Polan, "Globalism's Localisms"

Half a century after its independence from the United States, the Philippines is still very much in a neocolonial stage.[1] Epifanio San Juan Jr. notes that "the Filipino has been produced by Others (Spaniards, Japanese, the *Amerikanos*), not mainly by her own will to be recognized" (*Articulations of Power*, 118). Filipinos are transnational subalterns, used in many countries as cheap and temporary labor: the "'warm body export' of Filipino workers to the Middle East; Filipinas as 'mail-order brides,' ubiquitous prostitutes around enclaves formerly occupied by U.S. military bases; and 'hospitality girls' in Tokyo, Bangkok, Okinawa, and Taipei" (San Juan, *The Philippine Temptation*, 79). The more than six million Filipinos scattered around the world earn an average of "$3.5 billion a year for the Philippine government" (92) but at a great cost to Filipinos, especially to women and children.

Propelled by dire economic conditions in the Philippines and fed by the American dream of wealth and success, Filipinos migrate in large numbers and have become what Rhacel Parreñas calls "servants of globalization." The movement of people, goods, and culture in the new global capitalism entails, as Arif Dirlik writes, the "transnationalization of production, [...] the decentering of capitalism nationally," the increasing importance of the transnational corporation, and the "fragmentation of the production process into subnational regions and localities" ("The Global in the Local," 30). Negative effects of this migration and globalization include the separation of family members, perpetual states of exile and displacement, and self-hatred that results from the neocolonial mentality of seeing oneself as other. What faces Filipino immigrants in their adopted countries is often not a life of ease but of difficulties due to prejudice, racism, and alienation. Two recent novels by Filipino American writers, Brian Ascalon Roley's *American Son* and Han Ong's *Fixer Chao*, document these problems and reveal the ways in which global capitalism takes its toll on the young.[2] Roley's and Ong's narratives are told from the perspective of young adults whose familial and social lives have been changed by transnational migration, who see themselves as failures because their everyday lives do not match up to the high expectations of the American dream. Fueled by Hollywood ideals of glamor and power, various characters in these novels suffer and, in turn, lash out against others when they fall short of capitalist notions of success. Examples from these novels show the impact of global American culture on Filipinos and Filipino immigrants, problems in the construction of Filipino American ethnic subjectivity, and the violent effects of racial abjection on the body.

In general, these novels reveal a number of common negative effects of globalization on young Filipino Americans: (1) The overvalorization of and desire for wealth, First World products, and material goods. In these narratives, the children whose family members are separated often compensate for their lack of familial bonds and/or dysfunctional family situations by coveting, buying, or in some cases stealing, goods. Transnational production does not just affect people's work and labor conditions; it also affects libidinal desire. (2) Overdetermined and unattainable ideals based on Hollywood models of masculinity and beauty. Because "the global distribution of power still tends to make the First World countries cultural 'transmitters' and to reduce most Third World countries to the status of 'receivers'" (Shohat and Stam, "From the Imperial Family to the Transnational Imaginary," 147), the young protagonists in these novels identify with American images of success. These images affect the way one perceives one's own body and also affect one's romantic and sexual relationships. When Filipino American men find themselves unable to live up to the seductive or forceful celebrity images they see in films and on television, they frequently resort to violence or aggression against those around them. (3) Emotional and psychic transnationalism. Diane L. Wolf argues that "second generation Filipino youth experience *emotional transnationalism* which situates them between different generational and locational points of reference—their parents', sometimes also their grandparents', and their own—both the real and imagined" ("Family Secrets," 459). Children of first-generation Filipino immigrants and Filipino American children who belong to the 1.5 generation group are brought up "accepting patriarchal family dynamics and the predominance of parental wishes over children's voices, resulting in internal struggles and an inability to approach parents openly for fear of sanctions. Part of the struggle seems to stem from living and coping with multiple pressures and with the profound gap between family ideology and family practices" (473). Although this phenomenon is common for many immigrant children, it is particularly acute for those youths who not only feel the pressures from their family in their adopted country but are also burdened with the feeling accountable in some ways to their family, friends, and relatives "back home."

In *American Son* and *Fixer Chao*, Roley and Ong explore these various effects of globalization on young Filipino American men growing up in contemporary America. The authors show the emotional and psychic struggles of the protagonists as they negotiate the circumstances of their lives between the values of capitalist America and the self-sacrificing and self-abnegating attitudes of Filipino immigrants. Through the perspectives of these young men we see the damaging effects of small but repeated acts of racism, and we witness the ways their masculine subjectivity has been interpellated by Hollywood representations. In both novels the protagonists reveal how they have become abject others of the dominant culture that desires and yet abhors them. What we witness is the youths' disappointment with a society that invites them to be part of the nation yet refuses to accord them the same privileges as white Americans.[3] Through very different stories of growing up, Roley and Ong illustrate the complex ways in which cultural and racial marginalization, as well as a sense of failure that comes from being unable to live up to their own and their parents' ideals, lead young Filipino Americans to aggression and criminal behavior.

Celebrity Dogs

Brian Roley's *American Son*, set in California in 1993, depicts much of the disenchantment of Filipino American youths, revealing the "underbelly of the modern immigrant experience" (back cover). Told from the point of view of Gabrielito Sullivan, a fifteen-year-old American boy born of a white father and a Filipina mother, the novel presents a stark, unsentimental portrait of a family torn between the allure and wealth of America, exemplified by the rich celebrities who live in West LA, and the traditional, Catholic, Filipino values with their emphasis on filial piety, as voiced in the letters of Uncle Betino in the Philippines. Though Gabrielito (called Gabe), his mother, and his brother, Tomas, emigrated to America almost ten years earlier, they, like many immigrants, have had to struggle economically, socially, and culturally to survive in the multiracial and multifarious city of Los Angeles. They have settled in the United States, but they have not been completely uprooted from their home country and assimilated into the new society, as one might expect of immigrants who left their home more than years ago. Instead, they are what Glick Schiller, Basch, and Szanton-Blanc term "transmigrants," immigrants "whose daily lives depend on multiple and constant interconnections across international borders and whose public identities are configured in relationship to more than one nation-state" ("From Immigrant to Transmigrant," 48). According to Glick Schiller, Basch, and Szanton-Blanc, several forces lead these immigrants to settle in countries that are "centers of global capitalism, but to live transnational lives" (50). The reasons include a deterioration of social and economic conditions "in both labor sending and labor receiving countries with no location a secure terrain of settlement" and "racism in both the U.S. and Europe," which "contributes to the economic and political insecurity of the newcomers and their descendents" (50).

Gabe, his brother, and his mother all experience dislocations that are similar to those experienced by other Filipinos who work at low-paying or dead-end jobs in various parts of the world. As Rhacel Parreñas has observed of migrant Filipina domestic workers, the dislocations include "partial citizenship, the pain of family separation, the experience of contradictory class mobility, and the feeling of social exclusion or nonbelonging in the migrant community" (*Servants of Globalization*, 12). Gabe has not seen his American father since the night he got drunk after returning from his station in Germany. After hitting the children and "making fun of Filipinos and [his wife's] family," the father told Tomas that he married his mom because "he wanted someone meek and obedient, but had been fooled because she came with a nagging extended family" (*American Son*, 24). After his departure, the boys' mother used to telephone her brother in the Philippines for advice on bringing up the boys. Gabe reports: "Our mother had long, distressed conversations on the telephone [...]. Sometimes she would sob. Other times she simply wrapped a strand of hair around her finger" (22). Uncle Betino's letters repeatedly urge the mother to send the boys back to the Philippines so that they can be educated to be good Filipino Catholics, so that "some of the Asian virtues of [the] family heritage" (201) can be instilled in them. These plans never materialize, however. To maintain her household in America, she works at one point "sixty hours at a department store's shoe section" and has a "second job looking after an invalid Jewish lady in the Hollywood Hills" (160). She is caught in a situation of transmigrancy; she is not able to assimilate into American white society because of her accent, her diffidence, her difficult economic situation, and yet she feels that she cannot go back to the Philippines, where she complains of the heat and smelly showers, the insects, diseases, and relatives who make "tsismis about each other behind their backs" (33).

In the United States, the family is repeatedly reminded of their nonbelonging and otherness. These scenes reveal the ways in which exclusionary practices delimit and mark the subjectivity of the ethnic other. Gabe and Tomas demonstrate two different ways of reacting to the racist and discriminatory attitudes of the white majority. Initially the brothers are divided into a dichotomy representing the good and the bad. Gabe is the obedient child, "the son who is quiet and no trouble," who helps their "mother with chores around the house" (15). Tomas, the older brother, is the one who keeps their mother "up late with worry. He is the son who causes her embarrassment by showing up at family parties with his muscles covered in gangster tattoos and his head shaved down to stubble and his eyes bloodshot from pot" (15). As a way of defending himself against ridicule and prejudice, Tomas tried to cover up his Asian identity. At first, Tomas tried to pass as a white surfer and attempted to dye his hair blond, though it turned red in the process. Then he began "hanging out with Mexicans, who are tougher" (30).[4] If anyone tried "calling him an Asian he beat them up, and he started taunting these Korean kids who could barely speak English" (30). Significantly, Tomas inscribes his desired Mexican identity onto his body: "his tattoos are mostly gang, Spanish, and old-lady Catholic," Gabe observes: "As he leans forward, the thin fabric of his shirt moves over his Virgin of Guadalupe tattoo that covers his back from his neck down to his pants" (17). The tattoos remake his Asian features, reconfiguring his body from the feminized Oriental into the more macho Chicano Latino body.[5] At the same time, the Virgin of Guadalupe tattoo places the teachings of his mother, the Catholic Church, and the notions of sainthood and virginity in a new and potentially irreverent light. The markings on his body reveal the many ways in which contesting notions of racial identity are played out physically and corporeally on Tomas.

Seeing himself through the eyes of a dominant culture that views him as servile, feminized, and different, Tomas is ashamed of being identified as a Filipino American. To complete his public identity as a Mexican, he pretends to understand Spanish when people speak it to him. However, in his business, which consists of training attack dogs and selling them to "rich people and celebrities" (15) Tomas uses commands in German, telling his clients that the dogs have "pedigrees that go back to Germany, and that they descend from dogs the Nazis used" (20). Significantly, only by aligning his dogs—and, by extension, himself—with racist Nazis is Tomas able to claim power, legitimization, and recognition in contemporary American high-class society. Moreover, he claims that "this is a Teutonic art that goes back to the Prussian war states" (20). That his lies are so easily accepted demonstrates the extent to which contemporary society relies on racially and nationally based stereotypes. In contrast to the highly valued "Teutonic art," for both brothers being Filipino has demeaning associations, often linked to low-paying domestic occupations. Tomas tells his brother at one point, "If the client sees you standing there like that he's gonna think you're my houseboy" (18). Similarly, when Gabe runs away from home, he befriends a tow truck driver who, though kind to Gabe, makes derogatory remarks about the "fucking Mexicans," the "Cambodians, Vietnamese, Laotians," and the "mute Asians," who "won't even learn to speak English," who are everywhere in Venice and San Pedro (84). Gabe becomes embarrassed when the tow truck driver later sees his mother and tells him that the dark-skinned woman at the restaurant is their "maid" (116).

This scene, which is at the center of the novel, represents Gabe's betrayal, an act almost as hurtful as Tomas's many acts of disobedience and willfulness. The incident, though played out at the domestic level, is significant because it is suggestive of larger cultural issues and national politics. Gabe's mother represents the long-suffering Filipina who is abandoned by her American husband and protector. She believes in the Old World traditional values of the Filipino—filial duty and obedience to the Catholic Church and its priests. Yet as an immigrant and woman of color she is ineffectual in America and is left behind by her children. She is unable to help her children improve their marginal status through legitimate means. At one point in the novel, she goes shopping with Gabe down the promenade. Gabe notices that, unlike Tomas, his mother always "steps out of other people's paths" (179), and one man "in a yellow button-down shirt" sees her but "acts as if he does not notice her, and she actually has to squeeze beside a bench to let them pass" (179). At a makeup counter, a beautiful tall, model-like redhead in a white doctor's coat chats with another lady and ignores Gabe's mother as she waits at the counter to be served. Only with Gabe's intervention does the saleslady take notice of his mother, but, too shy at that point to make a scene, the mother pretends she is "just looking" (183) and walks away. It is this kind of self-abnegation and an inability to assert oneself that embarrasses the boys and leads them to react violently against those they perceive to be treating them as second-class citizens.

Asian American Masculinity

Masculine identity has been problematic for the Asian American male from the start (see Eng, *Racial Castration*; Goellnicht, "Tang Ao in America"; and Wong, "Ethnicizing Gender"). Historically, Asian males were subjected to exclusion laws, regarded as unassimilable (Takaki, *Strangers from a Different Shore*, chap. 3), and represented as threats to society because of fears of disease, miscegenation, and sexual corruption (Lee, *Orientals*, 76). They were also feminized because of their work in laundries, restaurants, and tailor shops. Today many Asian American men still work in poorly paid "feminized" service jobs. Cruise ships in the Caribbean and in Alaska employ Indonesian, Malaysian, and Filipino men and women as busboys, waiters and waitresses, and kitchen help. Filipino men work as houseboys, gardeners, orderlies, laborers, and cleaners in North America and the Middle East. In the popular media, Asian men are represented as hypersexual and dangerous because they were unable to consummate their desires through legitimate relationships, or else they are seen as feminine. Young Asian boys and Asian women are exploited as prostitutes and sex workers in many parts of the world. As David Eng notes, in "marvellous narratives of penile privilege, the Westerner monopolizes the part of the 'top'; the Asian is invariably assigned the role of the 'bottom'" (*Racial Castration*, 1).

The particular situation of powerlessness of Asian American men is not unlike that of black men, and their problems are similar to those of black masculinity in America. As Kobena Mercer and Isaac Julien note, "Whereas prevailing definitions of masculinity imply power, control and authority, these attributes have been historically denied to black men since slavery" ("Race, Sexual Politics and Black Masculinity," 112). In order to "contest conditions of dependency and powerlessness which racism and racial oppression enforce," black men develop macho attitudes. Macho is "a form of misdirected or 'negative' resistance, as it is shaped by the challenge to the hegemony of the socially dominant white male, yet it assumes a form which is in turn oppressive to black women, children and indeed, to black men themselves, as it can entail self-destructive acts and attitudes" (113). In Roley's novel, the difficulty Tomas encounters in constructing a viable masculine subject leads him to adopt a hypermasculine identity that manifests itself through violence and crime, as well as his identification with "tough" Mexicans. To make sure he is not teased as a weakling, as Asian, he takes on a macho identity, taunts others, and even beats his brother up whenever he is frustrated by Gabe's submissive attitude. His mother's pleas with Tomas do not stop him from a life of criminal activity, including breaking and entering, looting, assault, and robbery. Though Tomas and Gabe love her deeply, they respond with anger and outrage to their economic difficulties and her social helplessness. Their own place outside mainstream society and outside the capitalist system makes them resort to unlawful means in order to change the situation in their home. In the last part of the novel, Tomas takes Gabe along with him and they break into people's homes. While they steal most of the items for resale, they use some of them to elevate their mother's status. In one case, Tomas steals the brass sinks and faucets from an empty house and puts them in their mother's bathroom. He also replaces her couch and steals her a new bed. Breaking into a Hungarian lady's house in Brentwood Park, Tomas heads for the bedroom and tells Gabe, "Look for the pearls. Or anything with gold on it. Forget the silver stuff. It wouldn't look good on her brown skin" (*American Son*, 147). Because in America success is typically represented as the possession of economic wealth, goods, and objects, as the man of the house, Tomas mistakenly tries to show his love for his mother by obtaining items that are featured in advertisements and glossy magazines, on television, and in film.

The problem of being in one of the centers of global capitalism yet feeling excluded from full membership in it is that one always feels inadequate and lacking. In capitalist societies such as North America, clothes, cars, jewelry, and other possessions often serve to compensate for one's sense of insufficiency. However, for the dispossessed there are few legitimate ways to attain these goods. To borrow terms from studies on black masculinity, Tomas becomes a "hustler," not a prostitute like Han Ong's protagonist, but one who lives by dishonest means. As Mercer and Julien explain, "the figure of the hustler [...] is intelligible as a valid response to conditions of racism, poverty and exploitation, it does not challenge that system of oppression but rather accommodates itself to it: illegal means are used to attain the same normative ends or 'goals' of consumption associated with the patriarchal definition of the man's role as 'breadwinner'" ("Race, Sexual Politics and Black Masculinity," 114). Roley's novel becomes doubly tragic because not only do we witness Tomas becoming more and more involved in violent and criminal activities but we also see the way Gabe, who initially was the obedient brother, slowly succumbs to the gratification of violence and the deadening of emotion. It seems to be the only way to respond to the situation of his family's economic immobility and his own sense of powerlessness. Toward the end of the novel, the two brothers brutally beat up Ben, one of Gabe's schoolmates, the son of a rich woman who is threatening to collect eight hundred dollars from their mother because their mother has accidentally bumped the woman's Land Cruiser in front of the school. As Gabe swings a tire iron across Ben's legs, Gabe thinks, "I feel a rush not of anxiety but of confidence. In a scary way I realize I like it. Strangely, that only makes my stomach worse" (*American Son*, 215).

Ironically, it is only through violence that Gabe feels he can become an "American son," that is, a citizen of the United States, with authority and power. Because the narrative is told in the first person from Gabe's limited point of view, we are not given any further explanations about his psychic state after his first act of aggression against another human being. In the closing scene, Tomas puts his hand on Gabe in a way that their American father used to do with both of them. The gesture is suggestive and supposed to be reassuring. Together the brothers have survived displacement, prejudice, and dispossession but at a cost to their humanity. Unlike their mother, they may no longer be transmigrants, but in the process of transcending that role they have let go of the traditions and values she was trying to instill in them—respect for others, obedience to authority figures, and deference to the church and to the law. They have become American sons, not by being hardworking immigrants as their mother expected, but by becoming outlaws and urban cowboys.

Abject Subjects

In a similar way, the protagonist of Han Ong's *Fixer Chao* gets himself into a "complicated, manufactured" life (133) when he agrees to embark on a scheme of revenge for another's wrong. In Ong's novel globalization—in particular, the movement of culture, people, and goods from the Third World to the First World—is viewed with much irony and skepticism. *Fixer Chao* tells the story of a Filipino hustler, a former prostitute, William Narciso Paulinha, who is remade into Master William Chao, a revered feng shui expert from Hong Kong, with the help of Shem C, "a disreputable, social climbing writer embittered by his lack of success" (inside cover).[6] William Paulinha is lured deeper and deeper into a life of fraud and crime for many of the same reasons that Tomas and Gabe are: racism and a sense of self-abjection, the gap that he sees between the life of rich New Yorkers around him and his own hand-to-mouth existence. Like Tomas and Gabe, William is a Filipino who lives on the margins of society, never fully integrated into American culture because of a sense of rootlessness and class and racial difference.

Like Roley, Ong depicts social and economic inequities that have resulted from the global migration of Filipinos. Racial prejudice is a theme that is present, though muted, in the novel, for the book is largely a satire of the life of the privileged. As in Roley's novel, the characters in Ong's "view America through the fractured lens of its broken promises" (Freeman, Review of *Fixer Chao*). As John Freeman notes, "The nation invites them in, only to deny them the privileges of comfort in their own skins." As the novel begins, William Paulinha tells us that in his twenties he worked as a small-time prostitute in the Port Authority Bus Terminal. After that, he drifted from clerical job to job without much drive or success, working as a typist, a telephone receptionist, a mail clerk, and a data entry clerk. Except for the clerical positions, the jobs in which William has found himself are directly linked to his identity as an Asian man in a predominantly white society. He is chosen by Shem to be a feng shui expert because of his Asian features. Shem thinks that he is Chinese, even though William is Filipino. In his younger days at the Port Authority Bus Terminal, race also played a part in his career. He had to "compete with frisky Puerto Ricans and athletic black boys for a cut of the overweight white businessman business" (*Fixer Chao*, 12). His typical client was a "portly white gentleman, with a bald spot in the middle of his head [...] on [his] way home to the suburbs" (12). Young Asian, Latino, and African American boys serve to boost the egos of these businessmen and enable them to reassert their position of dominance in American society. As William says,

> They've had disastrous days and want to take out their frustration on someone. I'm perfect, a skinny colored kid, almost like the ones they see a lot of nowadays on TV, except shabbier. They're witnessing their time in the spotlight stolen by a whole crew of new, mystifying faces. Or so they think. And they want somebody to pay, be humiliated, physically put under them like restoring their natural position in the world. (12)

For these white businessmen, these young colored boys function as abject others, those who are like themselves but have to be expelled. Abject figures are abhorred, yet they remain desirable. Julia Kristeva's definition of the abject includes those objects, persons, things that have to be ejected or excluded, "what disturbs identity, system, order. What does not respect borders, positions, rules. The in-between, the ambiguous, the composite" (*Powers of Horror*, 4). Because he is gay and Asian, William is doubly abjected and othered by his race and gender. His bodily differences function to reassure the white businessman of what the white male subject is not.

As David Leiwei Li argues, Asian Americans in the last half of the twentieth century, though no longer excluded by law, were still perceived as not "competent enough to enjoy the subject status of citizens in a registered and recognized participation of American democracy" (*Imagining the Nation*, 6). Li notes, "The law cannot—even if it is willing to try—possibly adjudicate the psychocultural aspects of subject constitution; neither can it undo the historically saturated epistemological structures, and structures of feeling, which continue to undermine the claims of Asian American subjectivity" (11). In Roley's *American Son* and Ong's *Fixer Chao* we see the repercussions of this inside/outside position on Filipino Americans who are "formal nationals and cultural aliens" (Li, *Imagining the Nation*, 12). Though as immigrants they are ostensibly part of American society, there are many reminders of their status as subcitizens. These sometimes overt, sometimes subtle, repeated racist incidents and reminders of their otherness cause them to respond with violence and misdirected aggression to those around them.

As Master Chao, the feng shui expert, William uses what little knowledge he has of mystical harmony to help his clients. However, the first house he decides to deliberately sabotage is that of Cardie Kerchpoff, a woman who complains endlessly about her Indian nanny at a party. Cardie states that "Third Worlders" do not understand "American nuances or Western nuances," and she believes that her domestics should just take what she says as "divine truth" because they live in her house, where she has "sovereign rights" (*Fixer Chao*, 102). In the conversation someone suggests that she should get "a Filipino. They make the best servants" (103). This comment enrages William so much that he cannot help repeating it in his mind as he is fixing her house, and he cannot help adding, "Why? [. . .] Because they [Filipinos] kneel by instinct and bend over like clockwork" (104). He then proceeds to "do everything wrong" (104) in Cardie's house so that harm will befall the arrogant woman. This damaging set of actions starts a series of others that escalate into more serious acts of violence. Even though his reputation as a feng shui master earns William money, fame, and invitations to wealthy people's homes, he often identifies with the maids, doormen, and houseboys of the homes rather than with their white owners. He calls the doormen at the homes of rich people his "peers" (269). At one award ceremony he noticed that "the doorman of that building kept regarding me quizzically, not certain why I wasn't carrying the Chinese food he was sure I'd come to deliver" (197). Like the adolescents in Roley's novel, he becomes disillusioned with a society that still bases its expectations and values on one's appearance, one's race and ethnicity, while claiming to be open and democratic.

What is significant about the way Ong deploys criticism of globalization and global capitalism is that he does not just look at the way transnational labor and people figure in the United States but also gives a wry and humorous view of the way culture from the Third World has been received, marketed, and commodified. In *Fixer Chao* the clients easiest to dupe are those, like Lindsay S., a poet, who are Orientalists. Lindsay loves Oriental art and has a collection of beautiful Chinese scrolls, "teapots and teacups, Japanese swords, calligraphic ink sets, [...] hundreds of Buddhas of dazzling variety" (71). Lindsay believes that the "Chinese and the Japanese" have the "two greatest cultures in the world" (79). His appreciation of these cultures is shown mainly through the acquisition of objects and commodities from the East. The East has become a large marketplace for people like Lindsay, a shopping paradise he uses in order to enhance his own stature as consumer and collector. Hence, he willingly buys the services of Master Chao, who is supposed to bring him the gift of Eastern harmony in his life.

Just as William's young Asian body made him a suitable object of sexual desire for white businessmen at the Port Authority Bus Terminal, his seemingly asexual Asian masculine body now makes him an ideal feng shui master. Hsuan Hsu notes that William is adept at mimicry, and it enables him "to mock people preemptively before they can mock his poverty, his ethnic difference, his homosexuality" ("Mimicry, Spatial Captation, and Feng Shui in Han Ong's *Fixer Chao*," 680). In order to play his role as counselor, he has been made over with the help of Shem. William has a "handsome and conservative" (*Fixer Chao*, 63) haircut, wears "kung fu shoes" (97), and in a fake magazine article about him looks "Chinese [...] mysterious, gifted with powers" (87). He pretends to be "offhand, serene, gifted" (86), qualities that are often ascribed to inscrutable but clever Asians. Significantly, now that he presents himself as a feng shui master, his queer sexuality is no longer visible to the rich New Yorkers. Instead he successfully mimics the handsome poses of pop stars, "whose aura was white rather than black, sexless and filled with wisdom" (87). Significantly, here Ong points out the links among sexuality, race, and economic status. While working as a homosexual prostitute, William saw himself as a "colored" kid, aligning himself with Latinos and African Americans. But in his upwardly mobile shift to membership in the Manhattan elite, he affiliates himself with whites and, at the same time, becomes "sexless." Asian American queer sexuality disappears after the first third of the book, which is indicative of the way asexuality is still so easily written onto respectable Asian male bodies.

For people in developing countries, globalization and transnational trade have also created a skewed version of the West as a place of unlimited wealth, material goods, and promise. At one of the rare moments when William recollects his past, he tells his Filipino friend Preciosa that he came to America with his parents, who "wanted a better life" (262). The images of this "better life" were full of luxury items, "wall-to-wall carpeting," brand names like "General Electric, Sunbeam, Hoover, Proctor-Silex, Pfizer, Zenith" (263). He thinks, "They were all a shorthand for beauty, for quality, things that wouldn't break—as our appliances often did. That, for the longest time, had been my family's going definition of a better life: to own things that took a while to malfunction" (263). This dream, tied as it was to U.S. brand names, provides a telling comment on the global impact of American culture. People in the Third World are bombarded by American media and advertising so much that their desires are structured around these products. Hence, the worship of America and American consumer culture starts before one even enters America. Ironically, these products are now manufactured through transnational labor, so what William's family has long coveted is very likely produced using cheap laborers from his own country and from other countries in Asia and Mexico.

William's ten years in America have made him only too aware of the foolishness of those early dreams. In the bathroom of the Port Authority, "There had been a hyperactive automatic hand dryer which was a Proctor-Silex" (263). Recalling his family's reverence for the brand names before they came to America, William thinks he has finally understood the hidden meaning of Proctor-Silex, "as a shorthand for all the changes that are bound to happen in the process from wanting to get there to finally getting there, the process from dreaming the dream to eventually getting it—or some would say, killing it" (263). Wall-to-wall carpeting and the brand names do abound in America, but William and other Filipino Americans discover that they do not necessarily have the means to "walk on softness, coolness" (263), as they expected. Instead they find themselves cast as those who are expected to clean and maintain them for others to enjoy.

Desire and Women's Bodies

Another Filipino character, William's friend Preciosa, experiences a similar trajectory of disillusionment in America. Preciosa had aspirations of becoming an actress, and she never tires of seeing Barbara Stanwyck and Bette Davis when she goes to the movies.[7] When Preciosa does land a job as an actress at Lincoln Center in New York, it is for a play called *Primitives,* in which she appears, along with other dark-skinned men and women, wearing only a loincloth (42). Instead of being a sultry, beautiful actress like Stanwyck or Davis, Preciosa is cast in a play about white missionaries going to Central America. In the play Preciosa and the other "natives" only get to grunt and mumble gibberish. Her humiliation deepens when some of her Filipino friends come to see the play, witnessing her nakedness and loss of dignity. As the narrator says, for those in the audience, she is "as good as what the title of the damn thing had promised them: a primitive!" (313). In the penultimate scene, in which she is supposed to be possessed by a pagan demon, the audience and her co-actors mistake her anger for a convincing performance. Though not central to the main plot, Preciosa's story encapsulates many of the issues I have been raising regarding transmigrants. Like the dreams of Tomas and Gabe's family in Roley's novel and like those of William, Preciosa's dreams of a "better life" do not materialize in America. She succeeds only in occupations in which the dominant culture in America expects her to be good. Here she is cast in an undifferentiated pool of "native" women, easily passing for a primitive of Central America because to most white Americans, all dark-skinned people look almost the same.

Preciosa's history presents an important critique of the way the bodies of poor Filipina women are used both in their own country and globally.

Sent from the provinces to Manila to work as a maid in a Chinese household, she fell into the life of a prostitute for a while. After her escape from the brothel, she became a mail-order bride, from the writers of all the letters sent to her choosing to marry an old American man from Texas. Although he was kind to her and she found her feelings toward him growing tender, she remembers having to kiss his "frog face with its wrinkly, perpetually sweaty skin dotted with all those carbuncles" (311). When she had to gratify his sexual appetites, "Preciosa all the while thought of the dark blue cover of her new passport, thought of the Philippines as of a dilapidated building on the wrong side of town passed by without a second glance from a dark-windowed, air-conditioned car. [...] Even if the sex was disgusting, it was still sex in Texas, U.S.A." (311). The U.S. passport functions as the imaginary object of desire. Though globalization gives Preciosa a better set of living conditions, it still means sexual servitude, this time in the United States instead of in the Philippines. Her youth and beauty are the only commodities that she can use, and the passport becomes her way of escaping the Philippines and obtaining residency in America.

Immigration, however, does not necessarily mean a settled life in the States. After her husband's death, Preciosa finds herself moving from one low-paying job to another. She thinks of some of the dreary roles open to her as a Filipina: "frumpy nannies, matronly aides pushing wheelchair-bound wards on the streets, and nurses with the faces of servile dogs" (312). Her whole life in America is characterized by dislocation and displacement, because she never becomes fully integrated into the communities in which she finds herself. William remarks about her apartment:

> Even while Preciosa had lived there, it had already had an air of vacancy, of transiency about it, an air that I now realized was a transfer from its owner, who, even before she had revealed the story of her peripatetic life, had already had the look of someone who would make of her present address a somewhere else, another in a long line of somewhere elses like the country she'd just vacated to get here, on and on as if carrying out the directive of some deficiency encoded into her genes, a hunger, some basic discontent. This, being one more definition of immigrant—torn between the competing pulls of the fiction of the promised land, on the one hand, and the fiction of the sustaining mother country, on the other. (325–26)

This transiency characterizes Preciosa's life, as it does William's and those of many other global migrants. To go back home, however, seems unthinkable. As William puts it, "returning to the Philippines [...] seemed like an admission of defeat. Could you imagine the glee of relatives who would point you out in family gatherings, then launch into a story about going to live in the fabled United States only to crawl back with your tail between your legs—kicked out, in effect?" (308).

Underemployed in the United States, but too ashamed to go back home, these Filipino Americans remain in the place of in-betweenness and transmigrancy, always living in a state of nonbelonging even though they emigrated years ago.

In the novels discussed here, Roley and Ong reveal the many ways in which globalization affects Filipino Americans economically, culturally, and psychically. The new "borderless" world has produced uneven results for workers and for those who own and manage corporations. For those laborers from sending countries who leave their homes in search of a "better life," acceptance in the receiving countries has been mixed or half-hearted. The 1.5-generation children who grow up in these situations often resort to violence, fraud, and trickery in order to validate their sense of self, to gain acceptance into the dominant culture, and to obtain what they perceive to be the rewards of those who pursue the American dream. It is not surprising that at the end of both these novels the heroes are outlaws and exiles from society, distanced from their families. The children of this 1.5 generation, though burdened with the guilt and the ideological teachings of their parents, are unable to bear the hardships, the suffering, the humiliation of the first generation of Filipino immigrants. Unlike their parents, they want the fulfillment of the American dream of wealth and success, and they want it now. These novels by Roley and Ong show some of the desperate measures taken by these youths with thwarted dreams. Their Bildungen do not conclude in a state of epiphany, but, like their lives, are choppy, episodic, and nightmarish. Instead of finding happiness through acceptance and assimilation, they have, at best, only managed to survive the "rough draft" that has been their life (*Fixer Chao*, 377).

2
Recuperating Wretched Lives: Asian Sex Workers and the Underside of Nation Building

> To bring a past, in something like the fullness of its power or its horror, into the present in such a way as to force it to some restitution by making the people who read about it more thoughtful and less complacent [...]. To memorialize so sufficiently as to effect some always limited, always partial recuperation in the present, to make people *remember* what they do not know first-hand and to recognize in what they do know the dangers of the past that are alive in the present: this is one of the classic tasks of History.
>
> —Katherine Kearns, Psychoanalysis, Historiography, and Feminist Theory

This Place Called Absence, by Asian Canadian Lydia Kwa, and *Fox Girl,* by Asian American Nora Okja Keller, are novels that bear witness to the horrors of being a prostitute to foreigners either in one's own or in another country. Kwa's work recreates the lives of two young *"ah ku"* who work in the brothels of Singapore in the early 1900s, while Keller's book recounts the makeshift and desperate existence of two teenage prostitutes in Korea in the 1960s. Carefully researched by the authors, both novels attempt to give voice to women whose stories have not been well documented in history in order to "make people *remember* what they do not know first-hand" (Kearns, *Psychoanalysis, Historiography, and Femi-*

nist Theory, 22). Confronting us with details of the sordid and wretched lives of those who have been forced to sell their bodies for survival, Kwa and Keller perform the important act of witnessing, which Kelly Oliver describes as "the double sense of testifying to something that you have seen with your own eyes and bearing witness to something that you cannot see" (*Witnessing*, 18).

The subject matter in Kwa and Keller's works prefigured the kind of migration of women from Third World countries that has accelerated due to globalization in the past decade. Barbara Ehrenreich and Arlie Hochschild have written about the "female underside of globalization, whereby millions of [women] from poor countries in the south migrate to do the 'women's work' of the north—work that affluent women are no longer able or willing to do" (*Global Woman*, 3). They note, "The lifestyles of the First World are made possible by a global transfer of the services associated with a wife's traditional role—child care, homemaking, and sex—from poor countries to rich ones" (4). The imperialism of the northern countries is no longer just about extracting "natural resources and agricultural products [...] from lands they conquered and colonized"; today they are extracting "something harder to measure and quantify, something that can look very much like love" (4). Although the historical settings of both Kwa and Keller's novels predated the contemporary conditions of globalization that we have been looking at, their works reveal the beginnings of what has become a booming sex industry of Asian women in the late twentieth and early twenty-first centuries. In 1984, Elaine Kim noted the connection between military prostitution and the present-day global sex industry: "The transformation of wartime prostitution into the expanded peacetime sex industry of the 1980s should be viewed within the context of the international tourist industry, which has become an increasingly important part of the development strategy of non-socialist countries during the last two decades" ("Sex Tourism in Asia," 216).

Shannon Bell argues that "the prostitute" was "actively produced as a marginalized social-sexual identity, particularly during the latter half of the nineteenth century and the beginning of the twentieth century" (*Reading, Writing and Rewriting the Prostitute Body*, 40). Bell notes that "prostitutes were analyzed and categorized in relation to the bourgeois female ideals: the good wife and the virginal daughter" (40). The prostitute "was always the disprivileged other in relation to the determinant site: wife, mother, daughter" (40). Modern discourse further separated the female body so that "normal female sexuality was defined in terms of woman's reproductive functions, deviant female sexuality was defined in terms of prostitution" (41). Although most of Bell's examples are Western ones, her observations are applicable to the way prostitutes were described and represented in Asia in the twentieth century.[1] What happens is that the othering provides a kind of distance so that the everyday difficulties and realities faced by prostitutes are ignored by bourgeois society, which sees prostitutes only in terms of negativity and absence. In addition, because prostitution exists in the liminal space between acceptable social practice and the criminal, the working conditions and the social and familial situations of prostitutes are often simply overlooked or imperfectly recorded.

By focusing on prostitutes and using them as main characters in their novels, Kwa and Keller illuminate a facet of women's history that has hitherto been obscured from the imagination of the mainstream reading public. In the first chapter I discussed the way Roley and Ong uncover the ways globalization takes its toll on young adults. They depict some of the seedier sides of mobility and displacement. In *This Place Called Absence* and *Fox Girl*, Kwa and Keller deliberately obfuscate the boundaries between the respectable and society's abject, between normative female sexualities and deviant ones, between the privileged categories of wife, mother, and daughter and that of the disprivileged other. This connection between the prostitute and the domestic woman was present in the first chapter, but not as prominently figured as in this. In the subplot of Preciosa in *Fixer Chao*, Han Ong also reveals with irony the way a Filipina immigrant has to sell her body by becoming a mail-order bride in order to gain legitimate status and citizenship in the nation. In the works of Kwa and Keller, the links are more obvious and deliberate. By giving us details of the abuse, violence, and poverty of the prostitutes the authors enable us to witness what we normally would not see or experience about the underside of nation building. They show that love, motherhood, and daughterhood are not antithetical to prostitution but part of the subjectivity of these women, who are represented as heroic survivors and part of the nation. By depicting prostitutes in familial situations, by revealing the ways they negotiate their queer desires and aspirations and the way they reconcile themselves to their physical and material states, Kwa and Keller call attention to the absent voices in our trans-Pacific and transnational history, to the gaps in our understanding and knowledge of the postcolonial past and its neocolonial legacy.

Cynthia Enloe, a feminist scholar of international relations, notes that historical museums do not often tell the full story of war because they neglect to show crucial elements, such as the military brothel (*Morning After*, 145). She writes:

> War—and militarized peace—are occasions when sexual relations take on particular meanings. A museum curator—or a journalist, novelist, or political commentator—who edits out sexuality, who leaves it on the cutting-room floor, delivers to the audience a skewed and ultimately unhelpful account of just what kinds of myths, anxieties, inequalities, and state policies are required to fight a war or to sustain a militarized form of peace. (144)

Enloe points out that "much governmental authority is being expended to insure that a peculiar definition of masculinity is sustained. Military prostitution differs from other forms of industrialized prostitution in that there are explicit steps taken by state institutions to protect the male customers without undermining their perceptions of themselves as sexualized men" (145). Enloe's comments about war, government interventions, and the military brothel are applicable to colonial Singapore, which was not at war but had a similarly peculiar form of government-sanctioned prostitution in the late nineteenth and early twentieth centuries in order to bolster its economic development. Historian James Francis Warren writes,

> In the historiography of Singapore, there is a need to bring to the foreground the critical importance of the *ah ku* and *karayuki-san* in the sex and politics of the urban society [...]. The history of Chinese and Japanese prostitution in Singapore is a subject which not only raises issues of women's work and status but links these with the much less tractable questions of sex, race, and colonialism, as well as male sexuality and women's exploitation of other women. Prostitution in the period from 1870 to 1940 was determined by complex social and economic forces in Singapore. ("Ah Ku" and "Karayuki-san," 3–4)

The works of Enloe, Warren, and Katharine Moon (*Sex among Allies*) have provided good historical and sociopolitical accounts of the impact of government-sanctioned brothels in Asia in the twentieth century. In fictional form, Kwa and Keller similarly attempt to recuperate this history by giving shape and texture to the everyday lives of sex workers in these brothels. Their novels make vivid the stories of the anonymous women who were present and vital in these largely male-dominated segments of history.

The question is not simply that of historical causality, that is, how we have arrived in the twenty-first century with a global market of prostitutes exported from countries in Asia, such as Thailand, Burma, and the Philippines. The question is also about how our knowledge of the way politics and economic power in today's globalized world can illuminate history, particularly those aspects of history that do not figure in standard history books. What can globalization teach us about past practices? In his study of child prostitutes in Thailand, Kevin Bales explains that the "great transformation of industrialization" in Thailand in the past fifty years has created a flood of children sold into sexual slavery ("Because She Looks Like a Child," 211). Even in the less prosperous areas of the mountainous north of the country, consumer goods are "visible everywhere—refrigerators, televisions, cars and trucks, rice cookers, air conditioners" (211). Parents feel "a great pressure to buy consumer goods that were unknown even twenty years ago; the sale of a daughter might easily finance a new television set" (211). At the same time, in the central plain, "poor economic migrants from the rice fields now work on building sites or in new factories, earning many times what they did on the land. Possibly for the first time in their lives, these laborers can do what more well-off Thai men have always done: go to a brothel" (212). In the same way, economic booms and global conditions created a shift in labor patterns and migration in the late nineteenth and early twentieth centuries in Southeast Asia. Girls and women were bought, kidnapped, or enticed away from their families in the poorer areas of China and Japan in order to work as prostitutes servicing the growing coolie population in Singapore.

Unlike other scholars who focus mainly on globalization of the past twenty years, Andreas Wimmer and Nina Glick Schiller point out that the "transnational movement of commodities, capital, and labour reached a first peak" during this period before the First World War ("Methodological Nationalism and Beyond," 303). They argue that what we call globalization is "not in itself a new phenomenon" (302), and they explore the links between nation building, discourses of immigration, and global transformations over the past one hundred and thirty years or so. Of the first phase, 1870–1918, they write:

The *belle époque* was a time of dramatic growth with high demands for labour [...]. This was the epoch in which European states "scrambled" for Africa, as well as a time of heightened competition between European states and the United States for the control of raw materials produced in the Caribbean, Latin America, and Asia. It was also a period in which, as part of this effort to monopolize sources of raw materials and obtain labour for their production, imperialism was practiced and theorized. The result of these various and interactive developments, in a period that was simultaneously one of nation-building and intensive globalization, was wide-spread labour migration that spanned the globe with little or no restriction in most states. (312)

During this period Singapore was under British colonial rule and was rapidly expanding, becoming a major port, a world center for rubber planting and rubber export. Chinese and Arab migrants, mostly men, went to Singapore in search of work (ASNIC, "Singapore History").

Remembering the *Ah Ku*

In *This Place Called Absence,* Lydia Kwa links this early period of migration and intensive globalization with the present moment by evoking the lives of these Chinese prostitutes who lived in Singapore at the beginning of the twentieth century through the imagination and reading of a contemporary clinical psychologist, the book's protagonist, Wu Lan Lim. Kwa uses a double time scheme to suggest parallels between the lives of Wu Lan, a Singaporean immigrant who practices in Vancouver in the 1990s, and two *ah ku* women who lived almost a hundred years before her. Although Kwa herself says that she left Singapore in 1980 and does not return home often (Karamcheti, "Singapore on My Mind," 24), the protagonist of her novel maintains many ties to her family in Singapore, which are facilitated by globality. For example, Wu Lan makes and receives long distance calls from her mother and brother, jet travel enables her to attend her father's funeral in Singapore, and she is able to do research on nineteenth-century prostitutes in Malaysia in the state-of-the art Vancouver Public Library. In her mind, she constantly flits back and forth between her memories of her father and mother in Singapore and her present state of loneliness in Canada. She, like the two *ah ku* women, leads a transnational life, as defined by Basch, Glick Schiller, and Szanton-Blanc. For them, transnationalism refers to the "processes by which immigrants forge and sustain multi-stranded social relations that link together their societies of origin and settlement [...]. Many immigrants today build social fields that cross geographic, cultural, and political borders" (*Nations Unbound*, 7). Basch, Glick Schiller, and Szanton-Blanc develop the term "transmigrants" to describe "immigrants who develop and maintain multiple relationships—familial, economic, social, organizational, religious, and political—that span borders" (7). Like Wu Lan, the two *ah ku* women can be called transmigrants. They have vivid memories of their childhoods and maintain strong ties to their families back in their country of origin. Lee Ah Choi, for example, sends money to her family, taking her "packet to the remittance man" every month and watching him translate her words into "neat, black strokes and dots" for her (*This Place Called Absence*, 57). In spite of her unpleasant life as a prostitute, she notes with some pride, "I haven't forgotten my first family, their reliance on me" (57). Wimmer and Glick Schiller note that, in a pattern similar to that demonstrated by today's transnational migrant workers, during the first phase of globalization, "remittances from abroad were understood to be a significant part of the economies of many regions" ("Methodological Nationalism and Beyond," 315).

All three women in Kwa's novel—Wu Lan and the two prostitutes from a century ago—are transnational sojourners who have been separated from their families, have moved way from their birthplaces, but still maintain close ties to their homeland. They are all travelers but are marginal figures in their adopted countries because they are lesbians and do not conform to the Confucian patriarchal norms of being dutiful wives and obedient daughters. Their lives are touched in some form or another by suicide, violence, and death. This structure, using the mix of past and present, infuses a sense of contemporaneity and relevance into the historical narrative of the forgotten *ah ku* prostitutes, women whose individual biographies have not been included in standard historical or fictional accounts of Singapore. Kwa uses the voices of these three women, occasionally interspersed by the narrative of Wu Lan's mother, Mahmee, to tell intertwining stories of dislocation, desire, loss, and remembrance.

Although the life of contemporary Wu Lan in Vancouver is drastically different from the lives of the *ah ku* women in Singapore at the turn of the past century, Kwa links their narratives by employing a number of devices. She uses objects, such as the brocade slippers that appear in more than one narrative, and references to a time, such as the ghost month of August, or a place, such as a Buddhist temple, to link 1908 Singapore to 1994 Singapore and Vancouver. Additionally, motifs such as freedom, escape, and death recur. Family bonds—paternal and maternal love—are mentioned in each of the three narratives, but familial relations are depicted with some ambivalence. One central theme that further links the three stories is memory and remembering. When the novel opens, it is Remembrance Day 1994 in Canada, and Wu Lan is thinking about her father's recent death by suicide as well as the meaning of the holiday.[2] She says, "back home in Singapore, nobody commemorates the world wars" (*This Place Called Absence*, 3). Don Goellnicht insightfully notes: "It is not that Singapore did not experience World War II but that it did so as a colonial protectorate of Britain, occupied by the Japanese from 1942 to 1945; in other words it was doubly colonized during World War II, so military prowess cannot be manufactured into a national myth of maturing into a modern nation as it was in Canada" ("Forays into Acts of Transformation," 173). Both individual and collective memory is important to Wu Lan and in the novel, because it is only through remembering the past that Wu Lan and the two prostitutes are able to make sense of their lives and able eventually to reconcile their losses. Through Kwa's deliberate act of reconstructing this past, we become aware of these events in history. Significantly, the public act of remembrance does not always correlate with what one remembers in private. What Wu Lan recollects on Remembrance Day is not what the members of the Canadian Legion reflect upon, and what one remembers or knows about Singapore at the beginning of the past century is not what the *ah ku* women Lee Ah Choi and Chow Chat Mui are concerned about. What becomes important in the novel is the working of the characters' inner subjectivity, and by focusing on the private and the everyday Kwa provides a place for the psychic survival of lost subjects. Kelly Oliver notes that "to conceive of oneself as a subject is to have the ability to address oneself to another, real or imaginary, actual or potential. Subjectivity is the result of, and depends on, the process of witnessing—address-ability and response-ability" (*Witnessing*, 17). Thus, for Wu Lan the act of remembrance functions as an act of witnessing, for we become the listeners and witnesses to the connected narratives of trauma that unfold in the novel.

Wu Lan is a reluctant witness, haunted by her own troubles. On medical leave after her father's suicide, she is recovering from depression herself and questioning the validity of her career and life. She reflects, "I'd lost confidence in my ability to help people find a way past their powerlessness" (*This Place Called Absence*, 98). She feels that she has developed "an increasing resentment, an intolerance for the suffering of others," and is envious of "others' ability to express their needs" (98). On the brink of collapse and obsessed with ways to die, part of what haunts Wu Lan is a feeling of guilt, a nagging sense that she might have prevented her father's "wordless, private suicide" (17). This seemingly inexplicable death leads her to probe and imagine other people's wasted lives. She comes across James Francis Warren's account of prostitutes who were bought, kidnapped, or lured away from mainland China and Japan to work in the brothels of Singapore. Warren's version includes many facts and figures—on the extreme poverty in farming communities in southern China and in the Amakusa Islands of Japan, on the numbers of daughters sold to help the rest of the family survive; on the numbers of brothels and prostitutes in Singapore, on the numbers of those who became sick with diseases and why; and on those who committed suicide. In Wu Lan's fantasy and in her re-creation of the lives of two of these prostitutes, whose names are found in Warren's book, she not only changes the ending of the life of one of the prostitutes as given in the coroner's records but fills in details of the prostitutes' families, their past histories before arriving in Singapore, and their aspirations and yearnings while they work as *ah ku*. By so doing she preserves them from obscurity and rescues them from the seeming purposelessness of their lives as noted in the short entries on official documents. She renders nameless victims into heroes of a sort.

In his study of *ah ku* (Chinese prostitutes) and *karayuki-san* (Japanese prostitutes) in Singapore, Warren notes that more than three thousand girls and women were sent from China and Japan to work in brothels in the period between 1887 and 1894 (*"Ah Ku" and "Karayuki-san,"* 74). By 1894, an average of about nine hundred Chinese women were entering the city's brothels per year (74). Their working conditions were extremely poor; most of them were virtual slaves to their *kwai po* (brothel keepers), who were in charge of them and to whom they were indebted (53). Many of these women eventually caught sexually transmitted diseases such as gonorrhea and syphilis, and they were regarded as criminals. Warren notes that the medical profession at the time "showed little genuine interest or concern in the *ah ku* as real people, often condemning them as 'prostitutes'—women who were morally degraded and unfit, and as such not worthy of their help or consideration under the circumstances" (144). In their reports "there is no sense of compassion or pity" (144). The doctors described Chinese women who contracted venereal diseases as "beasts, mindless and sub-human" (144). The attitude of the colonial government was mixed: these women were necessary to meet the needs of the male Chinese coolie laborers, but British, Dutch, and other European soldiers and seamen were warned against contracting diseases from them. For the most part, the Chinese women were largely confined to their brothels; their pastimes were restricted to gambling, their bodily pains lessened only by smoking opium. A large number of them died young, from disease, violence, or suicide.[3]

In her representation of these *ah ku* prostitutes, Kwa combats the Victorian paternalistic attitudes of the medical profession and the colonial government by allowing the *ah ku* to speak for themselves. Kwa uses the factual information from Warren and weaves out of it a convincing, realistic background and life for the two *ah ku* prostitutes. The tendency to see them as distant others is minimized through their first-person narratives, enabling us to see the way they negotiate the distance between their own desires, the expectations of their brothel keepers, and the nineteenth-century view of them as dispensable commodities who existed in society's margins. For example, Lee Ah Choi, who appears in the appendix of Warren's book as a Cantonese woman of twenty-two who worked for a year at 61 Upper Hokkien Street and died in 1908 (*"Ah Ku" and "Karayuki-san,"* 391), has dreams of living another life in Kwa's version of her story. She is the eldest daughter of a poor farmer in a village near the town of Xiaolan who was sold for "three sacks of rice" (*This Place Called Absence,* 22). Although she is not proud of what she does, she does not wish to return to her village life of mosquitoes, caked mud, and watery gruel. She dreams of a life of luxury: "of saving enough for that lilac silk purse inlaid with pearls, eyes of the phoenix, and black velvet shoes from Shanghai, the kind women wear to banquets with their rich husbands [...], of gold bangles as thick as my thumb, of expensive hair ornaments that glitter like stars in my sea of black" (9).

Her closely guarded secret, that she has saved some two hundred dollars in tips underneath the straw mat of her bed, is her means of asserting her independence but later becomes a source of misery for her. Every month, even though she dutifully sends her packet of money to her family in China, she hopes that a man will take her away from her life as a prostitute: "either a man who adores me, or a man who makes me pregnant and will maintain his honour to me and his child" (77).

In actuality, the transition from prostitute to wife was not that easy. Although some prostitutes were bought by prospective husbands, Warren writes of many cases in which these types of marriages failed because of incompatibility, abuse, violence, and disease. The *ah ku* who were taken at a young age were often illiterate and not trained to be wives and mothers. Many adjusted with difficulty to the Confucian expectations of marriage and family. Some left brothels but could not discontinue their habits of gambling, opium, and alcoholism (*"Ah Ku" and "Karayuki-san,"* 332). Thus, Lee Ah Choi's dreams of being swept away by a gallant husband are more of a fantasy than a reality, as her friend Chow Chat Mui realizes. Chat Mui, who has been in the business longer, knows that not many "customers would want to marry an *ah ku*"; only the ones "insanely obsessed with their women" do (*This Place Called Absence*, 91). Chow Chat Mui also appears in the appendix of Warren's book, identified simply as a Cantonese prostitute who lived at 64 Upper Hokkien Street and died at the age of thirty in 1909 (*"Ah Ku" and "Karayuki-san,"* 392). In Kwa's version she, unlike Lee Ah Choi, is a voluntary prostitute, a *tap tang*, who enjoyed relatively more liberty than those sold by their families (*"Ah Ku" and "Karayuki-san,"* 56–57).

In *This Place Called Absence* Kwa endows Chow Chat Mui with an adventurous and a daring spirit that impels her to travel and seek other lands. Don Goellnicht, in an essay about the queer diaspora, observes, "The insistence on producing female protagonists with agency, however limited, [...] calls into question the masculinist root notion of 'diaspora' as a scattering of seeds from the father or the father-land. [The] lesbian diaspora is truly revolutionary, a blow against patriarchy and against the organicist metaphors that support patriarchy" ("Forays into Acts of Transformation," 160). Chow Chat Mui's life in the village with her alcoholic father, who physically abused her and her mother, was like that of a "captured animal, [...] a chicken in a wire cage, slaughtered nightly without bloodshed" (*This Place Called Absence*, 12). Like the contemporary protagonist Wu Lan, Chat Mui was a taller-than-average girl, an "anomaly" in the community because of her height (15). At twenty-one she grows tired of their complaints about her height, of waiting for a man to marry her; she disguises herself as a man and runs away with her cousin. On the boat to Southeast Asia, where she is crammed in with hundreds of sweating bodies, she feels no better than a pig being herded away. Her identity as a woman is discovered on-board, and she is raped by the seamen and human traffickers. After working for eight years as an *ah ku*, she has contracted a sexually transmitted disease and takes refuge in smoking. After meeting Lee Ah Choi, her secret desire is to be able to run away with her so the two can work independently and save money for themselves instead of working for their *kwai po*. It is through details like these that Kwa arouses our sympathy for and understanding of the difficult lives of prostitutes like Chat Mui in colonial Singapore.

Kwa's most brilliant and innovative invention, however, is Wu Lan's re-creation of these two *ah ku* prostitutes as queer lovers. Through this fictive intervention Kwa questions the heternormative assumptions about masculinity and femininity in colonial Singapore as well as in contemporary North America. She allows for the possibility that the prostitute's body can be something other than a heterosexual body and that there are alternative sexualities within the dominant discourse of nation building and masculinity. She goes beyond the traditional narratives found in official accounts and history by her inclusion of lesbian lovers. Someone like Warren, for example, although aware of nontraditional, adoptive, and makeshift families in colonial Singapore,[4] does not allude at all to queer sexualities or desires. The presence of queer sexualities, though imagined, in many ways subverts the unstated presumptions and fears of the colonial government. As revealed by the June 1894 document titled *Correspondence Regarding the Measures to Be Adopted for Checking the Spread of Venereal Disease, Ceylon, Hong Kong and Striats Settlements*, the government believed that in the absence of the possibility of marriage, prostitution or "unnatural and abominable vices" would proliferate, and it therefore represented prostitution as "a necessary evil" to save laborers from "something worse" (quoted by Manderson in "Colonial Desires," 377). One of the reasons for the existence of brothels in Singapore at the turn of the past century was to prevent homosocial relations between the coolie laborers, because the gender ratio was "1 female to 14 males in 1860 and this gender imbalance was to continue to exist for the next seventy years" (Warren, "Ah Ku" and "Karayuki-san," 34).

In Kwa's novel, when Chow Chat Mui and Lee Ah Choi reflect on how they give each other pleasure, when they think of the parts of their bodies—their tongues, breasts, lips, and feet—that are not in the service of their *kwai po* and for the men but for themselves, they are performing acts of resistance against history and the narratives of development and progress that accompany such accounts. Through Wu Lan's musings, Kwa enables them to retrieve the parts of their bodies that have been sold by their fathers and their brothel keepers, albeit temporarily, and use them as their own. What Gayatri Gopinath says of South Asian queer sexualities applies here:

> A queer South Asian diasporic geography of desire and pleasure stages this critique on multiple levels: it rewrites colonial constructions of Asian sexualities as anterior, premodern, and in need of Western political development—constructions that are recirculated by contemporary gay and lesbian transnational politics—while simultaneously interrogating different South Asian nationalist narratives that imagine and consolidate the nation in terms of organic heterosexuality. ("Nostalgia, Desire, Diaspora," 473–474)

In Kwa's version of the prostitutes' lives, although the dream of a safe haven for the two women does not materialize, nevertheless there is a hopeful ending for one of the prostitutes, Chow Chat Mui. Lee Ah Choi, her lover, is not so fortunate and meets a tragic end. When her *kwai po* discovers her hidden money, she is beaten in front of the other prostitutes in the house. Too humiliated by this beating and deprived of her means of escape, she commits suicide. Chat Mui, however, is of a more resilient spirit. She accidentally kills her brothel keeper and former lover when he intrudes on her and laughs at her efforts to learn to write. Because of this murder, she is compelled to flee her brothel. With the help of a scholar at the temple, whom she has befriended earlier, she is able to escape the city as his wife. This scholar devises the plan to marry her because he, himself, is queer and wants to please his mother, who is eager to see him married. Interestingly, this happy ending is possible only through the intervention of a gay man, which adds to the possibility that other queer identities existed at that time and formed communities with each other.

Before her escape with the scholar, Chat Mui, though illiterate, is fascinated by words and tries to imitate his writing. She is particularly fascinated by the character he writes to stand for her, a Chinese word consisting of a heart underneath a field and signifying "contemplation." This symbol becomes suggestive of the lives of the unnamed prostitutes and coolie laborers who were transported from mainland China and Japan to work in Southeast Asia during its time of development and modernization. Though these workers were largely from poor peasant families, they had hearts, minds, and spirits underneath their plainness and poverty. Symbolically, Chat Mui brings the scroll containing this character to Lee Ah Choi's grave as a sign of her love for her before she leaves Singapore. Wu Lan, concluding her imagined narrative of the prostitutes' lives with this memorializing gesture, is also able to come to terms with her father's death in the late twentieth century. She asserts: "I am Wu Lan, an exorcist of hidden demons. I am the discoverer of secrets [...]. I prepare the dead for release" (*This Place Called Absence*, 208).

On the Margins of Camptown

In the same way, Nora Okja Keller retells prostitutes' stories and opens up a largely secret aspect of Korean history. In an interview with Young-Oak Lee, Keller compared her first novel, *Comfort Woman*, to *Fox Girl*, saying, "It's that same kind of voicelessness that drew me to these women. Even the books that I read in English that dealt with American military presence in Korea, if they talked about the camp towns, it wasn't from the woman's perspective (Lee, "Nora Okja Keller and the Silenced Woman"). Both *Fox Girl* and *This Place Called Absence* acknowledge and give voice to women who played a part in world military history that has not been acknowledged by the East or the West. In *Fox Girl*, as in *This Place Called Absence*, two of the dominant themes are those of confinement and inevitability. Like Lee Ah Choi and Chow Chat Mui, the protagonists of *Fox Girl* also struggle with the difficulty of escaping the lives into which they were born.

In *Fox Girl*, a sense of futility and hopelessness pervades the destitute lives of girls and women like the character Sookie's mother who depend on military prostitution in Korea's America Town in the years after the Korean War (1950–53). Set in Korea in the 1960s, the novel depicts a multiracial world of Koreans; white GIs, called *"miguks"*; black GIs, called *"gomshis"*; and their mixed-raced offspring. They inhabit a borderless world of globalized American culture that is neither fully Korea nor America but both. Hyung Jin, for example, talks about the Juicy Fruit and Coca-Cola given to kids, as well as the "Touch and Glow base foundation, Beach Peach and Swinging Pink lipsticks, Coty puff powder" given to women by the GIs (*Fox Girl*, 11). At the same time, she is able to sing "*ka na da ra*," the Korean alphabet, and listen to her father's Korean tales of "bears turning into women fit to marry the king of heaven, of beautiful princesses trapped for three hundred years in the form of centipedes, of girls haunting the earth as nine-tailed foxes" (5, 8–9).

From the start of the novel, Hyung Jin, the protagonist and the girl who narrates the story and later becomes a prostitute, notes that she is marked or stained. She has a disfiguring birthmark on her face and is conscious of having to tuck the "stained side of [her] face into [her] shoulder" (3) in order to avoid the taunts of the neighborhood boys. Her playmate and best friend, Sookie, is also set apart from others, teased for being ugly because she is "bulbous eyed and dark skinned" (3). As a child of an African American GI and a Korean mother, Sookie is called "blackie" and "black dog" by the other children (4), placed at the bottom of their social hierarchy. Hyung Jin and Sookie are thus set at a distance from the rest of the community because of these physical markings or black stains, but the stains have deeper signification. Hyung Jin's birthmark and Sookie's dark features place them in a no-man's-land between white America and Korea. The physical marks on their bodies are inscriptions of their otherness and difference from the rest of the people in Korea. In the cases of both, their differences stem from the accidents of their births. The taunts directed at them reveal that even a society at the margins, such as that of America Town, had its abject figures. The people of this society, marginalized by the larger Korean community, nevertheless were intolerant of those who were either racially or economically and socially disenfranchised and indifferent to the plights. In addition, what Hyung Jin has to fight is the belief, articulated by her adoptive mother, that "it's in the blood. Everyone's life is mapped from the moment of birth" (50).

In her study of military prostitution, Katharine Moon writes of children like Sookie, who were of Korean–African American descent and were ostracized from the rest of Korea: "They were fully aware that there was no Korea for them outside the small camptown. Because of their black skin and racial features, their marginalization from Korean society was most severe" (*Sex among Allies*, 6). Camptowns such as the one described in *Fox Girl* are where the *kijich'on*, or military prostitutes, lived, a "place of self-exile as well as a last resort for earning a livelihood" (3). Mainstream Korean society viewed the *kijich'on* women as trash, "a disgrace to themselves and their people," because they had "mingled flesh and blood with foreigners (*yangnom*) in a society that has been racially and culturally homogeneous for thousands of years" (3). Once there, it was nearly impossible to reintegrate themselves into "normal" Korean society (3). Yet, as Katharine Moon argues, the work of the *kijich'on* women existed because of a complex web of international forces. Since the Korean War, the United States has stationed troops in South Korea and other parts of Asia. The Republic of Korea has been willing to allow its women to be "personal ambassadors" in order to improve U.S.-Korea civil-military relations and to secure U.S. military commitment to the Republic (12–13) in its efforts to combat the threat of North Korea.

What Hyung Jin's adoptive mother attributes to her "blood" is, in fact, more complicated. When Hyung Jin and Sookie turn to prostitution, it is not because it is in their "blood" but because there is very little else for a young woman to do in order to subsist in the camptown, which caters primarily to the needs of the U.S. servicemen. For Sookie it is a means of survival. Unable to feed herself when her mother goes away in order to have an abortion, Sookie accepts the offers of her mother's boyfriend, Chazu. In return for her sexual favors, he gives her American-style luxuries—candies, powdered milk, canned goods, and eventually a place to stay. Sookie is initiated into the ways of the club girls and stops attending school in her teens. For Hyung Jin, the turn to prostitution is part of a rebellious act of defiance against her parents, who already believe the worst of her because of her friendship with Sookie. Her life takes a downward turn in her teens. Initially, Hyung Jin was confident of her place in her middle-class family and in her society, taking pride in being "pure Korean" (*Fox Girl*, 4). However, when she discovered that her birth mother was actually Sookie's mother, a prostitute, she felt betrayed by her and by her father. At that point, she felt, "Everything, everything that had once belonged to my old life, my old self—the daughter of these parents—fell into the street" (125). After this incident, she feels that she has nowhere else to turn and agrees to work for her biracial friend Lobetto without really understanding the consequences of the kind of work he is offering.

Hyung Jin's first sexual experience is more like a rape than a trick. She is coerced into having sex with not one but three white GI Joes. Not knowing that she is a virgin, Lobetto sells her "three for the price of one" (151). One of the men who pays for the deal notices that "she looks young" but is reassured by the others that "them Orientals all look young" (151). Because of the culture of military camps, decent American men act like brutal animals toward Asian women. Katharine Moon notes that U.S. military officials and command policies contribute to the belief that prostitution in Asia is "a way of life for Asians and that Asians like prostitution" (*Sex among Allies*, 37). Contrary to the strict attitude of the command in places like Saudi Arabia, there is "overwhelming cultural pressure among enlisted men" to seek out prostitutes in places like the Philippines and Korea (37). Prostitution is even encouraged by some military officials, who have their own clubs and own women (37). Thus, even though Hyung Jin is whimpering and saying "Stop" in English and Korean, the men ignore her, believing that "it's part of the game" (*Fox Girl*, 152).

In that scene and in several other instances, Keller criticizes American GIs for their inability to see Korean women for what they are rather than simply as bodies for their use and pleasure. Sookie's mother says that it is possible for Korean women to be invisible to Americans: "*Miguks* [white foreigners] can't see us [...] Korean faces blind them" (23). She believes that when a Korean woman of any age uses makeup, it becomes "magic—a disguise that lets [them] move through their world safely" (25). Old Korean grandmothers can get young men who are not able to gauge their age, but unfortunately, at the same time young teenagers like Sookie and Hyung Jin are seen as part of the undifferentiated pool of available women, treated as older and experienced prostitutes rather than as schoolgirls just barely past puberty. Before the three GIs assault Hyung Jin, one of them says encouragingly to another, who is hesitant, "We don't need to look at her face" (151). It is not just because of her marked face that they feel they do not need to look at her; they also do not care about her pain or stop to listen to her wishes. It is this deliberate act of seeing only what they want to see that becomes symptomatic of much of the unequal relationships between

American servicemen and Korean prostitutes. According to Moon, the consequences of the war, "the accompanying poverty, social and political chaos, separation of families, and millions of young orphans and widows, 'mass-produced' prostitutes" (*Sex among Allies*, 28), who gave up "normal" lives and had to mold themselves to the desires of U.S. servicemen for their livelihood.

Hyung Jin eventually succeeded as a prostitute by doing the things that other women dared not or did not want to do. Because of her birthmark, she had to work harder at pleasing the men, who demanded new and different acts from the girls who danced at the clubs. Hyung Jin became the "Hunni Girl, the bar girl called on for requests, doing what the other girls didn't want to do—at least not on stage" (*Fox Girl*, 192). She says: "I was the GIs' life-size doll, always smiling, always bendable, always able. I had sex on stage with whoever and however many marched up. I poured beer and shot cherries from my vagina into men's mouths. I got pissed and shit on. I had oral sex with a dog that someone pulled in from the streets" (192). Her act worked because the GIs wanted to see her as the brazen freak who would do anything. For them, Hyung Jin's performance was the real thing. But what Keller continues to emphasize throughout the novel is what lies beneath or beyond the performance of the sex show—the physical pain in her body, the miscarried pregnancy, the struggle to continue with the improvised life she lived with Lobetto and his mother in their small house, and her friendship with Sookie.

Though she was able to earn a living as an entertainer, Hyung Jin was always conscious of her lack of status in the community as an "America Town girl" (192). She combated this sense of otherness and people's condemnation by showing off her wealth: "Though the fishwives would look at me as if I were trash—they in their grimy, gut-stained rags—I flashed my money. Enough of it to make them hide their scorn and smile at me. Enough to make them greet me like a celebrity, and to compete for my attention" (192–93). The sense of abjection from the community, however, was never far removed from the prostitutes' lives. They were treated like animals by the townspeople, by the U.S. servicemen, and by the government officials who ran services for them. In the novel, this debasement is evident in the discourse surrounding the prostitutes. The hospital where prostitutes went for abortions is called the "Monkey House" (46), while the shops in which the "hard-luck whores" danced are called "fish tanks"(77). The fish tanks, in which women were displayed, were really "rows of boxes" where women "danced naked in the glass doorways. As the GIs wandered in and out of the clubs, the women pressed themselves against the glass, and gyrating, touched themselves to get the men's attention" (114). The animal imagery is not only used for prostitutes and the places they inhabit but also extends, in a rather regrettable way, to their children. Unwanted babies are given away or drowned, like cats. Sookie, who never wanted to keep her baby, tries at one point to get rid of the child, saying, "she's better off dead than growing up as another black mutt in America Town" (223). The prostitutes' own marginal position in society, in which they experience life as a constant fight to survive disease, poverty, and hunger, does not allow them the luxury of developing a strong sense of attachment and familial love. Treated like animals, they respond by treating their offspring like animals.

Nevertheless, in spite of these conditions, Keller presents a number of scenes depicting Hyung Jin's maternal love and her efforts at mothering. She might not be a hero in the traditional sense, but she makes a heroic effort to create a decent life for herself and Sookie's baby. These scenes work to counter the representations of sex work that are present in the novel and to remind readers of the other side of prostitutes' lives. Hyung Jin is one of the few who defies the predictable pattern of the camptown woman. After having a miscarriage, she tries desperately to convince Sookie to carry Sookie's baby to full term. She works at the club so that Sookie can stay home; she goes to the market looking for the "choicest and most succulent offerings for Sookie: fetal octopus, sea cucumber, abalone, and oysters" (193) and massages Sookie all through her labor and delivery. Because Sookie refuses to name or care for the baby, Hyung Jin takes the baby as her own, naming her Myu Myu, feeding her by grinding rice pellets in her mouth "into a soupy mush" (202), and even taking her to work when necessary. Hyung Jin is not a great mother, but given her desperate circumstances, what she accomplishes is praiseworthy: she manages to keep Myu Myu alive in adverse circumstances and even takes the baby along with her to Hawai'i when she gets a chance to leave Korea.

Hyung Jin's transformation from "class leader" at school, "the one who led the line to the yard" (9) and knew all the answers, to the clever club dancer who can "work with the audience" (209), is both a story of victimization and a story of heroism. She is the "fox girl," the mythical creature that takes the shape of a girl in order to regain the jewel of knowledge that it possessed before it was stolen by a young male scholar (27). In the novel both Sookie and Hyung Jin are associated with the myth of the fox girl, with wearing disguises that become "a shield over tender skin" (27). Their masks are "cool and deadly," and they are "capable of swallowing the jewel of a man's soul" (27). In the myth the fox, in her disguise as a girl, eats before she is eaten. Fox girl can be viewed as a destructive, evil creature, but as Sookie's mother says, "It depends on who tells the story" (26). Sookie says, "The fox girl was only trying to regain what those boys stole from her" (26). Keller ends the novel with this note of ambivalence in the story that matches the myth. By the last chapter, Hyung Jin has given up prostitution and works legitimately as a gardener's assistant in Hawai'i. She acts as mother to Myu Myu, in whom she places all her hopes. At the end of the novel, she has thwarted her adoptive mother's warning about bad blood. Though born of a prostitute, she is able to live a decent life. In the child Myu Myu she sees "the best of Sookie, of Duk Hee [her birth mother], of Lobetto, of [herself]—everything [they] could have hoped for and wished to be" in the "jewel of a girl who holds the world in her hand and sees it, loves it, as her own" (290). In spite of those she has had to abandon and hurt to get here, Hyung Jin's story is a story of triumph over the devastating consequences of prostitution, a story of the loss of childhood and selfhood because of historical, political, and social circumstances. It provides an example of the possibility of transformation and liberation.

By writing about these prostitutes' lives, Kwa and Keller shift the focus of traditional historical discourse, which acknowledges the importance of the needs only of men, be they soldiers, sailors, or coolie laborers. Women, too, experienced mobility and were very much part of the building of the nation in the early to middle part of the twentieth century, but their pains, their desires, their dislocation from their places of birth, their estrangements from their parents and siblings were not areas of concern to the governments that were running the brothels, to the medical profession, to the history books, or to the field of international studies until very recently. Kwa's story about turn-of-the-twentieth-century prostitutes and their yearnings took place some one hundred years before today's growing sex tourism in countries such as Thailand, but the poignancy of the tale and the attempt to give voice to the unnamed are still very relevant in our globalized world. Keller's narrative of prostitutes in the Korean camptown of the 1960s resonates today, because the areas around U.S. military bases from Guam and the Philippines to Okinawa still experience high rates of sex crimes, including rape and pedophilia (see Transnational Institute, "Sex Crimes and Prostitution"). Masculinity and the needs of men still tend to take precedence in the construction of the nation and of militarization. Kathy Miriam, who takes a radical feminist abolitionist approach to prostitution, argues that "coercion, consent and agency are intricately bound together in a shared paradigm of *domination*. *Domination* can be best described, not as coercion or force, but as *a relation of access*, a relation that is embedded within a range of institutions that tacitly presuppose the *legitimacy* of this relation" ("Stopping the Traffic in Women," 13). For Miriam, what needs to be interrogated is "men's (and other dominant groups') politically and tacitly legitimized *demand* to have physical, sexual and emotional access to the capacities and bodies of other (e.g., gendered) groups of people" (13).

Although it is true that in almost all patriarchal societies the wishes of men are dominant in any case, in military prostitution and in colonial Singapore, femininity is hyperbolically reformulated to suit the needs of soldiers, sailors, and laborers. The desires of women to have children, to be wives and grandmothers, have no place in these societies created largely for the comfort of men. Although the soldiers and marines who use the brothels can always return home, there is no other home for the prostitutes. Admittedly, it was also hard for coolie laborers to establish traditional homes, but their lives were not as irreparably damaged by disease, by violence, by shame and abjection, as were the lives of the *ah ku* who serviced them. By incorporating the experiences of real women in their fiction, Kwa and Keller have performed the important act of revision. As Adrienne Rich writes, "Re-vision—the act of looking back, of seeing with fresh eyes, of entering an old text from a new critical direction—is for women more than a chapter in cultural history: it is an act of survival [...]. And this drive to self-knowledge, for women, is more than a search for identity: it is part of our refusal of the self-destructiveness of male-dominated society" (*On Lies, Secrets, and Silences*, 35).

II

Performing and Negotiating Transcultural Identities

3
"All of Us Are the Same":
Negotiating Loss, Witnessing Disability

> The body is never a single physical thing so much as a series of attitudes towards it.
>
> —*Lennard J. Davis*, Bending Over Backwards

That our bodies have been the site of various socially constructed meanings has been recognized by a number of feminist critics from Simone de Beauvoir to Judith Butler. In the past decade, cultural and race theorists have also argued that race is ideologically constructed and that racial identity is a process dependent on social and historical circumstances (see Omi and Winant, "On the Theoretical Status of the Concept of Race," 203). More recently, scholars who work on disability have contended that "disability is an unstable category" similarly dependent on material circumstances, social perception, and representation (Davis, *Bending Over Backwards*, 9). Lennard Davis points out that "disability studies demands a shift from the ideology of normalcy, from the rule and hegemony of normates, to a vision of the body as changeable, unperfectable, unruly, and untidy" (39).

He disagrees with the notion that the rest of society leads independent lives while those with disabilities do not. For Davis, in contemporary "dismodern" society we are all, in one way or another, dependent on things like cars, computers, microwaves, pills, body surgery, diets, dental work, hair color, eyeglasses, and so on, to achieve "normalcy" in our daily lives. In addition, half of us who are "able" today will not be so by the time we reach the age of sixty-five and beyond. The distinction between "us and them," between the physically able and the "disabled," therefore is false and needs careful rethinking (9 ff.).

Interest in and concern for people with disabilities have begun to increase in recent years in public discourse and the media. Although most of the discussion focuses on rights and accessibility, there are some works that attempt to use the body of people with disabilities to critique our current social practices and assumptions. Two recent plays by Asian Canadians feature protagonists with disabilities: Betty Quan's *Mother Tongue* and Sunil Kuruvilla's *Rice Boy*, respectively, depict Steve, a young man who is deaf and mute, and Tina, a young woman who cannot walk. What is significant about these works is that they offer us a chance to look at the way positions of otherness and marginality, such as those created by displacement, race, ethnicity, economic inequities, disability, and gender, intersect and constitute the formation of subjectivities in our contemporary globalized world. The plays reveal how discourses of race, otherness, disability, and gender are mapped onto racialized bodies simultaneously. This chapter explores these mappings and the role of memory, fantasy, and myth in the negotiation of loss and desire for Asians in the diaspora who have experienced transnational displacements. I argue that the liminal figure of those with disabilities works to delineate and challenge boundaries between dominant and minority culture, the ones with power and the disempowered, the voiced and the voiceless, the located and the rootless.

Over a decade ago, Misha Berson noted that the Asian American playwrights in his book collection had created characters who were caught "'between worlds,' suspended between countries of origin and adopted homelands" (*Between Worlds*, ix). In Quan and Kuruvilla's plays the characters are not so much "between" worlds as they are positioned in multiple worlds simultaneously. Both plays use double stages to signify the characters' transnational states of being. As they attempt to become assimilated citizens of Canada, the characters still maintain, either by their own efforts or through their parents, social, psychic, and even geographic ties with their countries of origin, China and India, respectively. The two plays use young protagonists to explore the theme of searching for one's identity within transnational families and communities, look at the ways in which language can and cannot express our dreams, and hint at various possibilities of escape and freedom. The character with a disability in each of the plays introduces an innovative aspect to the often-used and predictable plots of conflicts between the first and the second generation, the Old World and the New World. The presence of such a character in each of the plays accentuates the condition of being dislocated and disenfranchised. At the same time, this character reveals the ways in which marginality of various forms delimits one's identity and affects one's psyche and subjectivity.

Speaking in Tongues

Language and communication are central themes in Quan's *Mother Tongue*, a play that was a finalist for the 1996 Governor General's Award for drama.[1] Communicating with each other in three languages—English, Cantonese, and American Sign Language—the characters enact the linguistic, psychological, and social problems of what it means to be a displaced other or a perpetual stranger, in Etienne Balibar's sense of the term, in Canadian society. Balibar argues that *"foreigners* are those 'other humans' or precisely *strangers* who already belong to other spaces, who are citizens from different states, either by descent or by adoption" ("Strangers as Enemies," 4). He explains, "'Strangeness' and the various conditions referred to by the category of the Stranger are nothing natural, but they are produced and therefore also reproduced. They are not stable, but unstable and mobile" (4). As Chinese Canadians of varying ages and abilities, the three characters—the widowed immigrant mother; the young woman Mimi, who aspires to study architecture; and Steve, the sixteen-year-old who cannot hear—are all trapped by their fears, the expectations of the family members both in Canada and beyond, their pasts, and their linguistic disabilities. Steve, the figure with a disability, is the one most obviously unable to express himself, but the mother is, too, because she speaks mainly Cantonese and is not able to communicate with her son or with the social workers she has to deal with. Although Mimi is the most versatile of the three and is fluent in English, can understand Cantonese, and can sign, she, too, is hesitant about articulating her desires. She is burdened by her sense of family responsibility, with the guilt of her brother's deafness, and fears that she will be unable to pursue her career freely. As Asian Canadians, all three characters have to struggle not only with their individual fears and inadequacies—those of growing up, losing a husband, pursuing a career—but also with ethnocultural differences that add another layer of complication. Their linguistic difficulties, in the cases of Steve and his mother, exacerbate the problem of being strangers or being different in their community.

To illustrate the difficulties of communication and the borders created by linguistic differences, Quan does not translate many passages for the audience.[2] The mother speaks mostly in Cantonese, while the brother signs. When Mimi talks to them, she repeats enough of their words for us to understand what the mother and the brother said. On this issue of what is not translated, Julie Byczynski argues that "in the theatre, where language is normally shared by actors, and audience, dialogue spoken in minority languages can function in ways that upset the position of the dominant language *as* dominant [...]. Foreign dialogue has the potential to call into question the seeming authority that the English language has" ("A Word in a Foreign Language," 33). The foreign dialogue is disconcerting and somewhat confusing, mimicking the state of the characters who cannot use English well. This inability to communicate and to be heard is also expressed repeatedly through imagery of drowning. Early in the play the mother says, "I speak Chinese. Your voices. Your words. You drown me out" (scene 1). For the mother, who came to Canada when she was eighteen, not speaking a word of English, the English babble of her children as well as the people in her community is overwhelming. Even though she has spent more than thirty years in Vancouver, English continues to be a threatening language. It is the language of officials, of government forms, and she is constantly afraid of losing the social assistance she receives. Similarly, Steve feels that his condition of not being able to hear at all or not speak well is "like liquid. Drowning [...]. The waves of air [...] circulating. It's like that inside my head. Air floats inside me. The sound of ether rising [...]. Air forming into sounds I can't hear. Into words I can't speak. Into sentences no one will listen to" (scene 2). For Steve, losing his sense of hearing after a bout of high fever at age eleven has meant years of struggling to stay above the water, to not be swallowed up by nothingness.

As Lennard Davis has pointed out, impairment becomes a disability only because of the lack of resources of the person affected. Davis says, "In the social model, disability is presented as a social and political problem that turns an impairment into an oppression either by erecting barriers or by refusing to create barrier-free environments" (*Bending Over Backwards,* 23). For example, many of us are nearsighted. But having impaired vision is not considered a disability in our society because we have access to relatively affordable glasses or contact lenses. Steve is able to communicate as long as there are people around him who understand his signs. As his sister points out, "He's deaf, not retarded" (scene 7). But because there are not enough people in our community who are trained to communicate with those with deafness, it becomes a disability that is terrifying, rendering him helpless. Hence, he associates it with drowning. In his own family, though his mother cares for him, she has not taken the trouble of learning sign language. She says, "I have to learn English. Too late now" (scene 3). Steve's sister, Mimi, is the only one who understands him and is able to translate his desires for him. Upon discovering that Mimi is planning on moving to Kingston to study at Queen's University, he is almost frantic with despair and pleads, "Don't go, Mimi. Don't leave me all alone" (scene 2). Her mobility will become his immobility, because without her his impairment will become a major disability.

For the mother, the lack of English skills is also threatening because it is associated with powerlessness in a predominantly Anglo, logocentric culture. Like many immigrant parents, she relies on her daughter to be the "translator," to fill in government forms, answer phone calls, talk to doctors, and pay bills. Mimi becomes her link to the world outside as well as her link to Steve, who can speak only in American Sign Language. English is the language that her children speak, and she feels isolated from them because along with the loss of their Chinese language has come the loss of heritage and customs. The mother is particularly anxious because her children may or may not practice the Chinese traditions she values, such as *Chingming,* that of honoring one's ancestors (scene 3). In a monologue she says, "I often feel as if I bore strangers who have my eyes, my skin, my hair, but whose souls have been stolen by invisible spirits" (scene 3). Part of the mother's fears stem from her traumatic experiences in China, where, she says, "every night we would turn out the lights, draw the curtains. We waited for the knock at the door. It could be a friend, a neighbour—wearing a Red Army badge, ready to take everything away from us. To take everything away from me" (scene 7). She has brought this terror of authorities with her to Canada, still relives it frequently, and feels that she cannot trust anyone—neighbors, friends, or government agencies. The death of her husband has only added to her insecurity. The play overtly links her dislocation and sense of being a perpetual foreigner with disability at this point, for the mother's apprehension about her daughter's departure parallels her son's fears of losing his sister, his translator.

As is typical of immigrant families with limited resources, the eldest child is saddled with many of the responsibilities of the family. Often the eldest is required to perform tasks that are carried out by adults in other families. Portes and Rumbaut, who have studied second-generation youths from different national origins and class backgrounds, describe the kind of experience Mimi has with her family as "dissonant acculturation" rather than the more ideal "consonant acculturation" (paraphrased by Levitt and Waters in the introduction to *The Changing Face of Home*, 17). "Dissonant acculturation occurs when young people quickly adopt American ways and the English language and their parents do not move as quickly. This is the trajectory that leads to role reversal: Children must translate for their parents, and they become more worldly and sophisticated about American ways, leaving their immigrant parents relatively powerless and often dependent on them," whereas in "consonant acculturation" the parents and children "learn the new culture and abandon the old one at the same pace" (Portes and Rumbaut as paraphrased by Levitt and Waters, 17). Levitt and Waters suggest that the level of transnational involvement of the parental generation influences the way second-generation youth are acculturated (17). In Mimi's family the parents maintain a high level of cultural and emotional transnationalism, as reflected by the two-location and double-time stages, but the second-generation youths have not had as much opportunity to learn or interest in learning about their cultural heritage or in maintaining transnational networks as their parents have.

One of the adult "jobs" that Mimi had to take on as a teenager resulted in Steve's deafness. Years before, when Steve was sick with a fever, their mother had asked Mimi to take him to the doctor because she had to work overtime. At sixteen Mimi was more interested in attending the game at school than in her brother's illness. Her forgetfulness had dire consequences for her brother, and this failure to act is something she has been unable to forget. In a flashback dream scene where we see the past, she says, "For years I've been sorry. Make a fist and circle it on my chest. Sorry" (scene 4). The highlighting of her remorse through her statement, first in English and then in sign language, has a ritualistic and mesmerizing effect on stage. It is a kind of repetition and, like the repetition of certain dialogues in Cantonese and then in English, adds an element of the spiritual and the dramatic. Words accompanied by gestures—or, in the case of the mother's dialogue, Cantonese followed by English—produce a chantlike rhythmic effect, an otherworldliness that reminds us of other ways of communicating and speaking. Mimi lives in a transcultural world within her own family: she has had to negotiate with the diasporic Chinese culture of her mother, with the mainstream English Canadian culture and social practices by which she is surrounded, and with her brother's silent world of gestures. Through the repetition of sign language and spoken dialogue, through the repetition of Cantonese and English dialogues, we are shown some of the difficulties of a second-generation immigrant youth, as well as the troubles a racialized other with a disability has to deal with in the simple act of communication in his everyday life.

Although the problems depicted in the play are present in many Asian Canadian families and in the families of recent immigrants, the figure of the youth with a disability serves to intensify the challenges faced by these families. Steve's dependency on his sister and others to translate his needs and wants is a more acute version of what immigrants in Canada with little English (or French) experience in their daily lives. His frustration at not being able to say all the things inside his head is also reminiscent of those immigrants whose mother tongue is not English. Often what they can express is only a fraction of what they want to say. They, like Steve, have many words inside them, but their utterances, in broken or badly pronounced English, are heard by others as garbled and are not listened to closely.

The inability to communicate not only impedes a subject in his or her quotidian activities, such as shopping, banking, accessing health and social services, and so on, but it has psychic effects on the subject.

In her work on the formation of subjectivity, Kelly Oliver argues that our experience of ourselves as subjects is maintained "in the tension between our subject positions and our subjectivity" (*Witnessing*, 17). She explains: "Subject positions, although mobile, are constituted in our social interactions and our positions within our culture and context. They are determined by history and circumstance [...]. Subjectivity, on the other hand, is experienced as the sense of agency and response-ability that are constituted in the infinite encounter with otherness, which is fundamentally ethical [...]. Both are always profoundly interconnected" (17). In this play Mimi, Steve, and their mother all occupy subject positions that are marginal vis-à-vis the dominant white, patriarchal, able-bodied culture. For them, becoming full subjects requires "encounters with others" that are positive. In theories of identity based on recognition, Oliver says, there is the sense that "individual identity is constituted intersubjectively; that we come to recognize ourselves as subjects or active agents through recognition from others; that a positive sense of self is dependent on positive recognition from others, while a negative sense of self is the result of negative recognition or lack of recognition from others" (4). Oliver goes a step further and argues that "subjectivity is the result of the process of witnessing" (7). Witnessing means both "eyewitness testimony based on first-hand knowledge" and "bearing witness to something beyond recognition that can't be seen" (16). Oliver places emphasis on understanding those who are different from us: "There is a direct connection between the response-ability of subjectivity and ethical and political responsibility. The way in which we conceive of subjectivity affects the way that we conceive of our relationships and responsibilities to others, especially others whom we perceive as different from ourselves" (19).

What we have in *Mother Tongue* are two characters, Steve and his mother, who have difficulty in addressing others, in what Oliver calls witnessing. According to Oliver, those who have been othered have experienced trauma, and "witnessing works to ameliorate the trauma particular to othered subjectivity" (7). The number of people who actually listen to and can understand either Steve or his mother is limited. For this reason, the play *Mother Tongue* is important because it bears witness to their trauma of being culturally, linguistically, and racially different—as well as their trauma of being less than able economically and physically in a globalized world that emphasizes ability; linguistic competence, particularly in global English; technical competency; and literacy. Steve and his mother have difficulties acquiring and using these skills. In our position as audience members, we are the ones being addressed, and we are those who have the "response-ability" and the "ethical and political responsibility" (19) of seeing those who have been othered in our society with "love," a term Oliver uses to denote an attitude of "openness to otherness and difference" (20). Oliver believes that "we are fundamentally connected to our environment and other people through the circulation of energies that sustain us" (15). She states, "We are obligated to respond to our environment and other people in ways that open up rather than close off the possibility of response" (15). Significantly, at the end of the play Steve, like Oliver, also refers to the unseen things in our environment that connect us. His inner voice says:

> Can you see the words as they float in the air? My hands release them—out, out to be heard. Can you see the wind? The branches bending, the wind's fingers drumming against the window. There—thunder. The vibration crosses my spine. I can hear it. Yes, there's lightning. Music, music touches the floorboards, rises through my feet. My body hears all these sounds. Listen to my hands as I speak to you. Listen to me. Please. (scene 10)

This passage suggests that other forms of communication are possible through feeling, intuition, and gestures. It suggests that nature and even inanimate objects can offer connections. Steve's appeal is uncannily similar to philosopher Kelly Oliver's "new conception of vision," which is based in part on Luce Irigaray's theories. Oliver writes, "Imagining vision as circulation of energy through connections and touch, even caress, allows us to imagine our fundamental dependence on each other. Subjectivity is not the result of a war against all others. Rather, it is the result of a process of witnessing that connects us through the tissues of language and gestures" (223). It is this process of witnessing and communication that we experience when we watch this play about a racialized other with a disability.

Connections, communication, and transculturalism are further highlighted in *Mother Tongue* through its stage set and playing areas. In the Factory Theatre production in Toronto in 2001, there was a split stage: the realist scenes of present-day Vancouver in front and to the left of the audience and the dreamlike flashback scenes toward the right side and back of the audience. This set caused several critics to complain. For example, Glenn Sumi of *Now Magazine* in Toronto humorously wrote,

> That's [looking at one's watch is] better than looking at Glenn Davidson's set, though, which requires turning your head about two dozen times, tennis-match style. Director Jim Warren has staged the play, which explores the difficulties of communication and language in an immigrant Chinese family, on several playing areas. That's to underscore the theme of bridging gaps. And who's gonna pay my chiropractor bill?

As Sumi notes, the set symbolically suggests the need to build bridges, but, more important, it adds a surreal element to the play. Unlike the primary area, which represents the interior of a home, the other area, painted blue, suggests water, waves, and a more abstract space. Through this split stage the director is able to provide a dreamlike visual backdrop for the sections of the play from the characters' memory and for the sections dealing with Chinese myths and their past. The stage evocatively suggests the strong presence of the past and the continuing influence of their originary culture in the lives of these diasporic Asian Canadians.

The story of the bird Jingwei, a well-known Chinese myth told to children, is alluded to several times in the play. It is a story that reminds the two children, Mimi and Steve, of happier times, before the sudden death of their father and before Steve's deafness. Their father used to tell Mimi of the beloved young daughter of the emperor who drowned one day while playing in the sea. She was supposed to have been changed into a bird with a colorful head, Jingwei, who would carry bits of twigs and stone from the mountains to the sea in order to fill it up. The story suggests love and loss, transformation and heroism. Jingwei is associated with all three of the main characters in the play. The mother uses "Jingwei" as a term of endearment and calls Mimi by that nickname (scene 3). Mimi's role as translator, mediator, and eldest daughter of the family is an endless and difficult one. She is like the bird, who every day "would pick up pebbles and twigs in her beak and drop them into the water" in order to fill up the sea (scene 12). Although the bird's task seems like an impossible one, one admires its persistence, effort, and endurance.

Because both Steve and the mother have also suffered sudden loss, it is possible to link the myth of the drowned girl to them. Steve's deafness is figured as a kind of drowning, and the mother's departure from her family and homeland at age eighteen can be seen as a kind of loss. Her displacement, like that of many first-generation immigrants, has been a kind of exile and sacrifice. Their struggles to cope with their loss are as heroic as Jingwei's attempt to fill up the sea with her sticks and stones. All three characters in *Mother Tongue* attempt in their own way to defy the Sea God, who says, "You can never fill me up in a million years" (scene 12). But according to Jingwei, "Every day for a million years I will do this. Every day until one day there will be no more water between me and my family. I will build a bridge, a bridge that they can walk across" (scene 12). Steve, the character with a disability, struggles with such epic tasks daily, but the task of building bridges is also something that his mother and his sister, as marginalized figures in Canadian society, also face to a lesser degree in their lives. *Mother Tongue* reveals the difficulties of those who have been produced as "strangers" to cross borders and bridges in order to become full citizens of their adoptive community.

Ethnicity and Disability

Sunil Kuruvilla's *Rice Boy*,[3] a play that was also nominated for the Governor General's Award, similarly uses a character with a disability to illustrate parallels between disability and ethnic identity. The action takes place in 1975 in two distant locations—Kitchener, Ontario, and Kottayam in south India. Like *Mother Tongue*, it is a play about displacement, loss, and desire in an extended Asian Canadian family. It is more layered than *Mother Tongue* because, in addition to the main story of Tommy, a twelve-year-old Indian Canadian, there is a corresponding story of his Indian cousin, Tina, a sixteen-year-old girl who cannot walk, and a subplot involving a fish seller and a servant girl in India. One reviewer, Lisa Rabie, notes,

> *Rice Boy* does not imitate the inveterate models in western theater, and Kuruvilla breaks almost all of the golden rules. He allows the play to wander along lyrically between two continents and two different time periods with sporadic flares of dramatic action that seem somewhat disjointed and jarring. But, the episodic nature of the play allows *Rice Boy* to spend less energy on plot and more lovingly create vivid and profound characters ("*Rice Boy* Explores Search for Identity").

Rice Boy, Yale Repertory Theatre, New Haven, Connecticut, October 2000. Angel Desai as Tina; Wayne Kesserman as Tommy. Photograph by T. Charles Erickson; used with permission.

The two settings, that of Canada and that of India, are held together by the presence of the boy Tommy and his father. The disjointed narrative and the loosely connected plot are suggestive of the condition of both Tommy and his father as diasporic Indians. The scenes flit back and forth between present-day Canada and vignettes of the previous summer, spent in India. Like many Asian Canadians and Asian Americans, Tommy and his father inhabit a transcultural space, not fully belonging to one or to the other. Cheap means of transportation in the age of globalization allow them to travel between the two worlds, but their visits to India do not resolve their problems when they return to Canada. At the beginning of the play Tommy feels that his father is not Canadian enough, while his father does not think that Tommy behaves in an appropriate way as an Indian son. Tommy complains to his father: "All you do is sleep [...]. We came back from India six months ago! You're going to lose your job again" (*Rice Boy*, 4). His father, fighting depression, shows his displaced state by sleeping on the kitchen counter and remembering what he used to be and what his life was like. He reminds his son, "I was a math professor once" (5), but in Canada he has been able to find work only in various menial jobs, including a factory job at Kitchener Datsun, and more recently at Mother's Pizza. His difficulty in finding suitable employment equivalent to that he had in India is a common problem of educated immigrants who leave Asia only to have to take blue-collar jobs because they lack North American experience or because their degrees are not recognized. Studies of the adjustment of Asian Canadian immigrants and refugees show that "perceived discrimination, unemployment, and language difficulty each had significant and positive associations with depression" (Beiser and Hou, "Ethnic Identity among Southeast Asian Refugees in Canada"). In her study of Asian American immigrants, Yen Le Espiritu notes that frequently

> the patriarchal authority of Asian immigrant men, particularly those of the working class, has been challenged due to the social and economic losses that they suffered in their transition to the status of men of color in the United States. On the other hand, the recent growth of female-intensive industries—and the racist and sexist "preference" for the labor of immigrant women—has enhanced women's employability over that of some men. ("Gender and Labor in Asian Immigrant Families," 628)

Although Tommy's father is not competing with his wife, he is haunted by memories of her, for she supposedly drowned or disappeared while swimming in a river in India. He tells his son: "When you get older you stop thinking. All you do is remember" (*Rice Boy*, 5). This inability to go forward and to embrace what the future has to offer becomes a theme that is echoed by a number of characters in the play. Tommy's father; his uncle; his cousin, Tina; Mr. Harris; and even the Mennonite farmer are all circumscribed by the past, their cultural traditions, and their fears of the future. Through the stories of these disparate everyday characters, Kuruvilla gives us a glimpse of the difficulties of dealing with loss and change—whether from migration across the globe, growing pains, or the shifting roles and expectations of women. As in *Mother Tongue*, the figure of the person with a disability shows in a physical and literal way what other characters experience psychically and internally.

Rice Boy begins with an elaborate ritual performed in India by women. Tina is practicing how to make rice kolam patterns, the south Indian tradition of drawing patterns based on geometry on the entrance of a house (see Aparita, "Review of *Rice Boy*"). These patterns, made of the powder from ground rice, disappear within hours, and as Kuruvilla notes in the introduction to the play, "The creation and destruction of the kolam enacts the struggle to find pattern and stillness amidst the flux of life" (*Rice Boy*, n.p.). Kuruvilla says that the characters in his play "find it difficult to accept the kolam's message: all things are impermanent and should be celebrated for being so. But they try" (n.p.). However, the making of the kolam patterns is also about ritual, tradition, the creation and loss of beauty, and discipline. For Tina, who is unable to walk, it is a way to demonstrate her "normalcy." As Granny teaches her how to put water into her palm and water onto the floor, she says, "You will do this every morning like the other wives in this village" (7). Granny sees it as part of the marriage ritual, linking it to other pleasures and comforts that an Indian wife provides for her husband. Performing the ritual is one way that Tina will become "eligible" to wed her prospective husband. For a few hours every day, she is able to create an artistic showpiece as do other women of the village.

However, because Tina cannot walk, she is not like the other women of the village. She is at once the same as and different from other women. Kuruvilla uses her body with its disability to comment on and contrast with the bodies of those around her. Her physical limitations mirror the limitations of various characters in the play, suggesting parallels between characters, between disability, ethnicity, race, and other forms of otherness. Kuruvilla invites his audience to think of similarities through repetitions of scenes and motifs. For example, in one of the early scenes set in India, Tommy climbs up a coconut tree and describes what he sees to Tina, who remains below. Tina encourages him to climb higher and higher, saying, "Describe. Keep going. What do the houses look like? Are they different from this one? You can be my eyes. How wide is the road? What do the buses look like? And the trucks? They paint big names on the front, don't they? I've heard them drive by all my life" (10). Tina has been restricted to her house for much of her life, and only with Tommy's visit does she venture beyond her patio. Tommy says to her, "I can see the whole world. What can you see?" Tina says, "The bottom of your feet" (12). Tommy later encourages Tina to leave the house with him in the night and go see the city. Tommy's seemingly limitless view is an illusion, however. Even though Tina cannot see far away, she sees what matters. Unlike Tommy, she remembers Tommy's mother's death, and when Tommy is up in the tree, she sees his blood on the ground, dripping from Tommy's nose. What Kuruvilla is suggesting is two different types of vision—one that sees the outside globalized world of commerce, progress, and industry and the other that sees the seemingly insignificant details of everyday domestic life. Encounters with others bring out different ways of seeing and viewing the world, as this scene between Tina and Tommy shows.

This scene is repeated later in Canada when Tommy meets a Mennonite farmer in the countryside. Again Tommy climbs up a tree and looks out at the world. The Mennonite farmer tells him that he was born on the farm and has never "gone past that road" his whole life (20). Each sees the other as a curiosity. Tommy says to the Mennonite: "You wear black and don't believe in electricity" (19), while the Mennonite says to Tommy, "I've never seen a brown fella before" (19) and inspects him. When Tommy is up in the tree, the farmer, like Tina, asks Tommy, "What do you see?" Tommy answers with "A big field. Snow," which leaves the Mennonite unsatisfied (20). As in the scene with Tina, young Tommy's curiosity and spontaneity act as a catalyst for the Mennonite farmer, triggering in him desires that he has not yet fulfilled. The Mennonite, someone who has consciously retreated from capitalism and technology, ends up by climbing the tree himself at the conclusion of the scene, gazing outward. But the encounters go both ways. The Mennonite's austere life inspires Tommy to confide in him and confess his past misdemeanors. Tommy tells him, "When I see nice pictures in a magazine, I eat them. I steal jam from the grocery store and drop the bottles from the bridge near our house" (19). Tommy's difficulties come from his family's displacement as well as from having experienced racism as a child. He says, "At lunchtime the children chase me round the school-house with a skipping rope and try to hang me from a tree. It's because my father's from India" (19). Because of his feeling of dislocation, Tommy spends a great deal of time searching for substitute father figures and ways to belong. The Mennonite farmer is one such father figure whom Tommy meets and then rejects. The similarities between this encounter and the one with Tina suggest that these characters offer different ways of perceiving the world. Both Tina and the Mennonite are circumscribed and limited in their own ways, but they are useful for Tommy's development because they serve to bring out his own inadequacies and fantasies and help him see where his strengths lie.

The motif of the lost father is brought out more overtly in another scene set in Canada. Tommy reads about the disappearance of a twelve-year-old-boy, Doug Harris, from St. Jacobs, Ontario, on the back of a milk carton. In a rather surreal scene, he goes to visit Mr. Harris and offers himself as a substitute son:

> Mr. Harris. I don't have blond hair or blue eyes. I'm taller than 4 feet 8 inches and bigger than 100 pounds but I can be your son. I'll shine your shoes Sunday mornings if you wake me up. I'll shovel the porch if you do the drive. I'll dry if you wash. All you have to do is feed me and take me for rides in the car wash. I'll be proud to eat with you at the A & W instead of making you do drive-thru. People won't stare at us when we buy our groceries at Zehr's. You won't talk with an accent. You'll teach me how to throw a spiral. You'll do oil changes in the driveway. (37)

This passage reveals Tommy's desperate desire for assimilation, belonging, and the erasure of racial difference. Comic and at the same time full of pathos, it shows the pain of always being marked as racially other and different. Tommy's desires to be "normal" are mundane and almost comic. He wants to have a father who does the kind of "manly" things one expects in a Western society—teach him to play ball, shovel the driveway, fix cars. Yet these are precisely the day-to-day rituals that are not performed by many ethnic or immigrant families. David Eng notes of psychic identification:

> We must remember that idealized images such as masculinity, heterosexuality, and whiteness also imply an obverse set of images such as femininity, homosexuality, and racialization. These culturally devalued images are ones that socially marked subjects are encouraged to loath. Even more, they are encouraged to disidentify with these images. When held to these unpleasant and devalued identifications, the subject experiences them as external impositions, which leads to a negative sense of self and psychic sense of dislocation. (*Racial Castration*, 115)

Tommy's father, though heterosexual, is feminized in North America because he cannot and does not do those "normal [...] Canadian things" like "camping," "mini-golf," and "water-skiing" (*Rice Boy*, 5). In addition, he is economically disenfranchised because of his low-paying jobs and associated with traditional feminine roles because he works for a restaurant and sleeps on the kitchen counter. Psychically, Tommy disidentifies with his father and searches for the idealized white, masculine father who is validated and upheld by Western culture.

Though Tommy and Mr. Harris play at being father and son for a while, the substitution does not entirely succeed. Tommy provokes Mr. Harris's fantasies of his son's return—he imagines taking Tommy to the farmer's market, to a hockey game, to the father-son Christmas dinner at church—but Tommy does not sound like Doug, and the reality of Tommy's identity keeps intruding into their playacting. The scene ends abruptly, in a way as unreal as it began, when Mr. Harris says, "For a few moments you made me feel better. Thank you. You should leave" (51). Through this scene Kuruvilla suggests that the kind of full assimilation Tommy craves will not be the answer to otherness and racial difference. Tommy needs to find another way of dealing with issues of identity and marginalization. He cannot just pretend that his past and his Indian roots do not exist, just as Mr. Harris cannot will away his past and the loss of his son.

In a similar way, Tommy and his cousin, Tina, play at being husband and wife when they go into the city together. Because of her disability, Tina, too, has to work through issues of subjectivity and otherness that others around her do not experience. She is a young woman yet not regarded by most people in society as "desirable" or attractive because of her inability to walk. The playacting of Tommy with the girl with a disability functions in a different way from his playacting with Mr. Harris. With Mr. Harris what Tommy was searching for was belonging, specifically to normative white Canadian culture. With Tina the experience contributes to Tommy's maturity and growth as a boy, his affective development and understanding of sexuality. Tommy conspires to roll Tina to the city at night, when the others are sleeping, saying, "You don't have to wait until you get married" (23). Though ostensibly about their night escapade, the language here and the activity are sexually charged. For Tina the clandestine trip is a big adventure, her chance to do what others have done. She says to Tommy, "I've never seen these many people in one place [...]. I want to do everything, Husband" (32). Though Tina is sixteen and older than Tommy, twelve-year-old Tommy is the one who takes charge of her. He introduces her to sights unseen by her previously and becomes somewhat dizzy himself with the experience. It is also around this time that Tommy becomes aware of his own body, of his reproductive capacity and his sexuality. In a rather bizarre scene set in a half-frozen Canadian cornfield, Tommy masturbates on the ground, determined to plant his "little seeds" in order to have a "baby. A new Tommy. Good Tommy. Canadian" (55). Tina's impending marriage and her role-playing with Tommy lead to his fantasy of a regeneration without the feelings of abjection and otherness he himself feels.

In a subsequent scene of bathing, Tina inadvertently awakens Tommy's sexuality, and together they enjoy a secret sensual moment. Tommy takes over the servant girl's job of shampooing Tina's hair while her eyes are closed and while she is not wearing her sari. Though her breasts are bare, they touch each other only with their hands, lathering her hair at the same time. This scene, though brief, is an important one because it is the first time we, as an audience, see Tina as something other than a crippled girl. On stage, it is an erotic and electrically charged scene. It effectively works to reverse our preconceptions of Tina's disabled body. Disability theorist Susan Wendell points out that "disabled women suffer more than disabled men from the demand that people have "ideal" bodies, because in patriarchal culture people judge women more by their bodies than they do men. Disabled women often do not feel seen (because they are often not seen) by others as whole people, especially not as sexual people" ("Toward a Feminist Theory of Disability," 268). Kuruvilla lets the audience see Tina as a sexual woman and allows her to articulate her fears, her desires to be like other women, and her wish to be loved and adored. She is afraid of disappointing her future husband when he sees her legs, afraid that he will find her ugly. At the same time, she dreams of being chosen to "read the news on state television" (*Rice Boy*, 44). She says, "My face is pretty enough. You wouldn't see my legs behind the desk. I'm going to wander the streets until I get picked" (44). Tina's excursion to the city and her role-playing with Tommy provide her with an opportunity for adventure, for fantasy and excitement, without the burden of responsibility and tradition. It is a moment when she can forget about her legs that do not work, her disability, and her otherness, which set her apart from the women around her.

The play is like a fable in many ways, with enigmatic meanings about loss, drowning, and death and unfulfilled dreams and romances. Disability is only one of the many reasons that the characters' hopes and dreams are not realized. At the end of the play we are left with a series of losses experienced by the characters both in India and in Canada. A number of women disappear unaccountably. Tina, like Tommy's mother, goes missing. When Tommy asks Granny where Tina has gone, for she has been missing for the last six months, he is given only a number of speculations—that she died, that she arranges shoes "when people go into the Taj Mahal," that she "lives in Vellore and eats rose water ice cream, for breakfast," and that "she was hit by a train" (63). Tommy thinks that it is possible that she is "sliding around" and wandering somewhere in the city (73). But the family and the audience never learn the truth about her. Tina's disappearance echoes that of Tommy's mother, who, according to Tommy, "drowned 10 years ago" when they went to India and she went swimming in the river (20). The fact that they never found her body, however, leads Granny to create doubts in Tommy's father's mind: "She sunk to the bottom of the river. Or was carried to the sea. Or did she just swim away? Is she in Cape Comoran eating beef biriyani in a five-star? Is she in Mysore sucking on a mango seed as she swings in a hammock? Your beautiful wife walks in the Nilgris wiping the soap from another man's ear" (35). Though we do not know much about Tommy's mother, she is associated through imagery and description with the sensuality and nostalgic feelings of India. The father remembers her hand: "It smelled like this skin. The gold sari she'd wear to church. Bright as a flag. We'd come home and I'd unwrap her. Going in circles, moving away from her body and then in the end, moving close. Rolling on the ground. Silk in the mouth. The taste like hair" (4–5). Granny insinuates that Tommy's mother, like Tina, may have desired another life other than what the family expected. Both Tina and Tommy's mother had their own dreams, and both of them mysteriously disappeared, leaving the audience to speculate about their ends. They have either died tragically or succeeded in following their fantasies of freedom from conventionality.

    The subplot involving the fish seller and the servant girl, his ex-wife, also echoes the themes of loss, thwarted desires, and belonging raised in the main plot. Like Tommy's father, the fish seller has only memories of his relationship with his wife. He remembers "taking lessons at the post office" in order to read to his wife (60), as well as the sensuality of their sexual relationship. But because of the servant girl's desire to move up in the world, to better herself, she has disassociated herself from the fish seller, who, she says, stinks and has filthy hands. She says: "Long ago, you spread your fish smell all over me, onto my body, into my hair. I am clean now. And beautiful. But I'm always sad"

(72). In response, the fish seller reminds her, "We are not like them. But you think that you are" (72). The cost of her desire for social mobility has meant loneliness and estrangement from the one who loved her.[4] By the end of the play, the fish seller drowns, leaving the servant girl waiting in futility for his return.

The various vignettes, plots, and subplots of the play suggest the inscrutable and ineluctable nature of happiness. Like the kolam patterns, happiness is fleeting, and beautiful patterns, though desired, do not last long in this world. In Kuruvilla's *Rice Boy* the condition of globality is revealed by the many parallels of the characters from India and Canada. The young woman with a disability in India is shown to have many of the same longings and struggles as other characters in the play. She has limited access and experiences of the world, but so does the Mennonite whom Tommy encounters in Canada. She has unfulfilled sexual and emotional desires; so do other women, such as the servant girl and Tommy's mother. She feels marginalized and excluded from full participation in her society; so does Tommy as the son of an Indian immigrant in Canada. Kuruvilla is not negating the particular experiences and the extreme difficulties of the disabled body, but he is demonstrating how disability is an added factor in the way one is othered and becomes an abject figure in society. *Rice Boy*, like *Mother Tongue*, makes the link between disability and racialized or gendered subjectivity, revealing the potential and possibilities for disabled bodies. The disabled and racialized figures have aspirations that are rendered impossible to fulfill by cultural assumptions and material constraints in our present society. At the very least, the two plays allow these marginalized figures to articulate their frustrations and their needs, to look critically at the ways disabled figures are often ignored in practices and discourses of capitalist enterprises, migration, and global cities. Hence, they function as "witnesses" (Oliver, *Witnessing*, 7) to the plight of those with disabilities. Quan and Kuruvilla use what De Certeau calls everyday "tactics"—the untranslated passages, the two-world parallel settings—to subvert and question the "ways of operating" and the power of the abled (*The Practice of Everyday Life*, 37, xix). By placing figures with disabilities on center stage, Quan and Kuruvilla have taken disability and ethnic disability out of the shadows and the invisible recesses of North America, making them topics of concern in contemporary global society.

4
Feminist Subversions: Comedy and the Carnivalesque

Nina Aquino and Nadine Villasin's play *Miss Orient(ed)* and Deepa Mehta's film *Bollywood/Hollywood* (2002), both set in Toronto, use humor, irony, and parody to question and challenge the insidious effects of global American culture on Asians, particularly those in the North American diaspora. First performed in Toronto in December 2001 and then again in the spring of 2003, *Miss Orient(ed)* is a raucous and entertaining theatrical production featuring an all-female cast of Filipina Canadians.[1] Set in the world of the "Miss Pearl of the Orient" beauty pageant, the play reveals the ways in which contemporary Filipinas have been stereotyped, socialized, misconceptualized, and misoriented. *Bollywood/Hollywood*, though primarily farcical and fun rather than serious like Mehta's other films, has its share of subversive critical and feminist elements. Mehta uses a seemingly lightweight musical comedy rather than a dramatic art house film to respond to some of the prevailing racial, socioeconomic, and gender ideologies in contemporary North American culture. The film parodies and pokes fun at Hollywood and Bollywood filmic practices and provides what anthropologists call "rich descriptions" of the local South Asian diasporic community in Toronto (see Featherstone, "Localism, Globalism, and Cultural Identity," 48).

Beauty and Filipina Bodies

Miss Orient(ed) playfully but powerfully explores the construction of Filipina North American subjectivities. Filipina bodies in the diaspora are sites of contestation, used nostalgically as the embodiment of the lost motherland (see McClintock, *Imperial Leather*, 354) and, at the same time, used to personify the success of the American dream. The multiple and, at times, conflicting identities and ideologies in contemporary society "discipline" Filipina women (Foucault, *Discipline and Punish*, 187 ff), their bodies, and their desires, causing some women to collude with the colonizing gaze, the discourse of imperialism, and Hollywood's ideals of beauty. Success in North America is sometimes achieved at the expense of the female body and often results in the commodification and commercialization of "native" culture. *Miss Orient(ed)* exhibits various ways in which young Filipina Canadians react to, collaborate with, and resist these confusing ideals and negotiate with both internal ethnic practices and the dominant culture's assumptions about the "Oriental" girl. Through numerous short vignettes of three aspiring beauty queens and their mothers, it reveals the complex and sometimes confusing ideals and identities of the "modern Filipina" (scene 17). One reviewer notes, "If there's an image of Filipinas that hasn't made it into *Miss Orient(ed)*—from Imelda Marcos to babysitters to Mariah Carey-wannabes—it probably doesn't exist" (Al-Solaylee, "Review of *Miss Orient(ed)*"). Through songs, exaggeration, camp, and monologues, the play pokes fun at, but at the same time poignantly depicts, the aspirations and, often, the misplaced hopes of two generations of Filipinas in America.

That the site of a beauty pageant is the setting of *Miss Orient(ed)* is significant for a number of reasons. Beauty pageants play a large role in the cultural and psychic landscape of people in the Philippines. The crowning of a "Miss Philippines" or the year's "Miss Universe" is much anticipated and is a more publicized event there than it is in North America.[2] One of the mothers of the play's contestants, Conching, remembers winning "Miss Pearl Bicol" when she was young: "Winning the crown was a dream come true for us. Well you know, beauty pageants are so important to us Filipinos" (scene 11: Conching). As scholars of beauty pageants have shown, the beauty contest may appear frivolous and trivial, but it stages "complex struggles over power and representation" (Lieu, "Remembering 'the Nation' through Pageantry," 127). It is

Poster image for *Miss Orient(ed)*, Factory Studio Theatre, Toronto, Ontario, May–June 2003. Courtesy of Nadine Villasin. http://www.missoriented.com.

situated in "multiple systems of culture, struggles for power and control, and discursive fields of practice" (127). As it plays out in other parts of the globe, the beauty pageant is a site where dominant discourses of nationalism are articulated. In the Philippines, in addition to expressing national pride, reinforcing "dominant constructions of gender and idealized forms of femininity" (127), the beauty pageant is also a version of the American dream. Contestants, their families, and spectators look to beauty pageants as an easy way to success, fame, wealth, and a passport abroad. Because beauty can supposedly break down barriers created by social class, education, and economic status, winning a pageant is like being spotted by Prince Charming at the ball.

Filipinos in cities such as Toronto, Vancouver, and San Francisco have recreated "Miss Philippines" or "Little Miss Philippines" beauty pageants in their communities (see Islanders BC, "Non-profit Society Launches 'Little Miss Forever Young Philippines' Beauty Pageant."). As in the home country, these beauty pageants in the diaspora stimulate national pride and build a sense of community. But, more important,

Beauty queens from *Miss Orient(ed)*: *(clockwise from left)* Christina Florencio, Nadine Villasin, Marie V. Cruz, and Nina Aquino. Courtesy of Nadine Villasin. http://www.missoriented.com.

these pageants and, by association, the contestants become the embodiment of the now distant "Pilipinas," the imagined beloved motherland. There is an added element of longing and nostalgia in these contests. Regarding this nostalgia, Susan Stewart says, "Hostile to history and its invisible origins, and yet longing for an impossibly pure context of lived experience at a place of origin, nostalgia wears a distinctly utopian face, a face that turns toward a future-past, a past which has only ideological reality" (*On Longing*, 23). This ideological reality presents challenges to Filipina women in the diaspora who have to measure up not only to their parents' past experiences and memories of the Philippines but to what Salman Rushdie calls the "fictions, not actual cities or villages, but invisible ones, imaginary homelands" of their minds (*Imaginary Homelands*, 10). To become "Miss Philippines" in Toronto or Vancouver, or to have to measure up to them, is to have to embody the symbol of the impossibly pure utopian homeland. At the same time, these contestants are often dealing with the quotidian pressures of their transnational family, assimilation, and the trials of growing up.

These difficulties, as well as the issue of ethnic female subjectivity, are brought to the foreground by *Miss Orient(ed)*. In the play, the character called the "beauty icon," who acts as the master of ceremonies, says with some irony that the requirements for the "Miss Pearl of the Orient" contest are, "number one: you must be female, was born female and have always been female"; number two: "You must have a minimum height of 5'4"''; number three: "you must be free of any involvement in any act of moral turpitude"; and "the last and most important requirement, number four: You must be Filipino!" (scene 2). These requirements, seemingly simple, are not as straightforward and innocent as they seem. These requirements function to discipline Filipina bodies and to produce them, in the Foucauldian sense, as Victorian feminine subjects. Ideal femininity is associated with the sexually innocent, while the height requirement implicitly ensures that the winner will conform to Western standards of beauty—tall like a European, not small like Asians. Although not explicitly stated here, later in the play contestants are assigned ratings based on their appearance, their abilities, and their backgrounds. The beauty icon explains that "bonus points are given to candidates who [...] are tall, have a lighter shade of black hair, have a waist that measures twelve inches smaller than her bust and hips, can speak and write fluent Filipino, can speak the English language without a Filipino accent, have a Spanish last name, can sing karaoke, can dance the tinikling, live in Mississauga, and are still virgins" (scene 6). Bonus points are even given to contestants with white boyfriends. Playwrights Aquino and Villasin note, with tongue in cheek, that to be the perfect Filipina beauty queen, a young woman has to be able to speak fluent Filipino yet look as European or North American as possible and efface traces of her Filipinaness in her speech when required.

In a similar way, the requirement of being "Filipino" is more complex than it looks. For example, contestants in the "Miss Philippines" contest that is part of Mississauga's Carassauga festival compete with other contestants from seventeen pavilions representing other countries such as Egypt, Greece, India, the Caribbean, Latin America, China, and Portugal (see CPO News, "March 22, 2003"). But because one can no longer simply use citizenship to demarcate the boundaries between the contestants from the seventeen pavilions, one has to create new rules. Identities cannot be taken for granted. Whereas in the Philippines all the contestants are Filipino citizens and presumably speak Tagalog or another of the many dialects of the Philippines, in Canada the identities of Filipinas have to be defined. Because citizenship, place of birth, and knowledge of a "native" language cannot be counted on as the markers of a real Filipina, what indicates that a contestant is a real Filipina? What makes "Miss Philippines" in Mississauga different from other girls in Mississauga? Is it the simple fact that, as most contests' rules specify, "at least one of the parents must be of Filipino descent"?

These are some of the issues facing the protagonists of *Miss Orient(ed)*. Faced with the question, "What does being a Filipina mean to you," one of the contestants, Jennifer, says to herself:

> Being a Filipina means [...] that I am from the Philippines...means that I am a woman...who is Filipino...means that I am a good daughter to my mother [...] means that I am an obedient daughter who enters beauty pageants so that her mother can be happy for once in her life [...] *(catches herself)*. I don't know, I don't know. I mean, how am I supposed to answer that question? I've never even been to the Philippines. (scene 5)

This passage raises important questions that confront many Asian North Americans, particularly those second-generation youths whose parents engage in transnational practices. Can one who does not speak Tagalog and who has never been to the Philippines be a "Filipina"? Is the Filipina part of one's identity the residue that remains in one's blood, in one's physical appearance, or does it reside in cultural practice? Here Jennifer's definition of "Filipina" slips from place of birth and origin to fulfilling one's familial responsibility. Part of her definition of Filipina includes not only morally good behavior but filial obedience. She experiences what sociologist Diane L. Wolf terms "emotional transnationalism," which is common to children of Filipino immigrants ("Family Secrets," 459). Wolf suggests that second-generation Filipino youths are situated "between different generational and vocational points of reference—their parents', sometimes also their grandparents', and their own—both the real and the imagined" (459). Strong familial ties create pressures on these youths, who struggle to negotiate between their parents' ideals and their own "hyphenated and hybrid identity" (475). Significantly, unlike the motives of the other contestants, Jennifer's motive for entering the contests is not vanity or her desire for the prize money but a desire to please her mother.

Following this passage, Jennifer gives an interesting if somewhat sardonic description of the typical life of a young Filipina in the North American diaspora. She says that her upbringing has not followed the predictable patterns of a "modern" Filipino girl in Toronto. She muses:

> I played tennis and went skiing instead of hanging out at the mall and going to debuts like other Filipino girls. I went to private French immersion instead of Catholic school, I lived in the city not the suburbs, I listened to Pink Floyd instead of Mariah Carey, I did 'shrooms instead of getting pregnant, I took marketing instead of nursing, and no, I have never been interested in becoming the world's next big pop star. (scene 5)

This catalogue of the usual habits of Filipina girls in Toronto verges on the comic stereotype, yet it does reveal much about the dreams of Filipino youths and their families. Filipino Canadians' dream of a good life means sending children off to Catholic schools, living in the suburbs, and choosing a safe career traditionally occupied by Filipina women, nursing. At the same time, this catalogue mocks such aspirations and behaviors as wanting to be a pop superstar and attending debut parties. The comedy of *Miss Orient(ed)* comes from this blend of self-deprecating humor and observations of daily ethnic life.

Aquino and Villasin employed a device that, as scholars of the genre point out, is central to comedy, the mocking of norms and stereotypes (Finney, "Introduction" to *Look Who's Laughing*, 7). What is notable about their humor is their use of what Bakhtin calls the "double-voice discourse" (*The Dialogic Imagination*, 324). Judy Little argues that "double-voiced discourse" is "especially prevalent in comic writing by women, which often interweaves elements of a subversive discourse into the language of the status quo—the discourse of power and control—using the former to ridicule, subvert, or deconstruct the latter" (as paraphrased by Finney in "Introduction" to *Look Who's Laughing*, 7). Although Bakhtin was analyzing novels in his *Dialogic Imagination*, his observations about the way language and voices function are applicable to the way discourse is deployed in comedy. For Bakhtin, "Every utterance participates in the 'unitary language' [...] and at the same time partakes of social and historical heteroglossia" (272). Heteroglossia, in low genres such as "street songs, folksayings, anecdotes," was "parodic, and aimed sharply and polemically against the official languages of its given time" (273).

In *Miss Orient(ed)* there are several scenes in which Aquino and Villasin created humor from the juxtaposition of serious and parodic discourses, thereby critiquing official discourse or practices. For instance, Angie, the mother of one of the contestants, comes out at one point to talk about her experiences of being Filipina in Canada with a deliberately exaggerated Filipino accent:

> But let me be frank in saying—Filipinows don't know how to integrate in Canadian society! And let me tell you why. Well, first of all, they don't improve their English pro-nun-ci-a-shan! They don't improve their ed-u-ca-shan, for goodness sakes. Because they stick to each other and don't have a chance to practice speaking correct English with a Canadian accent, eh. I have been here long enough to know that the only way to get ahead in this country is to be better than other Filipinos. That's why I studied hard to become a registered nurse. That's why I worked very hard in the hospital and didn't complain when I always got the graveyard shift. That's why my husband and I really saved and saved our money so that we could move out of St. James Town as soon as we could. And this is a secret, but I'll tell you. That's why I had my nose fixed. My nose job changed my life! My nose before was not so bad. But it's a Filipino nose, you know. It was a little flat and a little thick. I was starting to be really unhappy with it, because it was the only thing that was keeping me from being a true Canadian. I was tired of being constantly asked where I am from—originally! Now look at my nose. It is taller and smaller, right. Look... am I right? Yes, indeed I get better treatment from more people now. At the Intercontinental Hotel the other day, the doorman opened the door for me and was very polite and said "Good morning, ma'am." (scene 9)

Here Angie echoes right-wing conservative sentiment in her complaint about Filipinos' not knowing how to "integrate in Canadian society," but this discourse is tinged with irony. Although she professes to be critical of Filipinos who are not assimilating well into Canadian society, through double-voiced discourse her speech actually points out some of the ways Filipinos have been discriminated against and what they have had to do in order to be perceived as good citizens. As Angie notes, immigrants are not viewed as proper Canadians as long as they still speak with foreign accents. They have to work harder than others in order to be successful. This work ethic means competing against people in their own ethnic community, taking the shifts no one wants, seeing themselves as imperfect imitations of European Canadians. Angie has even had to undergo surgery in order to make it as a Canadian. Regarding herself through the gaze of the dominant white culture, she sees herself as inadequate. What she describes is the process of psychic disavowal and mimicry. Her nose job reveals her desire to be an "authentic" Canadian through the process of what Homi Bhabha calls "colonial mimicry." Bhabha notes that mimicry produces a subject that is "almost the same but not quite" the same as the white subject (*The Location of Culture*, 88–89).

In addition, Angie reveals the degree to which she has abjected her own community in her effort to become integrated into society. She tells us that her family saved money in order to move away from Toronto's Filipino town, as if it is only through ethnic disavowal that one is able to move up in the world. David Eng notes of this phenomenon,

> The untenable predicament of wanting to join a mainstream society that one knows clearly and systematically excludes oneself delineates the painful problem of becoming the instrument of one's own self-exclusion [...]. In other words, the minority subject must, in the vein of the fetishist, simultaneously recognize and not recognize the material contradictions of institutionalized racism that claim his inclusion even as he is systemically excluded. (*Racial Castration*, 22)

This partly unconscious desire to dissociate oneself from one's ethnic community, to be part of the dominant culture, to no longer be asked where one comes from, is echoed by Angie's daughter, Caridad, a vain teen who calls herself Carrie.

Carrie, like her mother, has internalized a degree of self-hatred and, in the course of the play, reveals many of her insecurities about her ethnic and gendered subjectivity. In the Factory Studio production Carrie was played by a young woman who had dyed blond hair. Of the three contestants, she is the one who is the most slavish to Western ideals and Western images of beauty. She has tried to make a career of beauty contests, placing eighth in Miss Canada, fifth in Miss Ontario, third in Miss GTA, and second runner-up in Miss Scarborough (scene 7: Backstage). For her, winning a beauty contest is the way to self-fulfilment. Through exaggeration and parody, Aquino and Villasin highlight the way girls and women are made to embrace global (American) ideologies of "beauty" and femininity. Carrie's discourse echoes the views of fashion magazines and advertisements targeted at women. Proud of the way she puts on her makeup, she tells the other girls with a keen sense of her own superiority that Bobby Brown, "a makeup artist to the stars and owner of one of the most hottest makeup lines" says that "90% of putting together a flawless face comes from knowing how to use the right tools: brushes, sponges" (scene 7: Backstage). She transforms herself into what current fashion deems beautiful with the help of padding in her bras, Vaseline on her "eyelids, cleavage and teeth" (scene 7: Backstage), and brand-name items—clothes and shoes from The Gap, Prada, and Sketchers. Feminist critic Sandra Lee Bartky points out that "in the language of fashion magazines and cosmetic ads, making-up is typically portrayed as an aesthetic activity in which a woman can express her individuality. In reality, [...] making-up the face is, in fact, a highly stylized activity that gives little rein to self-expression" ("Foucault, Femininity, and the Modernization of Patriarchal Power," 70). She argues that such disciplinary practices "are part of the process by which the ideal body of femininity—and hence the feminine body-subject—is constructed; in doing this, they produce a 'practiced and subjected' body, that is, a body on which an inferior status has been inscribed" (71).

What becomes problematic for the Filipina woman is that this inferior status is doubly inscribed. Not only does Carrie have to contend with the ideals of feminine beauty; she also has to grapple with her non-Western features, which are deemed inferior by Western standards. With an attitude of mock seriousness, Carrie says that on August 13, 1993, she decided to "become a true Canadian. Inside a 24-hour Shopper's Drugmart" (scene 14: L'Oreal). Her becoming Canadian costs her "twenty-two dollars and eighty five cents, six hundred Shopper's Drugmart Optimum points," and it is through L'Oreal's "Feria Champagne Cocktail, Number 91" (scene 14: L'Oreal). Although it is humorous to think that the simple act of coloring one's hair can turn one into a Canadian, this passage does illustrate how much our notions of the Canadian are still predicated on the European, white subject. To at least have this subject's hair color is one step closer to being a white Canadian. However, Carrie is told by the sales clerk that it is not enough to simply purchase the hair coloring; she has to "strip the black out" of her hair first in order to look like the perfect blond white woman pictured on the box (scene 14: L'Oreal). Symbolically, what is being required of the non-European subject is a stripping off of her ethnic and physical difference before she can be recognized and accepted as a Canadian subject.

The play relates this personal debasement of having to erase one's ethnicity or culture in North America to the way the Philippines as a nation has also been stripped of its heritage or traditions by its colonizers. In one scene of the play, the beauty icon takes a moment to "acknowledge and applaud those pioneering Filipinas who paved the way for modern Filipino women everywhere" (scene 8: History). What we see is a series of slides of "Pearls through the Ages" featuring a combination of important historical female figures with popular icons. The first Filipinas, the "Babaylans" or indigenous priestesses, were "women who governed pre-Spanish, pre-civilized, pre-enlightened, communal society." They engaged in trade and industry and enjoyed the "right to own and inherit land" (scene 8: History). However, the Babaylans were erased by three hundred years of Spanish colonial rule and by the "power and influence of the Catholic Church," which replaced the figure of the Babaylan with the model of "Maria Clara," who was as pure "as the Virgin Mary" and was expected "to be shy and modest, with fine manners and delicate expressions" (scene 8: History). Then, in the twentieth century, America brought other images of women to the Philippines. These included heroines of romances, the bakers of Betty Crocker cakes, electrical appliance owners, and beauty queens. The humor of this catalogue comes from the comic inflation and deflation of Filipina women who climb "to the summit," including those of Miss Universe of 1969, Gloria Diaz; Imelda Marcos, who taught women how to "put their best foot forward"; Miss World; Miss Universe; Lea Salonga as Miss Saigon; and finally, Filipina domestic workers and caregivers (scene 8: History). Of these various images, only that of the Babaylan was indigenous to the Philippines. The others are all corrupt versions of Spanish and American ideals or else they arose as a result of Western capitalism and the recent globalization of labor.

To include Filipina domestic workers in this catalogue of heroines at first seems ironic; yet, as many scholars have shown, Filipina domestic workers constitute a large proportion of the Filipino migrant workers who help support the Philippine economy through their remittances (see Parreñas, *Servants of Globalization*, 51). The beauty icon notes that the Filipina domestic worker is the "dirty little secret" or the "dark side to the modern Filipina" (scene 8: History). These "servants of globalization," as Rhacel Parreñas calls them, are our silent heroines: "the domestic Filipina climbs a mound of dirty dishes, diapers and depraved employers as she takes care of the young and elderly, and saves the Philippine economy with her dollar remittances" (scene 8: History). More often than not, these women have to strip off or leave behind their identities as mothers, wives, and daughters in order to become a foreign family's nanny or caregiver to the elderly. Pauline Barber notes other contradictions in this type of transnational work. She writes:

> In the Philippine economy the significant influx of migrant remittances contributes to the national balance sheet and enables new forms of consumption and migration-related industries to flourish. However, the benefits of such changes are precariously tied to volatile labour market conditions beyond the control of Philippine policy. And, [...] for migrants themselves [...], migration enables new forms of consumption, economic subjectivity and class agency—but in problematic ways given the nature of their typically de-skilled employment, and the transnational location of their work and political expressions. ("Agency in Philippine Women's Labour Migration and Provisional Diaspora")

Like the play's contestants, who have been "misoriented" and interpellated by Western ideals of beauty, they, too, have been misoriented into an acceptance of themselves as docile transmigrant workers, allowing their bodies to become commodities for export.

Beauty contests, which have become so integral to Filipino life at home and abroad, were not originally part of Filipino culture but are part of the colonial heritage. Nanay, the mother of one of the contestants, who resides in the Philippines, objects to her daughter Twinkle's participation in the competition. Significantly, the mother still exerts a strong influence on her daughter even though they are separated geographically. She tells her daughter on the telephone that beauty pageants are simply stupid: "Mga ulol lang ang naniniwala diyan" (Only fools believe in them) (scene 16). For Nanay, beauty pageants, with their bathing suit parades, go against the values Filipinos cherish, such as respect, honor, humility, and modesty: "respeto, dangal, pagkamababang-loob, kabanihan" (scene 16). This dialogue, the only extended one in Tagalog, is delivered over the long-distance telephone, and in the stage production is deliberately muffled. The mother's lecture about standing by one's values is interrupted by static, and she is disconnected abruptly. The scene, one of the few that is not funny, reenacts in a poignant way the disappearance of Filipino values and traditions. The mother reminds Twinkle of the important qualities she was brought up with—dignity and pride in herself and the sense that she is already a "winner" in the game of life. She does not need such a pretentious event as a beauty pageant to make her happy.

In the final scene of the play, Twinkle, who has just been given the lecture by her mother over the telephone from the Philippines, sees the pageant for what it is and cries out: "This is a sham! A joke! Can't you all see this! Everybody! It's all fake!" (scene 17: Finale). What she recognizes is that although the pageant purports to search for the "ideal modern Filipina," what the judges are looking for is an Americanized version of beauty: someone tall, with bleached hair, a "Western nose. And above all, fair, fair skin" (scene 17: Finale). Intelligent, confident, short, and stocky, with jet-black hair, Twinkle realizes that in fact she is the "ideal modern Filipina" but will never be crowned as such. Her moment of insight, though briefly staged, nevertheless mars the superficial buoyancy of the pageant. Her outburst provokes a moment of uncertainty and self-awareness in one of the other contestants. Jennifer also decides that she cannot be the "modern Filipina" that her mother wants. She says, "I don't know how to speak Tagalog [...] and I can't sing the Philippine National Anthem or dance the tinikling [...] and I can't cook adobo" (scene 17: Finale). Modern Filipinas in the diaspora will have to carve out different identities for themselves, ones that are not necessarily based on the traditions their parents brought with them when they immigrated. Although the play does not outline what this identity will be, it definitely shows what it will not be. The "ideal modern Filipina" will not be the demure Oriental woman, a symbol of femininity and exoticism, nor will she have to be a pale imitation of the white European Canadian in order to succeed. She will be, as Twinkle is, a "spunky little fighter" (scene 16: Nanay), and she will not make a career out of dancing the "tinikling" or "cooking adobo."

Ultimately, though the ambitious Carrie is declared the "winner of the 2003 Miss Pearl of the Orient" contest, it is an empty and Pyrrhic victory. Carrie has had to "whiten" herself as much as possible to resemble a Barbie doll, with her lightened hair, blue contact lenses, fake breasts, and excessive makeup, in order to fulfill the beauty contest's ideals. But the fact that she has won the contest is also a rather sad and ironic commentary on some members of the Filipino community. Many Filipinos in Canada, in their struggle for acceptance, assimilation, and upward mobility, have internalized their own inferiority, accepting many of the fantasies and ideals of the dominant culture. What *Miss Orient(ed)* depicts is the comic effects of such institutionalized racism and cultural abjection on Filipinos in North America. But it also sends a strong message about the dangers of "misorientation."

Empowering the Local

Indian Canadian Deepa Mehta's *Bollywood/Hollywood* is also about the assimilationist and upward mobility desires of South Asians in Canada. Following serious social dramas such as *Fire* (1996) and *Earth* (1998), Mehta's *Bollywood/Hollywood* (2002) was not as well received critically as her first films.[3] *Toronto Globe and Mail* film reviewer Rick Groen says that "there are enticing glimmers, there are worthy moments but, in the end, the result is disappointing" ("Fusion Fare"). Others note that it is "trivial, and trite" (Hornaday, "Bollywood") and that "any viewer who has seen *Fire* or *Earth* will refuse to believe that this is a Deepa Mehta film" (Planet Bollywood, *"Bollywood/Hollywood"*). Mehta produced the movie when she could not complete the filming of the third part of her trilogy, *Water*, because of waves of protests in India. In an interview she said, "There was no other way. It was great therapy. I got to play. I got to realize that there is more to life than just pain. And, if it wasn't for the catharsis of *Bollywood/Hollywood,* I would be in agony right now because I was really down" (Kirkland, "Filmmaker Mehta Has a Love for Canada").[4] However, following the Bakhtin-inspired work of Peter Stallybrass and Allon White, I want to argue that Mehta's film, with its Bollywood and Hollywood musical style of dancing and singing and its colorful sets, creates a carnivalesque atmosphere in which a politics of transgression becomes possible within a popular genre. Instead of viewing it as a failed Bollywood or Hollywood imitation, as some critics do, I see the film as a product of Asian Canadian transnational subjectivity in which hybridity, borrowings, and transcultural exchanges generate energy, self-examination, and new identity formations. *Bollywood/Hollywood* successfully works through localized community settings and sensibilities and yet is able to venture forth and resonate with global spectators.

Mehta employed the traditional Cinderella rags-to-riches plot of a beautiful but poor girl who is swept off her feet by a rich prince, but uses it in a self-conscious and parodic way. At the same time, as some critics have noted, the movie "has a *Pretty Woman* twist to it, but done with much humility, charisma and class" (Gawle, "Bollywood Film with Hollywood Humour"). In her study of twentieth-century art forms, Linda Hutcheon points out that parody "is a form of imitation, but imitation characterized by ironic inversion, not always at the expense of the parodied text" (*A Poetics of Postmodernism*, 6). Mehta, I argue, is using what Hutcheon calls "repetition with critical distance, which marks difference rather than similarity" (6) to explore, albeit with humor, the vicissitudes and the pleasures of diasporic South Asians in Canada. Her deliberate echoing of the Hollywood romantic blockbuster featuring Richard Gere and Julia Roberts shows her familiarity with, her tribute to, and her mockery of the conventions of romantic comedy as well as offering the stories of diasporic South Asians as a legitimate subject of mainstream North American spectatorship. That is, Indians in the diaspora are no longer marginalized as the subjects of "ethnic" art house films or in Indian national cinema but are placed at the cinematic threshold of global audiences. Significantly, in this film, set in Toronto, diasporic South Asians are represented as economically successful citizens who belong to an upper-middle-class affluent community with large houses in the suburbs. Although scholars such as Vijay Mishra and others have noted the "massive size of Indian cinema,"[5] for many people in North America, *Bollywood/Hollywood* and films such as *Moulin Rouge* were their first exposures to Indian cinema (*Bollywood Cinema*, 1). Like Gurinder Chadha's *Bend It Like Beckham*, which came out the same year, *Bollywood/Hollywood* participates in the work of what Ella Shohat and Robert

Stam call "unthinking Eurocentrism" in their book of that name, because it places the everyday stories of diasporic Indians on center stage in a commercial film marketed for Western audiences.

The choice of locales featured in the film is another way of rejecting U.S. global hegemony. The film is set in Toronto, and indeed, one irascible critic says, Toronto herself is the "most memorable character" in the film, because she has received "quite the cinematic face-lift" (Groen, "Fusion Fare"). Rick Groen writes, "Mehta does for the city what Woody Allen did for Manhattan, and what she can't do for the comedy—glamorize her and stylize her and make the old gal sparkle." Although Toronto has been the location of a number of Hollywood films, in most of these films the location is not highlighted. The city is usually being passed off as another North American city.[6] In Mehta's film, however, the city, with the views of the Skydome, Gardiner Expressway, and skyscrapers on the horizon, takes center stage. The particular storefronts and settings chosen are also important, for they are part of Mehta's repudiation of large capitalist corporations and enterprises and her celebration of Toronto's cosmopolitan cultures. Though Toronto, like other North American cities, has been invaded by U.S. chain stores, hotels, and fast food outlets such as McDonald's, Sheraton, Wal-mart, Chapters Book stores, and others, these do not make an appearance in the film. Instead, Mehta has close-up shots of independent South Asian stores and eating establishments. For example, when Sue and Rahul negotiate their contract, they sit in a small eating place, "Motionmahal," located in Little India, where Sue amazes Rahul by eating a plateful of chilis.

Audiences familiar with *Pretty Woman* will recall that when Edward (Richard Gere) hires Vivian (Julia Roberts) for the week, he makes her over. He takes her shopping on LA's fashionable and snobbish Rodeo Drive. There designer shops like those of Armani, Gucci, Christian Dior, Coco Chanel, Ralph Lauren, Valentino, Cartier, and Tiffany are located and featured. It is one of the most expensive streets in the world, reputed to be "where the stars shop." In Mehta's film, Sunita is transformed into an elegant and respectable woman with the help of clothes and jewelry bought not from well-known French or Italian designers but from a local transnational, diasporic Indian store. In her establishing shots Mehta pans a number of other South Asian storefronts—Pooja, a clothing store on Gerrard Street, and Shubi's jewelry—suggesting the vitality of South Asian diasporic communities in

Toronto as well as promoting these small, independently owned stores in the global medium of a full-length feature film. In another scene, at the engagement party of Twinky and her fiance, the festivities take place in a rented hall. When Sunita and Rahul go for a walk, we find out that the party has taken place not in a fancy hotel but at the Scarborough Towne Centre, a shopping mall located in the east-end suburban, immigrant, middle-class area of the city.

The sites featured in the film are important locales in the daily lives of diasporic South Asians in the metropolitan area. They represent places where they shop, eat, rent videos, meet, and interact with other diasporic South Asians. They show Mehta's effort to frame "the local as creative, resistant, and transgressive" (Desai, *Beyond Bollywood*, 14). By featuring them Mehta was resisting what Stuart Hall has described as the "new kind of globalization" that comes to people in the form of American mass culture ("The Local and the Global," 178). Yet, at the same time we can see the film participating in the reformulation of global mass culture, which, Hall points out, is centered in the West but "does not speak the Queen's English any longer. It speaks English as an international language, which is quite a different thing" (179). Hall links this reformulation to a number of recent processes, including "the return to the local as a response of globalization," as well as the "struggle of the margins to come into representation" (183). In this film, which depicts, albeit through comedy and occasional irony, the social and familial concerns of diasporic Indians, I argue that Mehta is attempting to return to the local as well as to represent and empower the margins. Her film makes Westernized audiences aware of a number of issues that face diasporic subjects, and it places them on center stage rather than using them as extras or secondary characters, as in most filmic productions from the Western world.

Aside from showcasing local shops and eateries, Mehta also pays tribute to a "local" Torontonian, internationally known filmmaker Atom Egoyan. There are at least three instances in the film in which Mehta repudiates Hollywood films in favor of independent ones. Initially, in the comic interviews with potential wives for Rahul set up by the matriarchs of the household, one of the women states that she cannot stand those independent films about incest, which often crop up in the work of Canadian independent filmmakers. Of course, she is rejected by Rahul. In contrast, when Rahul and Sunita are getting to know each other, they talk about their preferences in terms of cuisine and films. Although Rahul likes Hollywood blockbusters with stars like Al Pacino, Sunita tells him she prefers the films of Atom Egoyan. She has a poster of the film *Exotica* in her bedroom. And the nightclub where she is insulted by a former client is also called Exotica.[7] These allusions are playful and cursory, to be sure, but their presence in the film signals Mehta's admiration of a fellow Canadian diasporic director, as well as her awareness of the liminal space of what Hamid Naficy calls "accented cinema." According to Naficy:

> Accented films are interstitial because they are created astride and in the interstices of social formations and cinematic practices. Consequently, they are simultaneously local and global, and they resonate against the prevailing cinematic production practices, at the same time that they benefit from them [...]. They signify and signify upon exile and diaspora by expressing, allegorizing, commenting upon, and critiquing the home and host societies and cultures and the deterritorialized conditions of the filmmakers. They signify and signify upon cinematic traditions by means of their artisanal and collective production modes, their aesthetics and politics of smallness and imperfection, and their narrative strategies that cross generic boundaries and undermine cinematic realism. (*An Accented Cinema*, 4–5)

I quote this passage at length because much of what Naficy describes is what Mehta, and of course Egoyan, attempt to do in their films.

Like Egoyan's films, Mehta's *Bollywood/Hollywood* straddles that space between home and host societies, examining and critiquing both. Through its self-conscious metafilmic narrative structure and its pointed surtitles an ironic distance from both cultures is established. This attitude of irony and self-mockery was not present in Mehta's two films about India, *Fire* and *Earth*. But from the start of *Bollywood/Hollywood*, with the opening scene of the father dying on a dark, stormy night, we become aware that this is not a typical "ethnic" film that arouses nostalgia for the homeland. Rahul's Daddy-ji exhorts him to be a good son, but his dying speech includes humorous references to being the "team captain," and he asks his son to "remember the Blue Jays."[8] That the whole family lives in a cosmopolitan, transcultural space is further emphasized when Granny-ji and Mummy-ji invite Rahul's white pop star girlfriend to the house. Even though Granny speaks English perfectly and often quotes from Shakespeare's plays, she asks her daughter-in-law to act as a translator. Her questions to the European Canadian pop star include "What caste are you?" which renders rather absurd the way some diasporic people persist in clinging to traditional categories of difference in their host countries. At the same time, it is the very need to preserve categories and traditions that impels the plot of the film and demarcates one's ethnic identity. The younger brother of Rahul videotapes the whole interview with Rahul's girlfriend, and when she (Jessica Pare) is insulted and leaves, he says, "This is way better than any Bollywood movie," calling attention to the genre the movie is indebted to and, at the same time, is parodying.

In particular, the film crosses east-west divides by locating itself at the boundary between the extravagant, sentimental productions of Bollywood musicals and the predictable, feel-good plots of Hollywood romantic comedies. At Twinky's engagement party, one of the guests says, "Films made in India are better," as if anticipating the criticism *Bollywood/Hollywood* would be given by critics who find it not authentic or not as elaborate as Bollywood films from India. This self-conscious metafilmic trait of the film creates a constant distancing effect for the audience, so we are never quite fully in the realm of the Hollywood comedy or the Bollywood musical but always somewhere in between. But the point is that the film is not strictly a Bollywood film, and even Bollywood films themselves are increasingly becoming transcultural, influenced by American, European, and other cinematic traditions.[9] Mehta's version, as Bruce Kirkland points out, is a "mock-Bollywood picture, the melodramatic bits are heightened to farce" ("Bollywood High"). Rahul's mother acts as if she were the heroine of a Bollywood movie, forever breaking into loud sobs and wailing at her misfortunes. Yet her complaints, "Why am I so unlucky?" are not taken seriously by anybody in her family or in the audience. Rahul's pop star girlfriend, Kimberly, is killed in a freak accident while she is learning to meditate. Through this scene Mehta not only pokes fun at New Age practices but humorously relates them and the rather contrived device of killing off the undesirable other woman to Hollywood by having Jessica Pare fall right in front of the renowned Hollywood sign in the Hollywood Hills.

At the same time, Bollywood movies' practice of conveying the emotions of the characters through sentimental love songs is also used and parodied. When Rahul loses his girlfriend, the surtitles compare him to "Devdas: very tragic Bollywood hero." Yet at this point we feel no emotional empathy for him, so, rather than conveying sadness and loss, Rahul's song reminds us of a flashy MTV video rather than a serious Bollywood segment. In addition, the constant presence of Bollywood movies in the background, on TV screens everywhere in Rahul's mansion from the bedroom to the kitchen, remind us of the highly mediated world of diasporic South Asians. Because they are geographically distant from their originary culture, they rely increasingly on memory, fantasy, technology, and media culture to reaffirm their Indian identity. Yet what is authentic Hindu tradition versus what is performance is questioned. For example, at one point the grandmother is saying her prayers, presumably in a highly spiritual mood. At the same time, she interrupts her prayers and gives Sunita orders for the maid to get her food, specifying a mango lassi "with lots of sugar," in a tone very unholy, earthly, and commanding. The disjunction between the grandmother's supposedly spiritual state and her bodily needs is comic but reminds us of the performative aspects of religious and ethnic cultural traditions. A number of scenes in the film demonstrate what Judith Butler has called the "performative" aspects of identity. In *Bodies That Matter*, Butler explains her theory of the performativity of the subject in relation to gender identity. Butler argues that sex and sexuality are neither "constructed nor determined" (94), but rather are assumed in complex ways. Her points about the importance of "the forced reiteration of norms," which "enables a subject and constitutes the temporal condition for the subject," can be applied to the way ethnic or racial identity is also assumed in our society. Just as sex and sexuality are not biologically determined or simply constructed, ethnic identity is also "a ritualized production, a ritual reiterated under and through constraint, under and through the force of prohibition and taboo" (95). Similarly, Gayatri Spivak has observed, "What we call experience is a staging of experience, sometimes on the small screen. In this sense, an earlier experience is being staged in this new, displaced imperialist scene: the horror of an absolute act of intercultural performance. One of the many tasks of the activist intellectual is to offer scrupulous and plausible accounts of the mechanics of staging" (*A Critique of Postcolonial Reason*, 781). In the film, the character who repeatedly forces us to think about what or who constitutes a diasporic Indian is Sunita, or Sue. Through Sunita's role-playing and changeable identity, Mehta critiques conventional assumptions about South Asian subjects, about Hindu girls, and suggests a more fluid and malleable version of acceptable codes of behavior for Indian women.

Sunita's role-playing highlights the performativity of racial and gender identity as they are played out in North America. During Rahul's first encounter with Sunita, he believes that she cannot be Indian because she is working at a bar as some kind of hostess or prostitute. He tells her that "Indian girls don't do this." She, however, has a much more flexible notion of what it means to belong to a certain racial or national group. She playfully tells him, "I can be anything you want me to be," which echoes a line of Vivian's in *Pretty Woman*. When asked about her name, Vivian (Julia Roberts) responds repeatedly, "What do you want it to be?" Her identity, like that of Sunita's, is malleable and can be changed to suit her clients. Similarly, Mehta wants to confound stereotypes of Indian girls as uniformly passive and obedient, and she makes Sunita perform a number of different identities. She proves that Indian girls can be "anything" they want to be, especially when they are exotic looking and racially ambiguous.[10] Sunita lets Rahul believe that she is a poetry-loving Spanish girl, a philosopher, and an experienced prostitute at the same time that she leads Rahul's family to believe that she is a good Indian girl simply by "performing" these identities. Just as in a Bakhtinian carnival the world is allowed to turn upside down, during the week when Sunita performs her role as Rahul's girlfriend she indulges in unlimited luxury, treats, fine clothes, and the semblance of a rich, happy extended family.

This plot of misidentification is a device commonly used in romances from Jane Austen's *Pride and Prejudice* to today's Harlequin romances and is one that is picked up in Bollywood movies. The hero or heroine, or sometimes both, has been misinformed and believes erroneously that the other possesses undesirable qualities that make him or her unsuitable as a partner. This misinformation presents an artificial obstacle to the romance between them, but in most comedies, the truth turns out to be much more positive and pleasing than what the protagonist had assumed. Mehta uses this device, but with a critical difference. In *Bollywood/Hollywood* the female character is fully in control of the plot, possessing knowledge about her identity that is withheld from the male character and the audience. It is as if Sunita, like Mehta, is in charge of the development of the narrative. This is the difference between Mehta's film and *Pretty Woman*. Although the endings of both films are the same—that is, there is the anticipation of a wedding—the middles are worked out differently in terms of gender relations. In Mehta's film, unlike *Pretty Woman* or most Bollywood movies, the woman takes an active part in the control of crucial information, in role-playing, and helps to engineer the happily-ever-after ending.

Like Austen's Elizabeth Bennett and Vivian in *Pretty Woman*, Sunita is an intelligent and educated woman who stands apart from the many other women who are potential wives for an eligible, rich, young, and good-looking bachelor. Though she comes from an immigrant Sikh family, she works as a hostess not out of necessity but in order to spite her father. She is a modern woman who, though still stunningly beautiful in a traditional sari, drives fast cars and is capable of acting tough when the situation calls for it. Her education is transcultural: not only does she recite poetry; she has studied anthropology and knows some Spanish, as well as Hindi. Sometime before her meeting with Rahul, she has rejected her parents' effort to arrange a suitable marriage for her. She has refused to marry the world wrestling champ, Killer Khalsa, even though this marriage would have brought the family some economic security. Like the heroines in romances, she has integrity and a sense of self-worth that, despite some earlier evidence to the contrary, capture the hero's heart in the end. Mehta thus conforms to the sentimental plots of social comedy, the comedy romances of Hollywood, and what Vijay Mishra calls the "order of marriage" that is mandatory in Bollywood movies (*Bollywood Cinema*, 27).

However, though the plot structure and movement of *Bollywood/Hollywood* largely conform to Hollywood comedy romances and Bollywood movies, which have the form of a "sentimental melodramatic romance," as Mishra notes (13), I suggest that Mehta's film inserts subtle, small changes into typical scenarios found in traditional romances. One striking example is the penultimate courtship scene, in which Rahul goes to Sunita's house to ask for her hand in marriage. He receives permission from Sunita's father to court her, climbs up her balcony with roses, and, like Edward in *Pretty Woman*, makes a plea for Sunita's hand. However, she does not accept him at that moment, which is playfully reminiscent of *Romeo and Juliet*, but rather, to his disappointment, appears to refuse him. In the next scene, though, Rahul and the viewers are surprised to find that Sunita, not the regular chauffeur, is driving the limousine that takes him home. Though this scene can be read as yet another one of Sunita's various attempts at role-playing, it is important in various ways. Wearing the chauffeur's cap, Sunita crosses gender, not racial, boundaries this time. Though she agrees to marry Rahul, the scene suggests that this marriage will be based on her terms—she is at the wheel and Rahul is in the back seat. She will not be cowed by his millionaire status into playing the role of a submissive wife but will continue to negotiate, as she has, her place as a diasporic Indian woman in his life.

In the film there are many other moments at which questions of Indo-Canadian identity and gender issues are raised, albeit playfully. Indian diasporic identity is shown to be hybridized, with Indian customs and beliefs intertwined not just with Westernized culture but with globalized Canadian multiculture. In one of the early scenes in the film, Rahul's sister swears and says, "Jesus Christ." Chastised by her grandmother to not take the name of the lord in vain, she says, "But he isn't even our God." This remark reveals the ways in which the discourses and worldview of the dominant culture, English and Christian, have permeated the lives of diasporic Indians. In a later scene, when Sunita threatens to leave home and move to London—Ontario, not England—her mother tries to calm her by looking into the future. However, the answer to the future is not in Hindu spiritualism but in Chinese fortune cookies, which are commercially produced locally in the factory where the mother works. In another scene, Rahul's younger brother, Govin, is being teased by bullies at school. Mehta does not play off whites against ethnic minorities in the schoolyard scenes but shows the multicultural mix of Toronto city life by having the student group composed of whites, East Asians, and youths of other ethnicities. The bully, Brian, is Chinese Canadian. A similar confusion of ethnicities occurs in the closing scene, in which Rockini (the chauffeur in drag) sings a song in English and Hindi but is dressed in a traditional Chinese dress.

For Mehta Rockini, the chauffeur, functions as a way to queer or to critique the "normative, particularly the heteronormative," which may be "embodied in citizenship and nationalism, circulated through capitalism, and mobilized in the terrain of postcoloniality" (Desai, *Beyond Bollywood*, 30). This figure of the cross-dresser, or transvestite, comes from the tradition of the hijra, a "highly visible intersex persona often called a 'eunuch' in English," which has recently become a Bollywood stock character, according to Thomas Waugh ("Queer Bollywood," 283). For Waugh the marginalization of this figure is problematic, because the hijra remains as "background figure or low comic diversion" (286).

Although I agree that Rockini is mainly a comic figure in *Bollywood/Hollywood*, it is nevertheless difficult to condemn Mehta's depiction of homosocial relationships, given what we know of her previous experience with *Fire*, which depicts a relationship between two unhappily married women in India. If anything, I found that the Rockini character reminded me of the ways in which mainstream culture forces filmmakers to capitulate to nationalistic, generic, and capitalistic pressures.

These examples may seem trivial, but cumulatively they serve to exemplify the hybridized culture and global identities that are now typical of Canada. Mehta's film situates itself at the cusp of two or more cultures—Hollywood and Bollywood, white and brown, local and global, Canadian and American. The film does not fully belong to one world or the other but belongs to both. It reveals the deterritorialized characteristic of the filmmaker as well as the characters she depicts. However, instead of signifying conditions of exile and loss as do other diasporic productions, the film suggests the vibrancy of being between worlds—the humor, self-mockery, and self-awareness of being exotic and other to both the West and the East. As the film's subtitle proclaims, "Nothing is what it appears to be," and the surprises in the film are some of the ways in which new identities and new formations are being enacted in playful, powerful, and creative ways.

III

Future Perfect: Feminist Resistance to Global Homogeneity

5
Shape-shifters and Disciplined Bodies: Feminist Tactics, Science Fiction, and Fantasy

As I have argued, novels by writers of the first generation of Asian North Americans, such as those by Maxine Hong Kingston, Carlos Bulosan, and Joy Kogawa, though frequently infused with legends and myths, have tended to be mainly autobiographical and based on the realities of social history.[1] Writers of the late 1980s and 1990s, such as Amy Tan, Jessica Hagedorn, Gish Jen, Wayson Choy, Chang-rae Lee, and others, have continued this tradition but have incorporated postmodern techniques of intertextuality—the use of parallel and disjunctive narratives, dreams, and postcolonial history—in their novels. However, most of these works still tend to be mainly realist in form. Only in the last few years, with writers such as Japanese American Karen Tei Yamashita and Japanese Canadian Hiromi Goto, have novels by Asian North Americans used elements of the fantastic in a sustained way to tell their stories.

Two recent examples of Asian North American novels that use magic realism and fantasy as a primary way to challenge and critique normative and culturally dominant views of the feminine body, globalization, race, and technology are Asian American Chitra Divakaruni's *The Mistress of Spices* and Asian Canadian Larissa Lai's *Salt Fish Girl*.

Both novels feature female protagonists who are shape-shifters and are endowed with the ability to transcend geographical as well as temporal boundaries. Divakaruni and Lai use familiar cityscapes, such as Oakland, California, and Vancouver, British Columbia, respectively, but they defamiliarize the locations; in Lai's case, the city becomes a futuristic dystopia. They use myths and stories from their cultures and transport them into these contemporary or futuristic settings, thwarting readers' expectations of the genres of European, Chinese, and Indian myths and legends as well as our preconceptions of how females in these stories are supposed to act. For example, in *The Mistress of Spices* Divakaruni uses the figure of what Janice Crosby (in *Cauldron of Changes*) calls the "wise woman" to heal and solve some of the problems of the diasporic Indian community in Oakland. The mistress's knowledge of the potency of spices enables her to weave magic around those who come to her store for help. In *Salt Fish Girl* Lai reworks Hans Christian Andersen's mermaid fairy tale, as well as the Chinese story of Nu Wa, to express lesbian desire, as well as to critique technological advances such as cloning, the genetic modification of food, and the exploitation of Third World women's labor by large corporations. Often by blurring the division between fantasy and reality, between traditional practices and science, these authors create multiple-world structures that enable readers to read the novels "dialogically," in the sense used by Bakhtin in *The Dialogic Imagination*. Through the use of what Colin Manlove calls "secondary world fantasy" (*The Fantasy Literature of England*, 4), readers are constantly forced to look at the activities of one world through the lens or the value system of the other. The unsettling of the familiar in these novels encourages us to look anew at various aspects of our lives, particularly women's lives, their bodies, and their relation to feminized ideals of beauty and notions of motherhood, aging, and disability. What the novels provide are strong commentaries on and feminist alternatives to global capitalism, to contemporary affective ties, to the ways we conduct sexual, romantic, and race relations in our community.

 This chapter examines Divakaruni's *Mistress of Spices* and Lai's *Salt Fish Girl* in the context of recent theories of globalization and transnational feminism. I contend that through the use of elements of magic realism and science fiction, Divakaruni and Lai call attention to the challenges faced by racially and culturally displaced subjects in a globalized environment; to the ways in which the female body is "disciplined" and "coerced," in Foucault's sense of the terms (seen in *Discipline and Punish*), to conform to what Sandra Bartky calls the "ideal body of femininity" ("Foucault, Femininity, and the Modernization of Patriarchal Power," 71) acceptable to modern society; and to inequities of work and human labor caused by the global expansion of multinational corporations. Both novelists, in their own way, play with notions of origins, hybridity, and libidinal desire; both are concerned with what Arun Appadurai calls "ethnoscape," which, according to Appadurai, is "the landscape of persons who constitute the shifting world in which we live: tourists, immigrants, refugees, exiles, guestworkers, and other moving groups and persons [who] constitute the essential feature of the world, and appear to affect the politics of and between nations to a hitherto unprecedented degree" ("Disjuncture and Difference in the Global Cultural Economy," 297).

A History of the Future

Set in Southern China in the late 1800s and early 1900s as well as in a futuristic Serendipity in British Columbia between 2044 and 2062, *Salt Fish Girl* uses the dual time frame and multiple settings to demonstrate the connections between the past and the present, as well as the similarities between what has traditionally been divided into the East and the West. Instead of seeing a break between the myths, histories, and traditions of the past and the postindustrial, scientific, fragmented, and sanitized world of the postmodern, Lai stresses the parallels between them and shows the value of remembrance and unforgetfulness at the same time that she seeks to rework a past that effaces the histories of the dispossessed.[2] In an article titled "Political Animals and the Body of History," Lai points out the importance of not forgetting the past, as well as the need to rewrite it: "To claim a racialized space is empowering in that it demands acknowledgement of a history of racism to which the mainstream does not want to admit" (149).

In this politicized context, the theme of remembrance and forgetfulness becomes important in the novel. At one point, Nu Wa, the female protagonist of the early 1900s, is taken to the Island of Mist and

Forgetfulness, where she passes an indeterminate amount of time and ends up forgetting her native Cantonese dialect. This segment is a rather surreal and ironic echo of Christian's journey in *Pilgrim's Progress*, as well as the journey of immigrants who leave their homelands in search of a better life in the West. With a pale-faced foreign woman who smells of "expensive face powder and the kind of cologne that comes in crystal bottles" (*Salt Fish Girl*, 127), Nu Wa enters the City of Hope, "glinting pink and gold" on the island, through the east gate, marked "Progress" (125). The west gate is marked "Democracy." The City of Hope, like America, however, offers opportunities and pleasure only to selected people, not to foreigners. Nu Wa finds much wealth and indulgence but also experiences the hardships that immigrants experience once her rich companion abandons her. She does not find the hope or salvation that Christian finds. Some of the work Nu Wa is forced to take on, under threat of deportation "back to China" (128), includes that of "a toilet scrubber and bedsheet changer" (129), as well as that of a telemarketing salesperson who scams pensioners. Yet she is lulled by luxuries such as "shopping" and a "pedicure" (135, 137) from her companion when she becomes restless. Given the predominance of Asian and Asian American women in sweatshops and beauty salons, these two pleasures are rather ironic. Through this episode Lai critiques the unequal opportunities afforded by North America and the way its luxuries make us forget about the underside of the society—the hardships of immigrants, the poor, and criminals. At the same time, Lai also mocks the forgetfulness of immigrants, who, becoming caught up in the material life of their adopted country, too soon fail to remember the promises they have made to those they left behind, as Nu Wa forgot the promises she had made to the salt fish girl.

Remembering occurs in the futuristic narrative, too, but in that setting memories can be fatal. Miranda, the protagonist of the twenty-first century, finds that she is afflicted with the drowning/dreaming disease (108), a sickness that makes her see strange images from the past. It is this affliction that makes her interesting to the scientists and medical doctors who want to study and eradicate people like Miranda, who smell and have the dreaming disease, a form of disability in that society. Many of those afflicted cannot find comfort from their bad dreams except by drowning. For example, there was a "girl who smelled of cooking oil, who remembered all the wars ever fought. She could recall and recount every death, every rape, every wound, every moment of suffering that had ever been inflicted by a member of her ancestral lineage" (85). For those in control of Serendipity, these visions of the past only disrupt the seemingly seamless and orderly present, and they must be suppressed. The people who dream of the past carry their histories with them, in the same way that they carry their stinking smell, no matter how much they try to clean themselves.

Lai's insistence on the remembrance of atrocities past and on history counters what Fredric Jameson says of postmodernism. In his essay *Postmodernism, or The Cultural Logic of Late Capitalism,* Jameson argued that the main features of postmodernism include "a new depthlessness, which finds its prolongation both in contemporary 'theory' and a whole new culture of the image or the simulacrum; a consequent weakening of historicity, both in our relationship to public History and in the new forms of our private temporality [...]; a whole new type of emotional ground tone [...]; the deep constitutive relationships of all this to a whole new technology" (6). In particular, Jameson was critical of such postmodernist forms as architecture because "aesthetic production today has become integrated into commodity production" (4). In contrast to this view of postmodernism, feminist postmodernist critics Nancy Fraser and Linda Nicholson have pointed out that for feminists, "the question of philosophy has always been subordinate to an interest in social criticism" ("Social Criticism without Philosophy," 20). In addition, the feminist science fiction critic Jenny Wolmark argues that Jameson overemphasized the "hegemonic capacities of postmodernism," and the "negative capacities of science fiction" (*Aliens and Others,* 11, 10). Wolmark sees "the potential of science fiction to offer alternative and critical ways of imagining social and cultural reality," and she argues that "new and contradictory social constituencies have emerged within postmodernity to challenge existing hierarchies and subjectivities" (10, 11). According to Wolmark, "The formation of new subject positions in terms of race, gender and class, and redefinitions of identity as provisional and plural are an important and oppositional response to the disappearance of the unitary subject, and yet their capacity to forge new ways of conceptualizing the link between history and subjectivity is consistently underestimated by Jameson" (11).

To counter the omission of those forgotten by history and, hence, create a new subject position for them in history, Lai says, "My strategy in recent years has been to make a project of constructing a consciously artificial history for myself and others like me—a history with identified women of Chinese descent living in the West as its center" ("Political Animals and the Body of History," 149). She further explains, "I mean people who come from histories of travel and migration, people who are caught in various, often contradictory, positions with regards to the politics of race, class, gender, sexuality, the body etc., people who are somehow marked as 'other,' as different, whether that is through race, or a way of moving through space, or a way of speaking" ("Future Asians," 170). Lai inserts her Chinese Canadian protagonists into her postmodernist narrative, placing them into the historical consciousness of her Western readers at the same time. Unlike the early works of Asian American writers, who consciously wrote for a mainly white readership, Lai takes for granted the racial identity of her protagonist and does not go out of her way to describe her origins or to exoticize her and her cultural practices in the same way as earlier Asian American writers, such as Jade Snow Wong, Maxine Hong Kingston, and Amy Tan. For Lai does not spend time describing the different kinds of Chinese dishes prepared by Miranda's family or their quaint customs.[3] Instead, halfway through the first chapter featuring Miranda, her mother says of her, "It's hard enough that she's the only Asian child in her class, and surely she is aware of that" (*Salt Fish Girl*, 23). For the readers, this is the first indication that Miranda is Asian, that she is a member of a racial minority. But what is energizing about Lai's account of Miranda's activities is that in the world of Serendipity her racial identity is in many ways subsumed by other kinds of differences. There are so many other ways to be different—cloned of human and animal tissue, engendered from a durian seed—that to be Asian seems to be the least of one's worries. In this exaggerated ethnoscape, to be a hybrid means more than taking on bicultural practices; instead hybridity is used at the physical genetic or biological level. In addition, exoticization through foods, what Asian American critics have called "food pornography" (Wong, *Reading Asian American Literature*, 61), does not occur because there is so little real food prepared in Serendipity. However, when Miranda and the clone Evie do buy something to eat from the street outside of the regulated zone, they have buns, "cha siew bow" or "gai bow" (*Salt Fish Girl*, 155). What is interesting is that Lai does not pause to explain that these are Chinese buns stuffed with meat and vegetables. She simply assumes that her readers know what they are, just as she assumes that women of Chinese descent have a right to live in the West.

Though Larissa Lai has shown her concern for issues such as the writing and rewriting of history, queer Asian subjectivity, race and power since her first novel, *When Fox Is a Thousand* (see Goellnicht, "Forays into Acts of Transformation"), she more directly confronts recent issues of globalization, genetic engineering, cloning, transnational labor, and diasporic subjectivity in her second novel, *Salt Fish Girl*. Here, in both settings of the novel, she presents scenes that remind her readers of the consequences of the expansion of multinational corporations, export industrialization, and the feminization of industrial work. The fact that this poorly paid exploitative labor is found both in the nineteenth-century Asian segment and in the twenty-first-century North American segment of the narrative is suggestive of the process of industrialization that occurred all over the globe in the last half of the twentieth century. As Aihwa Ong notes, "Modernization models of capitalist development predicted an increasing adoption of mass-assembly production and the gradual decline of cottage industries in the third world" ("The Gender and Labor Politics of Postmodernity," 61). However, there is now a new mix of mass production, subcontracting, and family-type firms worldwide. "Flexible labor regimes, based primarily on female and minority workers, are now common in the third world, as well as in poor regions of metropolitan countries" (61). Furthermore, Arif Dirlik notes that "the transnationalization of production calls into question earlier divisions of the world into first, second, and third worlds [...]. Parts of the earlier Third World are today on the pathways of transnational capital and belong in the 'developed' sector of the world economy. Likewise, parts of the First World marginalized in the new global economy are hardly distinguishable in way of life from what used to be viewed as the Third World" ("The Gender and Labor Politics of Postmodernity," 31). In her study of Asian American women and transnational labor, Laura Hyun Yi Kang similarly makes the connection between Asian women in sweatshops in Asia and Asian American women working in garment shops in the United States, noting that "the deployment of Asian immigrant female workers in U.S. garment and electronics manufacturing suggests that the offshoring of production processes in Asian countries should be read in terms of increasing interpenetration across geopolitical boundaries" (*Compositional Subjects*, 183).

In *Salt Fish Girl*, young Asian women and clones perform labor-intensive work that is harmful to their health. In the nineteenth-century segment, Nu Wa sees women working at making paper products—lanterns, stationery, and brightly dyed cutouts of opera masks, palace ladies, luscious flowers and exotic animals:

> Younger women, their eyes still sharp, worked with tiny scissors under the low light, snipping away at the paper so that each figurine emerged in lacy detail beneath their hands. I did not linger long enough to notice their eyes growing dimmer, or notice the older women, nearly blind, wasting away in the dark corners of the factory mixing the colours and wheezing in reaction to the bright, powdery, dry chemical form of the dyes. (118)

Later she sees the salt fish girl wearing a tan-colored uniform with military-style pockets working in a factory. The conditions are similarly poor: "There she sat in the dim light, bleary-eyed and leaning over a scrambled mess of tin animal arms and legs, trying to nudge a spring into place with a pair of tweezers" (118). In order to earn a small living, the salt fish girl "spent all hours of daylight, and often many of darkness too, crouched under the dim lights of the factory, straining through a magnifying glass to attach tin torsos, wings, arms, beaks, legs, guns and bicycles to their springs and wind-ups with precise mechanical accuracy" (120). These descriptions of gendered labor are in keeping with the ethnographic accounts of women in factories in Taiwan and Malaysia, who also complain of being shut up all day and wasting the "spring" of their youth (see Ong, "The Gender and Labor Politics of Postmodernity," 80). Similar conditions of low wages, "hard physical labor, long hours, and an unhealthful shop environment" are reported in Chinatown garment factories in major U.S. cities (see Kang, *Compositional Subjects*, 181). The salt fish girl later becomes thin and "deathly pale," with "bruises on her legs and shoulders that [suggest she has] not been entirely passive in the goings-on at the factory" (123). Refusing to work under such conditions and for so little return, Nu Wa picks the pockets of Western tourists and businessmen on busy streets instead. Both these occupations are precarious and dangerous, and Lai links the lack of viable career alternatives in an economically impoverished country not only to poor standards of living and ill health but also to crime and despair.

In the futuristic segment, Lai warns us against the misuse and overuse of science and genetic engineering, particularly in conjunction with capitalism.[4] Tara Lee notes, "Late capitalism wants bodies that are controlled by the global market, and in the case of noncompliant bodies, it will not hesitate to suppress and reshape them into conformity. Science not only aids capitalism in regulating disruptive bodies, but it also provides the technology to enable the disassembly and the subsequent reassembly of these deviant bodies into a semblance of unity" ("Mutant Bodies in Larissa Lai's *Salt Fish Girl*," 94). Miranda finds out that in her "brave new world" of Serendipity, there are powerful companies that make not only products, such as shoes, but also people. She learns from Evie, who herself has been cloned from human tissue and "point zero three percent freshwater carp" (*Salt Fish Girl*, 158), that a company called Pallas, a thinly disguised version of Nike, has been cloning people for a number of years in order to keep its labor costs low.[5] These cloned people, all Asian or native in their features, form the ideal labor pool, because they are without family, without nation, and without history. They look identical to each other, and instead of names, they are given numbers, so that they are Sonia 116, Sonia 121, Sonia 148, and so forth.[6] However, though they are clones, they are not without the inclination to rebel. In her study of Malay and South Korean women factory workers, Aihwa Ong found that they used "a range of resistance tactics that silently negotiated the contours of daily work relations" ("The Gender and Labor Politics of Postmodernity," 83) and that these women had organized themselves and "developed a whole repertoire of tactics and images expressing their struggles" (85). Andrew Ross has also outlined a number of efforts at stamping out sweatshops, organizing coalitions, and staging boycotts by labor movements that have made some impact on the fashion industry (see the introduction to *No Sweat*). Similarly, in Lai's novel the Sonias, with a name provided to a particular kind of clone, have organized ways of resistance and made plans to build a "free society of their own kind from the ground up" (*Salt Fish

Girl, 256). One way they communicate their dissatisfaction is through the soles of the shoes they make: "The soles of the shoes functioned like rubber stamps" (237), with various messages, saying:

> What does it mean to be human?
> How old is history?
> The shoemakers have no elves. (237)

Another imprint reveals the huge profits made by the shoe company:

> Materials: 10 units
> Labour: 3 units
> Retail price: 169 units
> Profit: 156 units
> Do you care? (238)

It is the combination of exploitative labor practices with science that is particularly troubling in this dystopia.

In addition to the use of racialized and gendered labor by capitalistic corporations, another element of contemporary culture that Lai critiques is the excessive disciplining of female bodies. With some humor, Lai pokes fun at the way the ideal feminine body in our culture is purged of all associations with dirt, leaks, smells, and scatological functions, the qualities Julia Kristeva associates with the abject in *Powers of Horror* (chapter 1). For Kristeva, what causes abjection is "what disturbs identity, system, order. What does not respect borders, positions, rules. The in-between, the ambiguous, the composite" (4). Miranda, like the cloned Evie and the Sonias, exists in this abject zone of the in-between. Miranda emanates an odor "akin to cat urine," or "a stink of durian" (*Salt Fish Girl*, 69). She has some skin trouble, an "aggravated form of psoriasis" (69), that later causes her to shed scales, and has "two small fistulas, one above each ear" (69), which hold puss. She remembers things that went on before she was born, and "things that happened in other lifetimes" (70). Her very existence reminds the people in Serendipity of their origins, of their relation to the body, and of their mortality, and she becomes a threat to the false sense of serenity in that city. As Monica Chiu has argued in *Filthy Fictions*, there is a historical association of dirt and disease with the Chinese that "speaks more clearly to the nation's own preoccupation with moral and medical self-hygiene than to that of the Chinese and other immigrants" (7). Chiu notes that "the subtle and overt references to Asian Americans as filthy that fill the pages of contemporary Asian American fiction offer counterperspectives rejecting an Orientalism rooted in Yellow Peril rhetoric" (4). In Lai's book it is not so much dirt but smell that is the sign of the pollution and pathology.

Miranda, like the cloned Sonias, is aberrant and abnormal and deemed monstrous. Of the monstrous, Rosi Braidotti says, "Contemporary 'monstrous Others' blur the dividing line between the organic and the inorganic, thus also rendering superfluous the political divide between technophobia and technophilia" ("Cyberteratologies," 153). For Braidotti, "The monstrous expresses a deep anxiety about the bodily roots of subjectivity that foreground the material/maternal feminine as the site of monstrosity" (154). This figure becomes a "counterpart and counterpoint to the emphasis hegemonic postindustrial culture places upon the construction of clean, healthy, fit, white, decent, law-abiding, heterosexual, and forever young bodies" (154). In contrast to this clean, fit body that always needs to be disciplined by exercise, diets, deodorants, mouth fresheners, and sanitary products is Miranda's body, stinking and leaking fluid. In both the nineteenth-century Asian segment and the futuristic North American segment of the novel, what is emphasized are the smells of women: the salt fish girl smells of the salty fish that she sells, and when she smelled it, Nu Wa says, "the stink of it made me want to live more than ever" (*Salt Fish Girl*, 56). In the futuristic segment, Miranda is similarly attracted to Evie because of her salt fish smell. When they make love, their bodies exude pungent, earthy odors: "When she kissed me it was like both eating and drinking at the same time. The stench that poured from our bodies was overwhelming—something between rotting garbage and heavenly stew. We rode the hiss and fizzle of salt fish and durian, minor notes of sour plum, fermented tofu, boiled dong quai—all those things buried and forgotten in the years of corporate homogenization. Steam rose from us like water splashed on a hot pan of garlic greens" (225). This focus on stench has offended some reviewers of the book,[7] but in the context of Jameson's critique of postmodernity for its lack of history and depthlessness, these images are important. For the smells are all linked to Miranda's, and presumably Evie's, Asian past, a tactile, material, and significant past that has been buried by "corporate homogenization" (*Salt Fish Girl*, 225). The foods evoked by the lovemaking are all slightly smelly delicacies that bring back forgotten memories and emphasize Miranda and Evie's difference from the inhabitants of this "brave new world." For them there is no need to mask the smells with air fresheners or bleach. The smells suggest sexual defiance, pleasure, and female strength.

Healing the Community

Also using strong smells and tastes in a playful manner, Chitra Divakaruni raises many of the same issues addressed by *Salt Fish Girl* in *The Mistress of Spices*, a novel similarly concerned with global migration, history, and female bodies. Set in Oakland, California, with flashbacks to an island somewhere in South Asia, Divakaruni's novel is closer to fantasy and magic realism than it is to science fiction.[8] It is not as symmetrically divided between two locations as Lai's book; most of it is set in present-day California. However, the past and the mystical practices of the East are evoked through the first-person narrative of Tilottama (Tilo), the mistress of spices. Through special insights that enable her to see beyond the surface of things and into the hearts and minds of her customers, Tilo adds a textured layer of commentary to the otherwise everyday lives of diasporic Indians. With some of her customers she sees the history behind their frustration or anger; with others she acts as their confidante and finds out how their displacement has caused them trouble in their adopted country. Her remarks often provide readers with ways to understand the problems experienced by her customers not as the problems of an individual but as those of many, with roots in structural inequities in society or caused by institutional, legal, or political injustices. Like Lai, Divakaruni examines some of the evils caused by globalization, but she does so through the local. As Gita Rajan says, "By not attempting to effect huge changes through the usual tropes of history, politics, and fantasy as magic realism would, Divakaruni is able to work on a smaller scale and address the psychological needs of her disempowered cast of characters" ("Chitra Divakaruni's *The Mistress of Spices*," 217). The mistress of spices heals and helps her local community of Indians, Pakistanis, and Bangladeshis from within the very insular and small space of her spice store, not by attempting to kill the heads of corporations or the directors of scientific laboratories.

Through a detailed look at the Oakland neighborhood around the Spice Bazaar, Divakaruni shows that the transnational movement of people across the globe has not always had positive effects. The setting, though in the so-called First World, is rather indistinguishable from what earlier was called Third World landscapes. The store is described by Tilo:

> Perfect-fitted between the narrow barred door of Rosa's Weekly Hotel, still blackened from a year-ago fire, and Lee Ying's Sewing Machine and Vacuum Cleaner Repair, with the glass cracked between the R and the e. Grease-smudged window. Looped letters that say SPICE BAZAAR faded into a dried-mud brown. Inside walls veined with cobwebs where hang discolored pictures of the gods, their sad shadow eyes. (*The Mistress of Spices*, 4)

This description presents an image very unlike that in the film version (2006), in which the spice bazaar is set in a nice, upper-middle-class neighborhood. In the novel the residents of the neighborhood come from all over the globe, as the names of these establishments suggest, but their settlement and acceptance by their host community are unstable and inconsistent. Like the signs indicating the names of their businesses, which are cracked and smudged, their lives are in need of attention, repairs, and help. Globalization and global movements have improved the lives of many, but through this neighborhood that has seen better days we see that, in the words of Dirlik, quoted earlier, "parts of the First World marginalized in the new global economy are hardly distinguishable in way of life from what used to be viewed as the Third World" ("The Global in the Local," 31).

Although Tilo is not always able to help make everyone's lives better, her account of the experiences of these diasporic Indians serves to illuminate some of the "local" consequences of globalization and modernization. Dirlik has argued that one positive effect of attention to the local is that "it rescues from invisibility those who were earlier viewed as castaways from history, whose social and cultural forms of existence appear in the narrative of modernization at best as irrelevancies, at worst as minor obstacles to be extinguished on the way to development" ("The Global in the Local," 25). Through Tilo Divakaruni presents a number of vignettes of people who are "castaways from history" because, individually, they are too insignificant for postmodernism's grand narratives of development. One of the most poignant stories is that of Mohan, the proprietor of Mohan Indian Foods, who is badly beaten up by two young American skinheads in "tight-fitting camouflage jackets" (*The Mistress of Spices*, 179). They taunt and insult him, saying, "Sonofabitch Indian, shoulda stayed in your own goddamn country" (180), then proceed to destroy his store, "kicking at the cart until it comes crashing down and the kababs and *samosas* that [his wife] Veena so carefully rolled and stuffed scatter everywhere in the dirt" (180). In self-defense, he hits one of them with a stone that he happens to reach. Later the men hire lawyers to claim that the Indian started it all. Disabled, unable to walk or work, he loses his store and finds out months later that the men have been acquitted of all charges. Depressed, feeling helpless with rage at the injustice, he becomes unstable and eventually "doesn't speak another word" (182). Finally, neighbors "pool together ticket money to send him and Veena back home, for what else is left for them in this country" (182). Although globalization is supposed to create transnational subjects who are able to move back and forth between continents, the story of Mohan presents an ironic twist to global mobility. For Mohan the movement across the globe occurs because of desperate circumstances and with pain, not out of choice or for leisure. This incident turns him into a migrant laborer as opposed to a transmigrant worker.

Although focused mainly on South Asian characters, Divakaruni's ethnoscape, that of multicultural Oakland, enables her to include the problems of other ethnic groups that are similarly disenfranchised by the dominant culture. One of the most fully developed stories in the novel is that of Raven, the half–Native American, half-white man who falls in love with Tilo. Lara Merlin suggests that through Raven "Divakaruni meditates upon the meaning of the word Indian—signifying both the Native American and the subcontinental—in order to remark upon the creative power of language and to broaden the concept of what it means to be an American" ("Review of 'The Mistress of Spices,'" 207). The Raven subplot, which includes a flashback narrative about Raven's upbringing and the story of his mother, illustrates the effects of what I have called "the politics of the visible" on native and minoritized subjects in North America.[9] As I have argued in *The Politics of the Visible*, the gaze of the dominant culture and repetitive negative stereotypes exert a powerful influence on minority subjects that ultimately creates a debilitating psychic sense of otherness and abjection in racialized subjects (introduction). Raven's native mother, who for years has passed as white, has internalized the sense of shame and inadequacy that one acquires after years of seeing oneself through the eyes of whites. She sees herself and her native culture as deficient, dirty, and backward. Raven had believed that he was white "for a long time, growing up" and recalls the way his mother "was always cleaning, with an angry kind of energy" (*The Mistress of Spices*, 163). He is shocked to discover one day that "her hair wasn't naturally curly" (166), and he remembers how she always used to say she wished Raven's hair "was more like Dad's and not so coarse and coalblack" (165). At one crucial point in his life, she stops Raven from learning about and inheriting the "old ways" from his great-grandfather (213), because for her, native culture represents nothing more than drunks, fat women "eating chunks of fried dough," and a life of squalor (220).

The disavowal of native culture, traditions, and heritage by Raven's mother and many others of her generation of the 1950s through the 1970s in order to enter into middle-class capitalist mobility parallels the attitudes of the young South Asians who enter Tilo's store today. For example, Jagjit struggles with his Punjabi parents and longs to be part of the gang of big American boys who wear "blue satin jackets [...,] black berets," and "hundred-dollar Karl Kani boots" (126). They buy him "*stuff, clothes shoes food watches Nintendo games stereos with speakers to make the walls shake*" (127), and Jagjit believes that if he hangs around with them, one day they will give him, "cold and black-shining and heavy with power [...] pulsing electric as life, as death," a "passport into the real America" (127). In this case, as in that of Raven's mother, America is aligned with the fantasy of materialistic luxuries as well as the promise of psychic completion and identity, the "power" of being a real American. Indian immigrants wish for not only economic status and mobility but also sociocultural, political, and professional respect and mobility that seem elusive, granted only to white Americans. Similarly, in another instance, in one of Tilo's insights she sees a little Indian girl who wishes for "a house, a big two-story house with flowers in front and no clothes hanging out of windows, and enough rooms so we don't sleep two to a bed [... with] lots and lots of Barbie dolls," as well as for "American skin that American hair those blue blue American eyes so that no one will stare [...] except to say WOW" (66). This little girl, too, has learned to feel ashamed of the physical features and culture and practices of diasporic South Asians and longs to be white and rich.

Two critics of globalization, Jeremy Brecher and Tim Costello, point out, "It is often said that globalization is leading to a global village. It would perhaps be more apt to say that globalization in its present form is leading to a pillage of the planet and its people" (*Global Village or Global Pillage*, 33). In the illustrations given by Divakaruni, both Jagjit and the unnamed Punjabi girl are displaced, brought to America by their parents' desires for economic and social improvements. They learn to have desires that are influenced by American television, media, and consumer society, yet their abilities to fulfill those desires are limited. If wealth and power are tied in their minds to being white American, they have to dissociate themselves from their South Asian culture in order to find economic and psychoemotional fulfillment. One problem of globalization, then, is that it has succeeded to the extent that is has homogenized the desires of peoples across the globe without giving everyone equal access to the fulfillment of those desires.

Another important issue that Divakaruni raises in *The Mistress of Spices* is that of the ideology of female beauty and its relationship to age. Feminist critics from Simone de Beauvoir to Naomi Wolf have pointed out that there is a "beauty myth" that controls women: "strong men battle for beautiful women, and beautiful women are more reproductively successful," notes Wolf (*The Beauty Myth*, 10). De Beauvoir observes that women are "called upon for youth and health" as well as beauty (*The Second Sex*, 157). Both feminists remark that beauty is antithetical to age. Wolf says, "Aging in women is 'unbeautiful' since women grow more powerful with time" (14), while de Beauvoir says, "The old woman, the homely woman, are not merely objects without allure—they arouse hatred mingled with fear. In them reappears the disquieting figure of the Mother, when once the charms of the Wife have vanished" (160). Divakaruni attempts to problematize these myths of beauty by having her protagonist appear as an old woman through most of the novel. Unfortunately, this element of the tale is not featured in the film version, in which beautiful young Aishwarya Rai plays Tilo. In the novel the mistress of spices, a young woman in the body of an old one, has been forbidden to look at herself in the mirror, a prohibition that is significant because it prevents her from spending time on her hair, dress, or makeup, thereby liberating her from many of the beauty rituals and vanities to which contemporary women succumb.

In the novel the attractiveness and beauty of women come from their internal strength and powers. For example, Tilo observes that the old woman on the island was "at once oldest and most beautiful of women with her silver wrinkles, though later I would see that she was not beautiful in the way men use the word. Her voice, which I would later learn in all its tones—anger and mockery and sadness—was sweet as the wind in the cinnamon trees behind her. A yearning to belong to her buffeted me like the waves I had fought all night" (*The Mistress of Spices*, 34–35). Here Tilo expresses more than respect for the old woman; she actually expresses a yearning for her. Later Tilo herself attracts the libidinous attention of Raven, though she is poorly clad and appears to be an old woman. She describes herself as "bent woman with skin the color of old sand" (4). What Raven sees is something beneath the exterior, a sign of her spiritual powers. He feels a desire for her companionship, her sympathy, and her wisdom. In many ways this feeling of being loved for oneself is the dream of every woman, but it is a dream that is at odds with the ideology of beauty. In the novel Divakaruni shows that contemporary women, even someone as determined as Tilo, still struggle daily with notions of femininity and beauty, as defined by Western-dominated media and visual culture. After a meeting with Raven, Tilo experiences a longing to see herself, to learn the "secret" of herself that a mirror can tell (151). She decides to risk it all by exchanging one night with Raven, in which her body appears young and beautiful, for a hundred years on the island or a single moment of conflagration (278).

The story of Tilo echoes that of the Arthurian legend of Gawain and the Loathly Lady, a tale that is told by Geoffrey Chaucer's Wife of Bath but that also existed in different versions in the Middle Ages. In the last two hundred years, it has been retold and exists mainly as a children's story (see Susan Reed, "Re-telling of 'Sir Gawain and Dame Ragnell,'" and Thomas Bulfinch, "Sir Gawain"). Both Tilo and the Loathly Lady are beautiful young women who have become ugly and old because of magic spells or charms. They both encounter a young man with whom they have a relationship in which the lack of youth and beauty becomes an obstacle to romantic love. The Loathly Lady story is a female version of the tale of the Frog Prince, in which an ugly hag is transformed into a beautiful woman only after a young man has been able to conquer his aversion to her; in the Loathly Lady's case, the transformation occurs after the man has relinquished his "sovereignty" or need for control. In Divakaruni's novel the lady has become loathly by choice in order to gain the power to help others. Yet she, too, desires to be beautiful once she meets someone she wishes to please. In "Foucault, Femininity, and the Modernization of Patriarchal Power," Sandra Lee Bartky talks about the various ways women discipline their bodies—through diets, exercise, bodily gestures, facial creams, makeup, and so on. She says, "the disciplinary practices I have described are part of the process by which the ideal body of femininity—and hence the feminine body-subject—is constructed; in doing this, they produce a 'practiced and subjected' body, that is, a body on which an inferior status has been inscribed" (71). Women have been taught to believe that without self-discipline, exercise, and cosmetics their bodies are not good enough. This ideology of the inferior female body even affects Tilo. At one point, she disobeys the injunctions of the First Mother and goes to a department store. She is tempted to buy frivolous things, like

> a mirror. A color TV so I may see into the heart of America, into the heart, I hope, of my lonely American. A makeup-kit with everything in it. Perfume of rose and lavender. Shoes, several pairs, in different colors, the last ones red as burnished chilies, high heels like chisels. Clothes and more clothes—dresses pantsuits sweaters, the intricate, wispy mysteries of American feminine underwear. And last of all a bed robe of white lace like raindrops caught in a spider's web. (*The Mistress of Spices*, 138)

However, she stops herself from completing these purchases. This temptation scene reveals the pervasive power of consumer advertising, American media, and fashion, demonstrating how they affect even those who are determined to live outside of these systems.

Although the female protagonists in Larissa Lai's *Salt Fish Girl* are othered because of their peculiarities of origin and their partly inhuman attributes, in *The Mistress of Spices* the protagonist struggles with otherness that comes from age and from culturally defined notions of beauty and ugliness. The ending of the novel offers a compromise for the vexed question of female beauty. Tilo does not become youthful and beautiful, but neither is she old and ugly. Instead she is given a body that is not "in youth's first roseglow, but not one in age's last unflowering either" (325).

What is crucial about the resolution of Divakaruni's novel is that it refuses to fully succumb to the romance of the exotic or take refuge in the mythic goodness of native or Indian originary culture. Raven tells Tilo that he has always had a dream or vision of an earthly paradise: "high in the mountains' pine and eucalyptus, damp odor of redwood, bark and cone, a stream so cool and fresh to the mouth you feel you've never tasted water before" (211). He proposes to take Tilo there, to "nature undiluted, in beauty and harshness both" (212), to live "alongside the bear lifting his mouth to the rowanberry, the antelope standing tall, listening for sounds. The mountain lion springing upon its fleeing prey" (212). Such an Edenic life, however, is not feasible in a postlapsarian multicultural America. Instead of ending her novel with the couple in some mountain idyll, Divakaruni presents a more up-to-date and down-to-earth vision of happiness. Happiness, according to the novel's conclusion, is only to be found in the service of others, in helping others. Tilo finds herself unable to go with Raven to seek his paradise. The novel does not end with the romantic union of the heterosexual couple, as the film version does. Instead Tilo feels compelled to go back to Oakland to help those who have been devastated by an earthquake that might have been brought on by her disobedience. Tilo concludes, "There is no earthly paradise. Except what we can make back there, in the soot in the rubble in the crisped-away flesh. In the guns and needles, the white drug-dust, the young men and women lying down to dreams of wealth and power and waking in cells. Yes, in the hate in the fear" (336). For Divakaruni as well as for Larissa Lai in *Salt Fish Girl*, endowing a protagonist with the ability to transcend geographical boundaries does not mean that she is able to neglect or magically remove the problems of the here and the everyday. Their heroines are shown to struggle daily with the challenges of technology, globalization, and cultural differences. What fantasy does, however, is allow us to see these problems in a more acute and provocative way, presenting us with different possibilities for understanding and resolving these large issues.

6
Scripting Fertility: Desire and Regeneration in Japanese North American Literature

A number of Japanese North American novels have explored the traumatic experience of dislocation, internment, confiscation of property, and dispersals of the Japanese Canadian and Japanese American communities during and after the Second World War and the consequences of these events. The best-known example is Joy Kogawa's *Obasan*, which delineates the mostly silent suffering of Japanese Canadians during that period. Other works about Japanese Americans during the war include Monica Itoi Sone's *Nisei Daughter* and John Okada's *No-No Boy*. Recently Japanese Canadian and Japanese American novels have been moving away from focusing on that subject and have attempted to go beyond an ethnographic account of the way the issei, nisei, and sansei cope with the internment and dispersal. Two novels that have appeared in the last few years have employed a deliberately playful tone, focused on protagonists who are decidedly not silent, acquiescent subjects or model minorities and whose trajectories are not from the west coast to the camps but involve a great deal of displacement across North America. Hiromi Goto's *The Kappa Child* (2001) and Ruth Ozeki's *All Over Creation* (2003), though different in genre, share similar concerns and are noteworthy examples of a shift in tendency in Japanese North American literature.

No longer limited to a mainly realist account of immigrant experiences of assimilation and acculturation, Asian North American authors such as Goto and Ozeki take on wide-ranging issues, such as normative traditional family values, globalization, contemporary capitalist culture, ecology, sexuality, and desire outside of what Adrienne Rich calls "compulsory heterosexuality" in her book of that name. The protagonists of both *The Kappa Child* and *All Over Creation* are women who lead rather unorthodox lives. They do not follow the usual pattern of the immigrant character struggling to fulfill the American dream. They are not particularly interested in the corporate definition of success but instead attempt to find different ways of achieving wholeness and harmony in their lives. Coincidentally, they both come from dysfunctional families and, by the start of each novel, have escaped, at least physically, from their families, who are on farms. Much of the narrative of each novel is taken up with coming to terms with the heroines' painful pasts, as well as with their strong-willed patriarchal fathers, whose parenting skills, like their farming efforts, leave something to be desired. The protagonists' rejection of their fathers parallels their rejection of the values taught by them—rugged individualism, competition, the importance of profit and business, and eventually desirable assimilation as model minorities.

It might seem, at first glance, that questions of representation and stereotypes of Asian Americans and Asian Canadians—as model minorities or exotic Oriental dolls—do not have much to do with issues of globalization and globality. However, Asian female bodies have been consistently produced and reproduced in Western media and transnational culture in particular ways that have facilitated their work in specialized areas. As Laura Kang argues, Asian female bodies "have come to matter" in transnational labor: in "political economies of assembly-line manufacturing, military prostitution, and sex tourism" (*Compositional Subjects*, 165). Kang explains:"Through the attribution of such inherent characteristics as childlike innocence and docility, digital nimbleness, physical stamina, keen eyesight, sexual largess, and muscular flexiblity, Asian women have been figured as especially suited to conduct certain labor needs of transnational capitalism" (165).

In previous chapters we have seen how authors like Kwa, Keller, and Lai have highlighted and problematized the work of Asian women in military prostitution, in the sex industry, and in assembly-line manufacturing. In this chapter I argue that although Goto and Ozeki do not deal with these types of work, they intentionally and good-humoredly rework stereotypes of Asian women's docility, reliability, innocence, and sexual pliancy in order to challenge what is expected, and in some cases required, of Asian women globally. Thus, in their novels the representation of characters who might be considered "failures" in capitalist society, and also of Asian North American women who do not possess delicate, agile bodies or nimble fingers, becomes a tactic of subversion.

Alien Bodies

Japanese Canadian Hiromi Goto's second novel, *The Kappa Child*, features a female protagonist who has an "abnormal pregnancy" (12) resulting from a dalliance with a strange creature on an airport strip during the "last total eclipse of the twentieth century" (119). This stranger, with otherworldly features, appears in the narrative only briefly but is pivotal to the novel. The extraterrestrial figure, along with the mythical Kappa creature who results from the pregnancy, add an unexpected twist to the book, shifting it generically from a seemingly realist narrative about growing up on the Canadian prairies to a magic realist or science fiction novel. *The Kappa Child* was the winner of the 2001 Tiptree Award for a work "that explores and expands gender roles in science fiction and fantasy." Like Goto's first novel, *Chorus of Mushrooms* (1994), and recent works by other Asian Canadians, such as Larissa Lai's *Salt Fish Girl* (2002), it represents an attempt by a racially minoritized writer to go beyond the boundaries of the autobiographical or the first-person ethnographic text, a genre most frequently associated with ethnic and postcolonial writing before the mid-1980s.[1] In *The Kappa Child* Goto makes use of a form that until recently had been targeted to a primarily male audience in addressing the concerns of globalized and minority subjects.[2] Goto employs science fiction and fantasy not only to write about gender, as the Tiptree Award announcement notes (James Tiptree Jr. Award Council, "The 2001 James Tiptree Jr. Award"), but also to explore different forms of otherness. Instead of using the form of a traditional *Bildungsroman*, Goto uses a popular genre to look at some of the most pressing questions facing global and ethnic subjects today—gendered and racialized identity in a multicultural society, female selfhood, representation in an increasingly homogenized world, and the psychic consequences of being an other in North American contemporary culture.

Hiromi Goto says, "I have not been abducted by aliens but I live well aware of race, the alien space I inhabit in a colonized country. If you want out of alien space, you must pretend not to notice daily references to the fact that you are an alien" ("Alien Texts, Alien Seductions," 263). For people of color, the notion of the alien has a particularly negative resonance. No matter how long one has lived in North America, people with racialized bodies are "resident aliens" or strangers, always being asked to demonstrate their right to belong or else constantly being reminded of their status as Other in one's country. The heroine of Goti's second novel, aware of the corporeal dissonance between what is expected of Asian women and what she feels, says, "You go your whole life without seeing yourself as you really are. All you know is how you are treated" (*The Kappa Child,* 14). In *The Kappa Child* Goto literalizes[3] this condition of nonbelonging and self-estrangement by having her protagonist embody the state of corporeal anomaly by harboring another body, that of a strange creature, within her own. Expanding on the arguments of feminist science fiction critic Sarah Lefanu, Rosi Braidotti notes that there is a "deep empathy between women and aliens [...]. As a matter of fact, in science fiction written by women, women love aliens and feel connected to them by a deep bond of recognition" ("Cyberteratologies," 152–53). Braidotti explains that this feeling comes about because "of a structural analogy between woman as the second sex [...] and the alien or monstrous Other" (152). The same could be said of minority subjects, who are also regarded as others in a predominantly white cultural space.

The alien becomes a material and embodied reality for Asians in North America through the example of Goto's Japanese Canadian science fiction version of *Little House on the Prairie.* The heroine's seduction by the stranger and her pregnancy, which results in the birth of the Kappa, a water sprite from Japanese myths, bring out some of the concerns prevalent in Goto's fiction—that of the stranger within the self and that of racial alienation in North American. In addition, other themes found in her first novel, *Chorus of Mushrooms,* resurface here: food as a means of social cohesion, female bonding, and the importance of the small local community. Because of her problematic father and family life, the heroine of *The Kappa Child* has to find sustenance and emotional support from outside of her nuclear family. Wendy Pearson notes, "Thematically, [...] *Kappa Child* is really about families, both the ones you're born into and the ones you make for yourself; it's about the difficulties and joys of human relationships, of friendship, of sisterhood, and of love" ("Saturating the Present with the Past," n.p.). The protagonist finds support and forms ties with women who understand her invisible pregnancy and her craving for specific foods, such as the Japanese cucumber. In Goto's novel the heroine's unusual condition paves the way for an eventual scene of regeneration and reconciliation between the self and other, between reality and fantasy, between Asian and Canadian. The heroine aptly comments at one point, "Every event in my life has led to this. To normalize the incredible. And really, what other choices are there?" (*The Kappa Child*, 218).

In spite of the one crucial scene that involves an extraterrestrial encounter, most of *The Kappa Child* does not involve "extraterrestrial settings, futuristic technologies, alien creatures, and other strategies that defamiliarize" the fictional world (Hayles and Gessler, "The Slipstream of Mixed Reality," 482). Instead, the novel can be described as "slipstream fiction," which Bruce Sterling defined as "works that occupy a borderland between mainstream and science fiction because they achieve a science-fiction feeling without the usual defamiliarizing devices" (quoted by Hayles and Gessler, 482). The mystery that drives the plot of *The Kappa Child* is whether the protagonist is actually pregnant, as she believes, or not, and if so, who is the father of the child. Flashbacks present us with insights about her childhood and adolescence on the prairies and the ways in which the nameless protagonist's early life is so unlike that described in *Little House on the Prairie*, a book she reads when the family moves to Lethbridge, Alberta (*The Kappa Child*, 33). The intertextual references to Laura Ingalls Wilder's book are significant: Wilder's book is about moving a Euro-American family into new territory (Indian) and about settlement from the perspective of a female protagonist; Goto's novel is about moving a Japanese Canadian family into mainly white territory (formerly Indian). If the move westward by American pioneers of the nineteenth century greatly transformed America, Goto is suggesting that a similar kind of migration is happening today. Roy Miki has observed, "The influx of 'asian' capital, goods, and populations into the urban core of Canadian cities (more so on the west coast) is rapidly transforming the scripting of 'asian' in what is still a white man's country [...]. How these changes will reconfigure the lexicon of current cultural politics—and thus the mutations of racialization—waits to be seen" (*Broken Entries*, 214). Goto's novel suggests that this contemporary movement of Asian peoples will not become the kind of wholesome and adventurous family entertainment that Ingalls' move was. Before the end of the summer, the protagonist burns her copy of *Little House on the Prairie* as her reality falls short of that seen in the American classic.

Like Ruth Ozeki's *All Over Creation*, *The Kappa Child* is concerned with healing—the regeneration of individuals as well as humanity and the earth. Pregnancy and childbirth are offered as partial solutions to a broken world. In both books the protagonists are not great men but inconsequential, sometimes bungling and seemingly ineffective women. These heroines serve to debunk the myth of the Asian American model minority and the stereotype of the exotic Oriental, for both do not hold particularly good jobs, are not exemplary citizens, and are not "geisha-ized" Japanese women.[4] Goto remarked in an interview that even if her characters are "small and their power is defined within a finite sphere, they are capable of, first, really seeing their circumstances and second, making a self-award choice." She noted, "I'm a firm believer in the accumulative power of small actions" (Kong, "Sook C. Kong Interviews Hiromi Goto"). Hence, the unnamed protagonist of *The Kappa Child* is a bit of a drifter, suffering from a lack of self-esteem and possibly depression. She works as a shopping cart collector, a job that is hardly typical of Asian females and does not require delicacy, nimble fingers, or sexual largess. From her marginalized position, however, she sees that the world around her is in need of repair or help.

The imagery that permeates the first few pages of *The Kappa Child* is that of the wounded and hurt. Rather humorously, the protagonist tells her boss on her CB that she is bringing in some shopping carts: "I have incoming wounded. I repeat. I have incoming wounded" (10). Later she calls them her "maimed and scattered carts" (11). The evening is described as "the crest of night splinters" (11). This language of hurt and pain is continued in the descriptions of the protagonist's state of mind and body. She talks about the way she leaves "a huge trail of dispirit which meanders everywhere" she walks (11). Her life seems to be rather empty of passion, and she feels reluctant to go home at the end of the day: "There are no love stories waiting for me and I'm not up to invention. Too bad, barbed wire's always easier to crawl through when there's someone else to make the space wider with a helpful hand and foot" (11). Instead of one who is a full participant in capitalist consumer culture, the protagonist is one who does not use shopping carts but finds wounded carts. Her relation to global capitalism, like her relation to the rest of society, is that of an outsider, a retriever of the wounded.

The protagonist's sense of alienation comes from a strong sense of difference and otherness that she feels, partly because of things that happened in the past in her family and partly because of her perception of her Asian body. She says: "A child isn't born bitter. I point no fingers as to who tainted the clean, pure pool of my childhood. Let's just say that when I realized that I didn't want to grow up, the damage was already done" (13). Like her shopping carts, she and her sisters are "wounded" and "maimed." They have had difficulties dealing with their hybrid Japanese Canadian identity, and this problem is revealed by their awkward names or lack of names. The protagonist, as mentioned, is nameless throughout the book. Her sisters are known by demeaning and pejorative names because people around them could not remember their Japanese names. The narrator says, "Okasan gave us all Japanese names too, but folks couldn't remember for nothing, as the saying goes. Hard to know what was worse. Having names no one could say or being called names not our own" (15). So, according to the narrator, she makes up names for them, "based on the animal of our birth year, names that would disguise and protect us" (15). Her sister, born the year of the boar, becomes Pig Girl, or PG for short. Her other sisters are called Mice and Slither. These unfortunate names stick to them, and the negative qualities of the animals become linked to the women. They become associated with these animals, lower than humans on the scale of living creatures, living furtive, subterranean existences.

Another reason for the protagonist's unease with her self and her body is her childhood in a dysfunctional family. Having grown up with an abusive, temperamental father and a fearful mother, she has not had the love and nurturing that she ought to have had. At their Easter dinner, Mice accidentally drops some turkey on the father's lap. He yells and raises his hands, and the family cringes in anticipation of his blows: "We cringe to the thud of blood in our heads. Anything more and Okasan will shatter like a pane of glass, we will only slice our hands if we try to salvage her. Don't move. Be still" (27). However, as they are now adults, for the first time all the sisters stand up to face his rage, and he is unable to strike them. Instead he "grabs two fistfuls of tablecloth and pulls. Turkey, carcass, stewed cabbage rolls, buns, sashimi, sekihan, potato salad, peas and carrots. The hours of work Okasan has spent, wasted on the floor" (27). The narrator cleans up the mess while her sister, Slither, decides to run away. The narrator concludes: "There's no use in sitting here. And if we stick around, our mother might get it into her head that her children ought to notice her and give the love she always wanted but could never receive. Ha! That's a laugh. We can't even love ourselves" (31). This incident is indicative of many such incidents in her childhood and youth that contribute to the protagonist's disabling sense of herself.

This inability to love herself shows in the way the protagonist dresses. She claims to have "the most expansive collection of pajamas in the western hemisphere" (51) and wears nothing but pajamas every day. She describes her body as one atypical of exotic Asian women:

> I am not a beautiful Asian. I am not beautiful. There is a difference between being petite and short; one is more attractive than the other. Don't get me wrong, I'm not bitter about my lack of physical beauty. My beauty lies beneath a tough surface, like a pomegranate, my Okasan is fond of telling me [...]. Clothing does not fit me. My big-boned arms, my daikon legs, my beta-beta feet, and splaying toes. My bratwurst fingers and nonexistent neck. And my head. My poor colossal head, too huge even to dream of a ten-gallon hat. (51)

Comparing herself to the ideal Western figure, which in itself is an unattainable ideal for most Western women, the protagonist finds her body lacking. In her description of herself she uses food imagery—the pomegranate, daikon, and bratwurst. The protagonist feels that she will be consumed or fears being eaten up by society. Sandra Lee Bartky has argued that the ideal body in our modern society is a "practiced and subjected body" that needs to be "made-over" with cosmetics, exercise, and surgery ("Foucault, Femininity, and the Modernization of Patriarchal Power," 71). She writes: "The disciplinary project of femininity is a 'setup': it requires such a radical and extensive measure of bodily transformation that virtually every woman who gives herself to it is destined in some degree to fail. Thus, a measure of shame is added to a woman's sense that the body she inhabits is deficient: she ought to take better care of herself; she might after all have jogged that last mile" (71). This sense of failure can be exacerbated for ethnic and racialized women who live in North America. Their sense of shame and failure is even greater because they feel that they do not have the right color of hair, eyes, or skin or the right kind of nose, hair, or proportions compared to the Euro-American women on magazine covers, in TV commercials, and in Hollywood films.

Furthermore, the description of the protagonist's body is grotesque and hyperbolic. She talks about her "colossal" head and "nonexistent" neck. Mary Russo notes that one form of the grotesque is associated with the uncanny; the grotesque body is "doubled, monstrous, deformed, excessive, and abject" and is "not identified with materiality as such, but assumes a division or distance between the discursive fictions of the biological body and the law" (*The Female Grotesque*, 9). In addition, Russo points out that the sense of the uncanny was associated by the German Romantics with "a generalized *alienation* from the-world-which-has-become strange" (9). This sense of the grotesque is applicable to the condition of the protagonist, who sees her body as monstrous and deformed and who lives as if the world around her is not part of her but always laughing at her, ready to harm her, or about to eat her up. She lives alone in a basement apartment, and even when her own sister asks if she can spend a night at her place, the protagonist gets nervous. The protagonist thinks: "She's my *sister!* She's done nothing to hurt me! But she could hurt me all the same. She's so needy. [...] What if she wants me to save her and I can't? What if she tries to take more than I can give?" (*The Kappa Child*, 58). Unable to see her own strength and beauty, she is unable to offer love to anyone around her, even her needy sister. Having been rejected by her parents and abjected by society, the protagonist is jumpy and scared and fears that she experiences "paranoia" and "schizophrenia" (62).

In *The Colonization of Psychic Space*, feminist philosopher Kelly Oliver argues that blacks, minorities, homosexuals, women, and "those othered" who are "excluded from positions of power and not accepted as fully rational autonomous subjects" in our society experience a "colonization of psychic space" in which the "unwanted" and "negative affects of the oppressors are deposited into the bones of the oppressed" (87, xix). She explains, "Those othered within mainstream culture are excluded from the world of meaning except as abject or inferior [...]. The meaning of their own lives and bodies has already been defined as inferior, deficient, or sick; but more than this, they have been defined as incapable of defining themselves" (88). The result is a form of "social melancholy" that is characterized by "suffering, pain, depression, shame, anger, or alienation" (88).

In *The Kappa Child* the attitude of the protagonist toward her own body can be understood as a manifestation of this "social melancholy." She feels ashamed of her name, her nonexistent romantic life, and her physical features, a shame that "is the result of internalizing the contempt of others, which becomes contempt toward the self," to use Oliver's words (117). Oliver points out that in the United States the rates of depression and psychiatric disorders are highest among the lowest social classes and among blacks, Hispanics, and minorities.[5] She notes: "In a culture where women and men of color have been pathologized, abjected, ridiculed, and hated, it is difficult for them to avoid some incorporation of self-hatred or a sense of inferiority or lack of legitimacy" (122). In *The Kappa Child,* although Goto does not highlight scenes of overt racism, there are several small incidents that suggest the way the protagonist and her family are repeatedly rendered "other" by those around them. On the first page of the novel, a woman driving a minivan almost hits the protagonist and her shopping carts and yells, "May Jesus forgive your heathen soul!" (9). Later, in a flashback scene, the protagonist remembers that when they arrived in Alberta the man checking them into the motel wished them well and remarked, "I always thought it was terrible what was done to you people" (70). Although the comment is meant to be sympathetic to the plight of Japanese Canadians during the war, it reveals the way racialized bodies are always regarded as other, never just people but always bearing the mark of their ethnicity or race. The motel clerk thinks of them as "you people," assuming that they are non-Canadians, or aliens. The father replies with indignation, "We are CANADIAN!" (70). But the motel clerk can see only the family's Japanese features, which act as a mask or screen that covers up other aspects of their hyphenated Canadian identity.[6]

One way to counter the protagonist's sense of alienation is through fantasy and science fiction. Unable to connect to the people around her, she encounters a stranger during "the last total eclipse of the twentieth century" (119). This stranger encourages her to take off her clothes and to "be naked when the three celestial bodies align" (122). In the moonlight, the stranger looks "almost greenish, skin hairless and moist [...]. No nipples. Nor a bellybutton" (122). They suma wrestle, Japanese style, and both fall to the ground. At that point, the protagonist says, "something cool-wet spilled, covered me in liquid sweetness" (124), and the creature "came in waves of pleasure" (124). For the first time in a long time, the protagonist gives herself up sexually to someone else. The strange and ambiguously gendered creature touches her between her legs, and she notes, "Time spiraled and inflated, how could I know? A moon rising to seek the darkness, the earth just a mote in the breath of the universe. I wanted to laugh, to weep, to keep this moment forever" (124). Whether this scene actually took place or took place only in the protagonist's mind matters less in the narrative than does the restorative powers it seems to provide the protagonist. The scene marks a turning point in the protagonist's life. She remarks, "I wake up smiling for no reason" (136). She feels energized, thinking that she is no longer alone, because there is a creature growing inside her, even though her pregnancy test comes back negative. Jenny Wolmark says that feminist appropriations of science fiction are "cultural interventions which result in texts that are recognizably structured by partiality and difference, rather than unity [...]. What the narratives of feminist science fiction can do is to test the limits of the dominant ideology of gender by proposing alternative possibilities for social and sexual relations which conflict with the dominant representations" (*Aliens and Others*, 55). Here Goto envisions a situation in which pregnancy results not from a heterosexual sexual encounter but from a friendly, pleasurable encounter with a strange creature who is not clearly sexed. The encounter challenges patriarchal norms and heterosexist ideologies at the same time as it negates racial stereotypes and assumptions.

Another way to resolve the protagonist's feelings of disaffection in contemporary Canadian society and her social melancholia is through the use of poetic, lyrical passages that describe the process of her impregnation, gestation, and childbirth. These passages destabilize the narrative and disrupt the science fiction genre because they seem out of sync with the rest of the book. In contrast to the descriptions of the cold, concrete city and the sometimes angry and violent domestic scenes, these passages depict warmth and solidarity. For example, there is a section that is narrated from the point of view of the protagonist's egg: "I linger briefly in the waving cilia passage, easy as a speck of sand among undulating ribbons of seaweed. Lovely and rich. How wondrous, being an egg. I am surrounded by six thousand of my egg sisters. Laughing softly, their presence a comforting murmur of water. And how I feel! The perpetual sense of potential, vibrant and miraculous" (*The Kappa Child*, 18). This scene is evocative of the community, pleasure, and comfort that the protagonist does not experience in her daily life. In a different passage, this egg narrator highlights again the "six thousand sister eggs," their "comforting murmurs," and the way their "beautiful siren voices hum living songs in endless harmony" (30).

These passages about eggs, creatures "without skin" (30), and about swimming in a "watery place" (105) are rather surreal and redolent of another time and place. They lead up to or prepare us for the birth or appearance of the kappa. Goto takes the legend of the kappa, a water sprite, a froglike creature from Japanese folktales who can be mischievous but also has supernatural powers, and blends it with the other stories in the novel—those of an immigrant family's life in the prairies, of the protagonist's isolation in a modern landscape, of a real or imagined encounter with an alien, and the daughters' coming to terms with an abusive father. For the protagonist, who is isolated and disengaged with the world, the birth of the kappa, real or psychosomatic, is a way of getting out of her depressed state. Although a kappa can be evil, it can also be heroic and regenerative. At one point the narrator tells the story of a girl who coerces a kappa to teach her how to heal. She becomes a "famous bonesetter and many people come to benefit from her skills" (75).

The kappa is attributed with bringing life, hope, and energy. In another section of the novel, the protagonist recalls the only summer that her father's dream of growing rice on the prairies became a reality. It was a summer when the rains fell, and "the land flourished with greenage" (226). It was also the summer that the family saw a webbed footprint of a kappa in their fields. Later the protagonist's rebirth is also associated with the kappa figure. She imagines or sees a green face in the mirror one day. This stranger tells her to stop worrying about her pregnancy and get a haircut. This haircut changes the protagonist's sense of herself completely: "My pumpkin head. He's cut my hair short, shorter than it has ever been, and the weight is off my head, the bones in my face pronounced. My neck emerges from my shoulders, not graceful swan-like, never that, but a neck, definitely long enough to kiss. I shiver at the thought" (248). With her hair short she feels "a little jauntier" and even contemplates changing her wardrobe (249). She no longer sees herself as alien and strange. After this change, the protagonist is able to confront some of the ghosts of her childhood—making up with her childhood friend, Gerald, whom she had hurt because of her insecurity, returning to her father and confronting him with her anger, and finally getting enough courage to ask her female friend Bernie to come out with her. Her sisters also come to terms with their past, and by the end of the novel they symbolically shed their animal names for their given names. The last pages suggest that the protagonist and her sisters will be able to lead new, more empowering daily lives.

Organic Politics

Unlike Goto's *The Kappa Child*, Ozeki's *All Over Creation* does not use science fiction or fantasy. However, like Goto's novel, *All Over Creation* depicts protagonists whose lives badly need an element of magic or fantasy. Help does not come from aliens or strange creatures in Ozeki's novel. Instead it comes from a group of young activists concerned with the environment, ecology, and people's health, who happen to land in Liberty Falls, Idaho, the home of the Idaho potato farms. The description of their vehicle, the Spudnik, makes it sound like an alien spaceship in middle America:

> It had the unmistakable shape of a Winnebago, boxy and inelegant, but the body of the vehicle was covered with pop-riveted patches of tin and aluminum, like scales, while its roof had been shingled with some sort of dark, rectangular paneling. A conning tower rose from the roof. It looked like a robotic armadillo, a road-warrior tank, a huge armored beetle—it was the most radical thing Frank Perdue had ever seen. (*All Over Creation*, 47–48)

The members of the activist group, named the Seeds of Resistance, travel around the country targeting "a range of food-related issues" such as genetic engineering, biotechnology, and the use of pesticides on and in fruits and vegetables (52). The members and their strange beliefs and activities function in the same way as the strange creature in *The Kappa Child*. They are the means by which regeneration and hope are brought to two female protagonists, Yumi Fuller and Cass Unger, who were best friends and neighbors when they were young.

Through the group's activist work Ozeki is able to make her readers aware of a number of pressing issues concerning our food products and farming methods. For example, at a local supermarket the group presents shoppers with a lecture about the use of pesticides on and in potatoes; the use of genetically modified corn or soy in a range of products, such as "infant formulas, baby foods, pizza, soda, chips" (92); and the fact that manufacturers are not obliged to label genetically altered food products for their consumers. Scattered throughout the novel are lessons about the dangers and the potential destruction of our vegetables and fruits caused by commercial production. The activists become environmental gurus, while Frank, the foster boy who gets involved with them, functions as a naïve character, like the reader, to be educated. For example, group member Geek tells Frank:

> Did you know that the Aymara of Peru have hundreds of different kinds of potatoes, and they can tell them apart by taste, and they have names for each one? [...] We only have maybe a dozen kinds left in commercial production here, because engineers have decided that potatoes all have to be the same size. Diversity is inconvenient to mechanized farming. This is what happens when agriculture becomes agribusiness. (125)

Through these minilectures Ozeki is able to use her novel to critique current farming and business practices. Her novel is more than social comedy; it becomes a form of social resistance.

Although politics and resistance have always been part of Asian American literature, what is different about Ozeki's novel is the subject matter. It is no longer about dominant white culture against Japanese Americans but rather is part of a fight against global and transnational corporations and practices. Although the novel is located mainly in Idaho, its concerns have far-reaching implications. Rachel Kamel notes, "By understanding that every local story is part of a global 'big picture,' we can open up space for dialog and sharing of experiences—especially across barriers of language, nationality, gender, race and class. And as that process of communication moves toward networking and coalition-building, the vision of a multi-national movement can become a reality" (as quoted by Dirlik in "The Global in the Local," 37). Ozeki has had a history of consciousness-raising activities. Her first book, *My Year of Meats* (1999), was about the use of growth hormones in the American beef industry, and as Monica Chiu observes, the "slaughterhouse scenes reveal larger issues surrounding the rise of unions and prohibitions against child labor as well as more recent laws concerning safe and sanitary working conditions and the standardization of hygienic food processing" (*Filthy Fictions*, 139). In the same way, *All Over Creation* is concerned not just with how to grow potatoes but with a number of larger issues. In an interview Ozeki said of her second novel, "I wanted to bring in this idea of creation because that's so much what the book is about, generations and regenerations. But also it's about this need we have to imitate God and to impose our own creative will on nature" (Weich and Ozeki, "Ruth Ozeki, Bearing Witness," n.p.). She feels that biotechnology is moving at such a rapid pace that most people cannot keep up with it, so we end up like the protagonist of *All Over Creation*, Yumi, losing hope.

> So many of the troubles we have derive from fear: *It's too scary. It's too threatening. It's too complicated. It's too much to look at, so therefore I'm just not going to look.* We have a real bias in this country toward reductive thinking. The media certainly has created that. That kind of reductionism is a real problem. Yes, it's overwhelming, and maybe we can't do much about it—but I do think we can do *something* about it.
>
> As citizens in a capitalist culture, we vote with our dollar. The more we know, the more we can vote in the right direction. Consumers have an enormous amount of untapped power that we're just beginning to understand. We can only tap that through information, through really understanding some of the very complex issues that go into our food or our politics or our international policy. (n.p.)

All Over Creation thus goes beyond identity politics to tackle the complex problems of the food industry and international politics. Her books are Ozeki's way of lobbying her readers, not through the distribution of pamphlets and speeches but through a comic and entertaining narrative.

Ozeki's strategy is similar to those of a number of recent Asian American novelists who deliberately write against the stereotype of the model minority in order to point out structural racial inequities and/or class and global injustices. In addition to Goto's nameless protagonist in *The Kappa Child*, other examples of Asian North American protagonists who do not follow the ideal of the hardworking immigrant who rises up the economic and social ladder include Han Ong's William Paulinha in *Fixer Chao*, Brian Roley's Tomas and Gabe in *American Son*, Larissa Lai's

Miranda in *Salt Fish Girl*, and Ying Chen's protagonist in *Ingratitude*. Although it would be a dubious distinction to claim that these protagonists have "progressed," as they tend to be engaged in criminal and violent activities or to lead somewhat makeshift existences, in terms of issues of representation they demonstrate the ways Asian North American writers have felt more at ease about writing beyond the confines of the model minority myth.

The difficulty of the model minority myth has been articulated by a number of critics. Tomo Hattori points out the problematic link between the model minority and capitalism in America:

> The stereotype of the model minority as the ideal immigrant, often ascribed to Asians in America, predicates social acceptance upon exceptional capitalist achievement. Model minority discourse is the term that describes the Asian American psychic institutions that emerge from this predication and, to the extent that model minority discourse is the term that describes the Asian American culture and studies, describes the process of minority collaboration in dominant cultural motives within works and institutions allegedly devoted to ethnic and racial emergence, provocation, and resistance. ("Model Minority Discourse and Asian American Jouis-Sense," 231)

Ozeki's protagonist, Yumi, fails as a model minority because she has been a drifter since her affair with and pregnancy by her high school teacher, Elliot. In spite of the fact that she now teaches some English classes in Hawaii and sells real estate on the side, Yumi does not fit into the stereotype of the "good Asian." She lives dangerously and rather haphazardly as a single mother with three children from three different men. Her home is near a place

> where you can walk right out onto an active lava flow [..., where] the crust is so hot you can feel it burning through the rubber of your soles. If you go at night and look down, you can see cracks in the black crust and the red-hot molten lava flowing underneath, just inches from your feet. And you know that if you take a wrong step where the crust is too thin, your foot will go right through and that'll be the end of you. (226–27)

The description of this molten area is a rather appropriate reflection of Yumi's existence, always on the brink of self-destruction. She is not what Hattori ironically described as a "reliable middle-class consumer of Third World sweatshop products."

Just as Goto's protagonist seems alienated from the largely middle-class world in which she lives, so is she eccentric and out of place compared to her friends and family from her Idaho community. Yumi is like the prodigal daughter who has misspent her youth and talents, while her friend Cass Unger has stayed home and taken care of the farm and Yumi's aged parents. Yumi is quite irresponsible, gets depressed, and drinks, while Cass, who is unable to have children and adores babies, often takes care of Yumi's baby for her. In Yumi Ozeki has created a character with whom it is hard to sympathize or identify. As the hippie or the teenager who never matured, Yumi becomes an interesting example of the shift in representation of Asian Americans. No longer do Asian Americans have to constantly fit into certain expectations or fantasies of the dominant culture. Yumi's unpredictability and her unconventional behavior create instability in the category Asian American as conceptualized and understood by the dominant culture.

On the issue of minority representation, David Palumbo-Liu notes,

> It would seem that the task for minority cultures is not to lament their eternal marginalization, for the minor is always already located in varied positions within the hegemony; nor is it to accept defeat before an eternally evasive dominant, for the dominant always has constantly to renegotiate, to finesse its contradictions, and that maneuver in turn reshapes what one regards as the "dominant." The hard part is to insist upon a certain agency as minor subjects, to negotiate the status of cultural citizen, even given the ways that a dominant culture can absorb and domesticate the cultural production of minority culture. (*Asian/American Historical Crossings of a Racial Frontier*, 202)

Similarly, Hattori says,

> The last thing Asian Americans need now is a new face. It does not take criticism to tell us who we really are, what our cultural "truth" really is. Asian America does not need a face-lift: [...] Asian American culture needs to be liberated from the obligation of compulsory auto-ethnography. We need to be liberated from the endless rehearsal of the trauma of our identity, from the prison of the endless performance of the yellowness of our bodies. ("Model Minority Discourse," 244)

Even though stories about marginalization, exclusion, and problems of identity are extremely important and integral to the development of Asian Americans and Asian Canadians as a group, both critics emphasize the need today to break away from these positions, because the articulation of abjection and victimization, while a necessary form of identity formation and resistance, can also act as a form of containment, prescriptive representation, and misidentity. Ozeki and Goto, in representing their protagonists in their unconventional ways, are not simply responding to existing cultural expectations but taking charge of symbolic power, what Stuart Hall calls the "power of representation," including the "power to mark, assign and classify" (*Representation*, 259).

As an answer to the way Asian Americans have been homogenized, Lisa Lowe, in her oft-reprinted essay *Immigrant Acts*, stresses "heterogeneity, hybridity, and multiplicity in the characterization of Asian American culture" (66–67). Lowe uses the term "heterogeneity" to "indicate the existence of differences and differential relationships within a bounded category; that is, among Asian Americans there are differences of Asian national origins, of generational relation to immigrant exclusion laws, of class backgrounds in Asia and economic conditions within the United States, and of gender" (67). By "hybridity" she refers to the "formation of cultural objects and practices that are produced by the histories of uneven and unsynthetic power relations; for example, the racial and linguistic mixings in the Philippines and among Filipinos in the United States" (67). What is fascinating about Ozeki's novel is her exaggerated use of the notion of heterogeneity and hybridity. She takes the notion of hybridity and heterogeneity literally, with somewhat comic and ironic effects. First, Yumi is the daughter of a white father and a Japanese mother. Her three children are not only of mixed races; they all have different fathers of different racial origins. Baby Poo's father is a musician and Hawaiian; Ocean's father "sells surfboards in Waikiki," but because no racial origin is mentioned, he is presumably white; and Phoenix's father is a plant scientist who is Japanese (*All Over Creation*, 96). Ozeki seems to be self-consciously playing with notions of botany and race, using the comments made in the chapter called "The Promiscuity of Squashes" (111) to reflect the sexual propensities of human beings. In this chapter, which is a flashback to a scene in the past, Yumi's mother, Momoko, tells her husband, Lloyd, about her difficulties in "keeping her Shanghai squash from cross-pollinating with her Mammoth Kings, and her Sweetbush from her Whangaporoas" (115). In chapters before and after this one, we find accounts of Yumi's cross-pollinated family, as well as the sexual exploits of Charmey, a French Canadian from Quebec, and Frank Perdue, a local Idaho boy. Yumi's master's thesis, called "Fading Blossoms, Falling Leaves: Visions of Transience and Instability in the Literature of Asian-American Diaspora" (42), is "about the way images of nature are used as metaphors for cultural dissolution" (42).

Yet the novel is not a lament about the "cultural dissolution" or the profligacy of Asian Americans. The tone of the novel is more irreverent and farcical than it is moralistic or didactic. Yumi has not been the model Asian American, yet her one-time best friend and neighbor Cass, who has stayed home in Idaho, led a conventional life as a farmer's wife, and been faithful to her husband, has not fared much better in life. Cass is apparently infertile. It seems that being the home-grown, hometown girl has not made her the all-natural, healthy woman one expects. The inability of Cass and her husband, Will, to have children may be due to Will's exposure to Agent Orange while he was in Vietnam. But their health may have also been endangered by the couple's use of pesticides on their potato farm. The same company that manufactured the herbicide used in Vietnam, which contains dioxins and PCBs, are now manufacturing potatoes engineered with chemicals that make them bug resistant. Will remarks, "Cynaco made Agent Orange for the army. They make GroundUp and now the Nulifes, too" (219). Ozeki is not advocating promiscuity, but she is asking us to rethink traditional ways of farming, our relation to nature, and our familial structures. An important point to note is that the novel concludes with a happy regeneration brought about by an untraditional family structure. Cass and Will's longing for a baby is ultimately fulfilled not by artificial insemination or adoption from a Third World country but by the baby left to them by Charmey and Frankie. It is through the makeshift family or conglomeration of the Seeds of Resistance that baby Tibet is conceived and nourished. And Geek, one member of the group, is sufficiently committed to Yumi that he might follow her and her three children to Hawaii, again to help sustain an untraditional family.

The point I am making is that Ruth Ozeki consciously tries to confound any easy assumptions about home and away, about self and other, about white and nonwhite, about good and bad. Using botanical, gardening, and ecological metaphors, she demonstrates that there is no "pure" or authentic species, for plants and seeds have been transplanted, hybridized, cross-pollinated, or, more recently, genetically engineered. Of course the important message of *All Over Creation* is the need to resist excessive harmful biochemical intervention akin to colonization, but at the same time Ozeki shows that cross-pollination and hybridization have been occurring and do occur in nature, with or without our intervention. Her analogy of plants to the human world enables us to see Yumi and the other rebellious characters, like Charmey and Frank, in a different, perhaps more tolerant, light. Their rootlessness and mobility, their various sexual partners, their refusal to stay at home, their traveling across North America are all part of a process of evolution, of survival and collective human experience, especially for diasporic people. In his book *Routes*, anthropologist James Clifford writes,

> Diasporic cultural forms can never, in practice, be exclusively nationalist. They are deployed in transnational networks built from multiple attachments, and they encode practices of accommodation with, as well as resistance to, host countries and their norms [...]. Diasporia discourse articulates, or ends together, both roots *and* routes to construct what Gilroy describes as alternate publics spheres, forms of community consciousness and solidarity that maintain identifications outside the national time/space in order to live inside, with a difference. (251)

Hence what is suggested by the constant movement and displacement of many of the main characters of Ozeki's novel is not so much their otherness or nonbelonging; rather, they are part of culture, which is always in the process of crossing and interaction. Even those who remain steadily in town, like Cass and Will, are affected by "travel," for they inherit precious baby Tibet, who, as her name suggests, is a gift from afar. For Ozeki it is not only Asian American culture that can be characterized by what Lowe calls "heterogeneity, hybridity, and multiplicity"; it is all of America. When asked to identify a vegetable that looks something like a zucchini but feels like a squash, Yumi's mother, Momoko, looks at the large mutant squashes and giggles, "Maybe a little bit zuke, and a little bit Delicata, and little bit [...] whatchamacallit. Sweet Pumpkin." She points to Yumi's children Ocean and Phoenix and says, "Like them. All mixed up" (*All Over Creation*, 118). Ozeki's novel cautions us against playing God with genetic engineering and the natural world, yet at the same time demonstrates that natural processes of hybridization and being mixed up are already "all over creation."

Goto and Ozeki's novels both critique the normative structures of contemporary patriarchal society, with its valorization of competitiveness, power, consumerism, and capitalism. Incorporating fantasy and myth, these novelists tell stories of the lives of everyday women who challenge corporate notions of success, along with ideals of improvement and perfectibility through cosmetics, science, and technology. They refuse to be co-opted and hailed by the model minority myth, with its seductive promise of belonging and acceptance. Instead, both novelists rewrite the terms of what constitutes a good "family," what is acceptable behavior for a racialized female subject, and what our society means by progress. Uneasy about the well-being of our planet, Goto and Ozeki explore important issues of reproduction, fertility, and the responsibility that comes with our ability to propagate ourselves and other parts of our natural world.

Coda
Rethinking the Hyphen

Since the late 1970s and early 1980s, with the development of Asian American studies as a discipline and the Asian American movement as a panethnic coalition in the United States (see Espiritu, *Asian American Panethnicity*, 10), it has become common practice to refer to nonwhite writers in America, more recently in Canada and Europe, as African American, Asian Canadian, or in Britain, black British writers. This hyphenated status has been seen as a marker of one's belonging to two worlds, of one's hybrid identity, and has also been criticized as a sign of nonbelonging to the mainstream culture (see Ling, *Narrating Nationalisms*; Bhabha, *The Location of Culture*, 112; Miki, "Altered States").[1] A classic and often-quoted essay on the topic of Asian American identity is Lisa Lowe's "Heterogeneity, Hybridity, Multiplicity," which celebrates the heterogeneous character of Asian America.

Though liberating, Lowe's paradigm is still based on difference—within the category of Asian American and against a hegemonic other. The designation Asian American, although meant to be descriptive, presumes that to be just "American" means that one is part of the white majority. That is, Asian Americans continue to be excluded from the term "Americans." The hyphenated terms were good transitional designations for the last few decades of the twentieth century for writers whose works were concerned with "claiming America," as Maxine Hong Kingston's *The Woman Warrior* was, or with exposing the discrimination of the mainstream culture's treatment of ethnic citizens, as Joy Kogawa's *Obasan* did in the early 1980s. In the last decade or so, as I have argued, there have emerged a different group of Asian writers whose novels are not primarily concerned with the challenges of assimilation, racial prejudice, or with cultural hybridity. These novels have moved away from the *Bildungsroman* and the emigration narratives that negotiate problems created by the shift from the originary country to the adopted culture. The hyphenated designation is no longer adequate, particularly for writers like Salman Rushdie, Kazuo Ishiguro, Arlene Chai, Michael Ondaatje, and, to a lesser extent, Shyam Selvadurai, Ying Chen, and others. Their works fit uneasily into this hyphenated space of the Chinese American, South Asian Canadian, or Japanese British category because of the way they locate themselves and because of their subject matter.

A number of critics have attempted to redefine the place of these hyphenated Asians and to describe them in different ways. For example, Shirley Geok-lin Lim found it helpful to use the categories "immigrant and diasporic" ("Immigration and Diaspora," 290), Sau-ling Wong employed the term "denationalization,"[2] and Rocío Davis used "transcultural" (*Transcultural Reinventions*); later Lim and Inderpal Grewal and others have used "transnational" (Lim et al., *Transnational Asian American Literature*; Grewal, *Transnational America*), while others, like Chelva Kanaganayakam, talk about "moveable margins" (*Moveable Margins*). Instead of identifying them as ethnic, minority, immigrant, diasporic, transnational, or Asian American, Asian Canadian, Asian British, or Asian Australian, a term such as "Asian global narratives" might be a more appropriate designation for a number of works by these novelists.

In an issue of *PMLA* Paul Jay notes that "English literature is increasingly postnational, whether written by cosmopolitan writers like Salman Rushdie, Derek Walcott, Arundhati Roy, and Nadine Gordimer or by a host of lesser known writers working in their home countries or in diasporic communities around the world" ("Beyond Discipline?" 33). He argues that instead of using national categories, English as a discipline ought to emphasize "literature's relation to the historical process of globalization" (33). Writing about American literature after the destruction of the World Trade Center and after Hurricane Katrina, Wai Chee Dimock suggests that the very concept of "nation seems to have come literally 'unbundled' before our eyes, its fabric of life torn apart by extremist militant groups, and by physical forces of even greater scope, wrought by climate change and the intensified hurricane cycles. Territory sovereignty, we suddenly realize, is no more than a legal fiction, a man-made fiction" ("Introduction," 1).[3]

In dealing with recent narratives by Asians in the diaspora who have become unfastened from their territory, I contend that *global novelists* and *global writing* are more accurate terms for writers and for works that fall into one or more of the following three categories:

1. Works that overtly thematize globalization and transnational movement. A good example is Rushdie's *The Ground beneath her Feet*, which playfully deals with the power of rock 'n' roll music and rock stars as a global phenomenon.
2. Works that are authored by Asians in North America, Britain, or Australia but whose subject matters have little or nothing to do with the adopted country of the authors. These works are often set in the past and frequently deal with some element of history or political crisis, usually in the country with which the author is most familiar. Examples are Ha Jin's *Waiting*, set in China from 1962 to the 1980s; Arlene Chai's *The Last Time I Saw Mother*, whose main narrative is the heroine's discovery of events that occurred during the Second World War in the Philippines; and Shyam Selvadurai's *Funny Boy*, depicting the political and personal tensions in Sri Lanka during the seven years before the 1983 riots.
3. Finally, there are works by Asians in the diaspora that do not feature Asians as protagonists or deal with anything Asian, including films like *Sense and Sensibility* and *The Ice Storm* by Ang Lee, Michael Ondaatje's novel *Divisadero*, and the novel *The Remains of the Day* by Kazuo Ishiguro.

Instead of using the Asian American or the ethnic national paradigm, it is more fruitful to look at these works and these authors in terms of what Susan Stanford Friedman calls the "new geographics of identity" (*Mappings*, 17). Friedman argues that this "new geography involves a move from the allegorization of the self in terms of organicism, stable centers, cores, and wholeness to a discourse of spatialized identities constantly on the move [...]. Instead of the individualistic telos of developmental models, the new geographics figures identity as a historically embedded site, a positionality, a location, a standpoint, a terrain, an intersection, a network, a crossroads of multiply situated knowledges" (19).

Keeping in mind Friedman's model of the geography of identity, in this coda I look at a number of texts from the three categories listed. These global narratives highlight movement, instability, and the importance of standpoint or location. Their settings, unlike those of the novels I discussed earlier, tend not to be in North America or Britain but elsewhere. They reveal the ways globalization, colonialization, and media technology have shifted and changed the meaning and the signifier *Asian North American* or *Asian European*.

Before proceeding with an examination of Asian global narratives, I would like to briefly recapitulate the underlying assumptions behind my argument. Although a term such as *Asian American* is meant to include, as Shirley Lim and Amy Ling noted in 1992, "disparate peoples of different races and with diverse languages, religions, and cultural and national backgrounds" (*Reading the Literatures of Asian America*, 3–4), it still has the lingering denotation of a hyphenated identity. Lim and Ling explain:

> Once inside the borders of the United States, different Asian nationals share common experiences of immigration, discrimination, acculturation, conflict, and generational strains. Their originating cultures set them apart from the dominant Euro-American ones and become the basis for a sense of community both with each other and with other peoples of color. National, historical, and even class distinctions recede in the light of the experience of difference within a white-dominated society. (4)

What brings these people together, Lim and Ling argue, are their responses to American culture and society. Recent critical studies of Asian American literature have complicated the paradigm somewhat by adding several new dimensions to their reading: form and history (Jinqi Ling, *Narrating Nationalisms*); culture and nationalism (Li, *Imagining the Nation*); and gender (Lee, *The Americas of Asian American Literature*, and Eng, *Racial Castration*). However, these critics have not disputed the initial impetus, which was the claiming of America, or the "appropriative manoeuvres for an Asian American integrity in the historical, cultural, and ideological formation of the United States" (Li, *Imagining the Nation*, 63).

What I am speculating on in this concluding section are narratives by Asians in the diaspora whose works fall outside of this hyphenated paradigm of Asian plus adopted country. In the last few years, as I have noted, Asians in the diaspora have produced books and films that do not necessarily deal with immigration, citizenship, or being caught "between worlds." For these I propose the term *Asian global,* because these narratives arise out of and are contingent on globalization—the movement of people, capital, and production across the north and south— and because they are no longer located just in North America or Britain. They are contributing to the creation of what D. N. Rodowick calls a "globalized cosmopolitan public sphere," a "contradictory and heterogeneous transnational space" ("Introduction," 14). According to Rodowick, this space is being brought about by two factors: (1) the increasing importance of human rights as a transnational concept and (2) the global reach of electronic communication and entertainment networks (14). Because of these two factors, people are less dependent on the nation for their survival, and they look to other ways of forming community. Rodowick argues that "postmodern forces of globalization have shifted or, more precisely multiplied and complicated centers of power so as to diminish the forms of self-identity conveyed by nationality" (14) and that new media enable different "ways of forging political consensus and inventing strategies of action as communication networks connect local and transnational organizations" (15). These factors are creating mobile identities and mobile citizens, including not only the "expatriate intellectual," but the "new cosmopolitans—economic immigrants, members of diaspora communities, political refugees, and displaced person" (15).

Nowhere is this globalized cosmopolitan public sphere better depicted and mocked than in Salman Rushdie's *The Ground beneath Her Feet.* In this playful postmodern novel set in various cities of Mexico, India, England, and the United States, Rushdie remakes the myth of Orpheus through the love story of Vina Apsara, a pop star, and Ormus Cama, a songwriter and musician. In this novel it is rock 'n' roll rather than Hollywood films or the Internet that brings about the interaction of the transnational, the national, and the local. This work reveals the inadequacy of the hyphenated designation of Asian British or Indo-British, in part because of the wide-ranging locations and sites of the local in the novel, and also because of the overt thematization of the power of global media.⁴ The novel is not concerned simply with issues of immigration or hybrid cultures, though some issues about assimilations are raised. For example, in recounting Vina's past, Rai, the narrator, tells us that Vina, born in Virginia of a Greek American mother and an Indian father, is called "Blackfoot Indian" and "goatgirl" by her white school friends. However, the overall sense of the novel is that home is more of a transnational space. Music becomes the ubiquitous medium that links and is present in various cultures all over the world. Rai, a photographer, comments that "music, popular music, was the key that unlocked the door for [Vina and Ormus], the door to magic lands" (*The Ground beneath Her Feet*, 95). Instead of seeing pop music as "one of the great weapons of cultural imperialism," Rushdie deliberately obfuscates beginnings and boundaries, claiming that "the genius of Ormus Cama did not emerge in response to, or in imitation of, America" (95). Ormus claims "that his early music, the music he heard in his head during the unsinging childhood years, was not of the West, except in the sense that the West was in Bombay from the beginning, impure old Bombay where West, East, North and South had always been scrambled, like codes, like eggs" (95–96).

This theme of flux and mobility is echoed in the hit songs Ormus sings: "The earthquake songs of Ormus Cama are rants in praise of the approach of chaos [. . .]. The songs are about the collapse of all walls, boundaries, restraints. They describe worlds in collision, two universes tearing into each other, striving to become one, destroying each other in the effort" (390). The collapse of boundaries becomes a metaphor for much of what goes on in the novel: the blurring of real and fictional, East and West, inside and outside, home and abroad, private and public, divine and secular, love and hate, Asian and non-Asian identities. In this world national, sexual, and social identities are all being questioned. The popularity of Ormus's music comes from its deliberate hybrid and transnational quality. He adds "un-American sounds" to his tracks: "the sexiness of the Cuban horns, the mind-bending patterns of the Brazilian drums, the Chilean woodwinds moaning like the winds of oppression, the African male voice choruses like trees swaying in freedom's breeze, the grand old ladies of Algerian music with their yearning squawks and ululations, the holy passion of the Pakistani *qawwals*" (379). Mariam Pirbhai says,

In Rushdie's text, even the sounds that appear to be exotically foreign and "un-American" to American audiences are, in fact, the sounds of America. This is because "American" sounds are shown to be composed of various musical traditions that draw from a rich, diverse cultural background. Ironically, that which non-American audiences around the world receive as American music is, to some extent, the music of the world. ("The Paradox of Globalization," 62)

Not only does the music of Vina and Ormus break down national boundaries; their personal lives do not follow traditional divides. Vina decides "to live her private life in public" (*The Ground beneath Her Feet,* 384), letting her concert audiences know about her lovers and giving them details of her sexual preferences. At the height of the duo's popularity, they became a global phenomenon. Her friend Rai notes that Vina Apsara "became the world's most dreamed about woman, not just America's Sweetheart like Mary Pickford long ago but the beloved of the whole aching planet" (412). When she is accidentally killed by an earthquake, the world mourns in the same way that they did for Princess Diana:

> All over the world, when the news of her death breaks, people pour into the streets, whatever their local hour, pushed out of their homes by a force they can't yet name. [...] It's hard to mourn for strangers except conventionally [...]. But Vina is not a stranger. The crowds know her, and over and over again, in the streets of Yokohama, Darwin, Montevideo, Calcutta, Stockholm, Newcastle, Los Angeles, people are heard describing her death as a personal bereavement, a death in the family. By her dying she has momentarily re-invented their sense of a larger kinship, of their membership in the family of mankind. (480)

This feeling of identification with a superstar, which is shared by people from all over America, Europe, Africa, and Asia, shows the way a global community that transcends national limits has been created through rock music. Douglas Kellner has argued that "television and other forms of media culture play key roles in the structuring of contemporary identity and shaping thought and behaviour" (*Media Culture,* 237). Here it is the music and the public personality of Vina that have created a media community or media state. Their sense of community impels individuals to public spaces. Crowds begin to "gravitate to stadiums, arenas, parks, maidans,—the major venues. Shea Stadium, Candlestick Park, Soldier's Field, San Siro, Bernabeu, Wembley, Munich's Olympic Stadium,

Rio's fabulous Marcanà." The people are joined by this "single, uniting event: the miracle of the stadiums, the people gathered to share their loss" (*The Ground beneath Her Feet*, 481). What is created through mourning is a cosmopolitan public sphere.

I am using the term *cosmopolitan* here with the resonances defined by Kwame Anthony Appiah:

> The cosmopolitan patriot can entertain the possibility of a world in which everyone is a rooted cosmopolitan, attached to a home of her own, with its own cultural particularities, but taking pleasure from the presence of other, different, places that are home to other, different, people. The cosmopolitan also imagines that in such a world not everyone will find it best to stay in their natal patria, so that the circulation of people between different localities will involve not only cultural tourism (which the cosmopolitan admits to enjoying) but migration, nomadism, diaspora. ("Against National Culture," 175–76)

Appiah cautions that cosmopolitan is not the same as humanism, because "cosmopolitanism is not just the feeling that everybody matters. For the cosmopolitan also celebrates the fact that there are different local human ways of being; while humanism is consistent with the desire for global homogeneity. Humanism can be made compatible with cosmopolitan sentiments; however, it can also live with a deadening urge to uniformity" (178).

In this sense, one could say that Michael Ondaatje's *The English Patient* is also a cosmopolitan or global narrative by an Asian Canadian writer. In a novel that is ironically about war, there is nevertheless a feeling of cosmopolitanism in the small community consisting of the nurse Hana; the supposed English patient; Kip, the Sikh sapper; and Caravaggio. The novel deliberately confuses our sense of nation and nationality through various settings and references to locations past and present in Europe, North America, Asia, and Africa. Ondaatje refers to the nomadic Bedouin tribe, to Toronto, Tuscany, Cairo, and Westbury, as well as to Hiroshima and Nagasaki. At one point the English patient thinks, "What did most of us know of such parts of Africa? [. . .] But who was the enemy? Who were the allies of this place—the fertile lands of Cyrenaica, the salt marshes of El Agheila? All of Europe were fighting their wars in North Africa, in Sidi Rezegh, in Baguoh" (19). Though the context of the war seems an unlikely locale for what Appiah calls "cosmopolitan patriots," the novel focuses on the kinds of communities that form as a result of displacement. As in Rushdie's novel, Ondaatje wrote about global or mobile citizens. The members of the Geographical Society were "a small clutch of a nation between the wars, mapping and re-exploring" (136). Almásy, the English patient, says, "We were German, English, Hungarian, African [...]. Gradually we became nationless. I came to hate nations. We are deformed by nation-states" (138).

Although in Rushdie's novel it is music that unites people, in Ondaatje's it is the desert, which is larger than anyone or any nation.[5] Almásy says,

> The desert could not be claimed or owned,—it was a piece of cloth carried by winds, never held down by stones, and given a hundred shifting names long before Canterbury existed, long before battles and treaties quilted Europe and the East. [...] It was a place of faith. We disappeared into landscape. Fire and sand. We left the harbours of oasis. The places water came to and touched [...] Ain, Bir, Wadi, Foggara, Khottara, Shaduf. I didn't want my name against such beautiful names. Erase the family name! Erase nations! I was taught such things by the desert. (138–39)

These sentiments suggest the possibility of a cosmopolitan society that exceeds the boundaries of the nation, though it is one that is temporarily located between the wars and created by the shared love of the desert landscape.

My second category of global narratives consists of those texts written by Asians in the diaspora that deliberately position themselves outside of their adopted countries. Novels like *Funny Boy* by Shyam Selvadurai and *The Last Time I Saw Mother* by Arlene Chai and films like *Eat Drink Man Woman* by Ang Lee and *Earth* by Deepa Mehta are examples of works that are by Asians in the diaspora but do not fit into the paradigm proposed by Amy Ling and Shirley Lim. The authors of these works do not deal with questions of identity and assimilation of the Asian subject in Canada, America, or Australia but instead look back to the originary country as a location for the conflict or crisis in their fictional works. These types of novels may have some elements common to immigration narratives, but, more important, they relocate centers and redraw boundaries. Unlike in immigration narratives, in each of these works the author's homeland is not just a poor Third World country from which the protagonist must flee in order to have a better life. It becomes a site of intrigue, fantasy, and desire. These works create new or renewed interest in countries like Sri Lanka, the Philippines, Taiwan, and India by providing readers and audiences with an enhanced understanding of those cultural spaces and their histories. They bring a global perspective to the otherwise narrowly defined parameters of the hyphenated identities of Asian American or Asian Canadian. They force us, as Paul Jay notes, to bring a "transnational perspective to how we present the history of literature in the West, moving away from a traditional division of discrete national literatures into ossified literary-historical periods and giving the history of global expansion, trade, and intercultural exchange precedence in our curriculum over the mapping of an essentially aestheticized national character" ("Beyond Discipline?" 43).

In *Funny Boy*, for example, Asian Canadian Shyam Selvadurai's portrayal of Arjie Chelvaratnam's growing up in Columbo is set against the political tensions leading up to the 1983 riots in Sri Lanka. Almost all the action takes place in Sri Lanka, and Canada is mentioned briefly only at the beginning and the end of the novel as a place of refuge for the Tamils who were being driven out of the country. The narrator looks back fondly at his childhood: "Those spend-the-days, the remembered innocence of childhood, are now coloured in the hues of the twilight sky. It is a picture made even more sentimental by the loss of all that was associated with them. By all of us having to leave Sri Lanka years later because of communal violence and forge a new home for ourselves in Canada" (5). The effect of this structure is to place the West in a kind of parenthesis that is contained by the more important story of the protagonist as he struggles with his gender, sexual identity, and illusions of romance and as he becomes aware of the social and racial tensions between the Burghers and the Sri Lankans and between the Tamils and the Sinhalese.[6] Many of Arjie's childhood memories are linked to his identification with girls and women—playing bride-bride and watching his mother dress. Thus, as Gayatri Gopinath notes, "The narrator's evocation of these remembered instances of cross-gender identificatory practices and pleasures becomes a means of negotiating the loss of 'home' as a fantasied site of geographic footedness, belonging, and gender and erotic play" ("Nostalgia, Desire, Diaspora," 476). For the narrator, place and nation are less important than his memories of a period before what Adrienne Rich terms "compulsory heterosexuality" in her article of that title. At the same time, one becomes aware of the racial, religious, sexual, and political complexities underlying the *Bildungsroman* in much the same way that one learns of the racial, religious, political, and social tensions surrounding the partition of India in Deepa Mehta's film *Earth*.

I argue that Selvadurai's novel is better labeled global rather than Asian Canadian or South Asian, because in many ways it deals with the relationships between cultures, the effects of global tourism, homosexual identity, and the consequences of British colonialism. For example, in the story of Radha Aunty, which can be read as a kind of Romeo and Juliet romance, the family opposes the friendship between Radha Aunty and Anil because he is Sinhalese and they are Tamil. The young Arjie learns that in the 1950s "the Sinhalese wanted to make Sinhala the only national language," which was opposed by the Tamils and resulted in the killing of many Tamils (*Funny Boy*, 61). Instead of showing the protagonist's romance and passion, the story of Radha Aunty becomes a lesson about the interconnectedness between the self and the community, between the local and the global. Radha Aunty discovers from an older aunt that marrying someone not "their own kind" means ostracization and banishment from the family forever (54). For the older Aunty Doris, marrying a kind, gentle, and handsome man was not sufficient compensation for the loss of an eternity of isolation and silence from her own family. For Radha Aunty the dangers of his aunty and her lover's being from different backgrounds are made real when she is injured in an attack on Tamil people while on a train. Through this story both Arjie and the reader learn the relevance of history, religion, and politics and the way they make an inescapable mark on the particular, or on the individual.

Other global themes, such as the encroachment of the West and the effects of American imperialism, are evident in the chapter titled "See No Evil, Hear No Evil." Arjie talks about tasting such "exotic food as hamburgers and strawberry cake" (101). He finds out that his father has become part owner of Paradise Beach Resort, which is being marketed to European and foreign tourists. In this same chapter, his family's

Dutch friend, Daryl Uncle, who believed that he was impervious to the local unrest because he is white, is killed mysteriously in Jaffna, where the police had been hunting down Tamil rebels. Toward the end of the book, Arjie attends "Queen Victoria Academy," where his father feels that he will learn to "become a man" (210). What I am highlighting here through these seemingly small and unrelated details is the way the novel, though set in one country, demonstrates globality and the incursions of the Western world on Sri Lankan culture. The novel not only reveals tensions among race, ethnicity, religion, and class but sets them within the context of Western imperialism and overdevelopment. For the protagonist identity is based on both intracolonial and intercolonial dynamics. As Stuart Hall notes, "Globalized forces have [...] destroyed the identities of specific places, absorbed them into a postmodern flux of diversity. So one understands the moment when people reach for those groundings, and that reach is what I call ethnicity" ("The Local and the Global," 184). Arjie learns that although he belongs to a comfortable middle-class family, the fact that they are Tamil in a predominantly Sinhalese culture renders them vulnerable in their native country. Possessing money, culture, and a British education does not save them from racial conflicts, politics, and the fury of the mob.

My final category of Asian global narratives consists of those works produced by Asians in the diaspora that do not explicitly deal with Asian American or ethnic themes. In addition to Ondaatje's *The English Patient* and *Divisadero*, the latter set in California and France, novels such as *The Remains of the Day* by Kazuo Ishiguro, *Baroque-a-nova* by Kevin Chong, and *Other Women* by Evelyn Lau do not have Asian themes or explicitly Asian protagonists. A novel such as *Ingratitude* by Asian French Canadian Ying Chen uses Asian names but deliberately obfuscates its setting, so the novel's intense mother-daughter conflict could be set in any city in the world. Wayne Wang's film *Smoke* and other films such as *The Ice Storm* and *Sense and Sensibility* by Ang Lee are also examples of those works that fit uneasily into hyphenated categories of Asian American, Asian Canadian, or Asian British. These works challenge us to rethink categories and labels and force us to break the automatic association of ethnic authorship with ethnic cultural production. To use the example of Ang Lee, in America he is perceived as Asian American; in Taiwan he is seen as more American than Chinese; in

China he is regarded as a foreigner. When he was asked to direct the film version of Jane Austen's novel, he was a talented global artist, as capable as anyone else who has had film training and has lived with Englishness and English culture. He is, in many ways, one of those mobile, cosmopolitan citizens I alluded to earlier.

To conclude, I am not arguing for the abolition of the paradigm reflected by the labels Asian American, Asian Canadian, and Asian plus adopted country per se. As David Leiwei Li argues, "Retaining 'Asian' as a racial description and 'American' as a national signifier" is important politically as it returns "to the uneven historical opposition between citizens and aliens, and the contemporary contradiction between the legal assurance of equal rights and the cultural rearticulation of national competence" (*Imagining the Nation*, 203). What I want to call attention to in this final section is the fluidity of subjectivity and positions available to Asian British, Asian Australian, Asian Canadian, and Asian American people today. I come back to Susan Stanford Friedman's notion of the geographies of identity that articulates the "mapping of territories and boundaries, the dialectical terrains of inside/outside or center/margin, the axial intersections of different positionalities, and the space of dynamic encounter" (*Mappings*, 19). In particular, one of the discourses of positionality Friedman puts forward is that of relationality, emphasizing the epistemological standpoint for identity. She writes, "Identity depends upon a point of reference; as that point moves nomadically, so do the contours of identity, particularly as they relate to the structures of power" (22). According to her model, it is possible to highlight various aspects of one's subjectivity in different situations—to be part of the Asian American community in one situation, to feel allegiance with women of color in another, to feel "American" in another context, and to be part of the artistic Bohemian group in yet another. Friedman argues that these "scripts of relational positionality construct a multiplicity of fluid identities defined and acting situationally" (47), enabling subjects to go beyond static notions of identity. Adopting the notion that identities shift with changing contexts, we see why some works by Asian North Americans have Asian North American themes though others do not. Asians in the diaspora, like other cosmopolitans, are no longer bound simply by allegiances to nation, culture, and ethnicity but live plural identities shaped by many other factors, such as sexuality, gender, class, religion, education, health, and age. Stressing the global or cosmopolitan aspects of works by Asians in the diaspora is my way of pointing out the increasingly transnational, transcultural, and fluid potential that is seen in many recent works by Asian American, Asian Canadian, and Asian British authors.

Notes

Introduction

1. Ironically, the merger of Daimler-Benz with Chrysler has not been profitable. After ten years it pushed "healthy Daimler-Benz into a severe crisis" while making former CEO Jürgen Schrempp of Daimler-Benz into a rich man. Spiegel Online International, "Merkel Takes On Fat Cats."

2. Mississauga is a city of 400,000 people about thirty-five to forty kilometers west of Toronto.

3. In Canada, the live-in caregiver program allows women from countries such as the Philippines to work as live-in domestics. After two years, they can apply to be permanent residents of Canada. See Citizenship and Immigration Canada, "Working Temporarily in Canada."

4. Statistics vary because of documented and undocumented migrant workers. There are an estimated eight to eleven million overseas Filipinos, and 70 percent of those are women. Among the women, a large majority work as domestic workers. See Wikipedia, "Overseas Filipino," and Citizenshift, "Feminization of Migration."

5. Inter-Mares, a recruitment agency in Singapore, advertises, "We recruit Filipino nannies, Indonesian housekeepers and caregivers, Sri Lankan cooks and other nationalities while they are still in Singapore.... And when they have gained enough experience we send them to work for Canadian families" (Inter-Mares Management Services, "Inter-Mares Maid Agency").

6. Maria DiCenzo ("Editorial") has noted the same kind of mobility, and

later tensions, in the Italian Canadian community, a group that immigrated to Toronto earlier, primarily in the 1950s and 1960s.

7. Shaw argued, "It is no accident that globalization became a dominant theme in the 1990s after the Cold War ended. Although the term globalization, first used in the 1960s, has been in common use since the 1970s and became increasingly connected to the understanding of market liberalization in the 1980s, it is in the 1990s that it has dominated social-scientific and to a considerable extent political debate."

8. Miyoshi notes that a "truly transnational corporation [...] might no longer be tied to its nation of origin, but is adrift and mobile, ready to settle anywhere and exploit any state including its own, as long as the affiliation serves its own interest" (736).

9. Sau-ling Wong is echoing Janis Stout, who wrote that American literature has, from its beginnings, been a "literature of movement, of motion, its great icons the track through the forest and the superhighway" (*The Journey Narrative in American Literature*, 3).

10. Angel Island was an immigration station open from 1910 through 1940. It was designed to control the flow of Chinese into the country. Gary Okihiro says, "The migrants were carefully screened by U.S. Immigration officials and held for days, weeks, or months to determine their fitness for America" ("When and Where I Enter," 4).

11. Historian Henry Yu notes, "Canada had experienced a history of Asian migration strikingly parallel to the United States," but "that parallel can mislead us into thinking that the experience of 'Asian Canadians' is simply a variation of that of 'Asian Americans'" (*Pacific Canada*, xi). His introduction, "Towards a Pacific History of the Americas," to a special issue of *Amerasia Journal* outlines some of these similarities and differences.

12. Mexico falls under "North American," but because it is not a country that customarily receives immigrants, it does not have a substantial "Asian Mexican" community to date.

13. Lily Cho argues that diaspora "emerges from deeply subjective processes of racial memory, of grieving for losses which cannot always be articulated and longings which hang at the edge of possibility" ("The Turn to Diaspora," 15).

14. David Roediger has pointed out that in the process of becoming Americans, groups such as the Irish, Poles, Greeks, and Italians also acquired the status of white Americans (333). Myrna Kostash has also noted that "in 1908, Ukrainians were not white. Two generations later we are. How can this be?" (as quoted by Gunew, *Haunted Nations*, 26).

15. See my discussion of the implication of this classification in *The Politics of the Visible*, 5–11.

16. For a comparison of Asian Canadians and African Canadians as visible minorities, see Ty, "Complicating Racial Binaries." For a discussion of similarities between Asian Australians and Asian Canadians, see chapters 1 and 2 of Tseen-Ling Khoo's *Banana Bending*.

17. Parreñas notes, "The instabilities imposed by the political economy of globalization on Filipino households force a great number of families to send an able-bodied member outside of the country. According to one report, 'between 22 to 35 millions—34 to 54 percent of the total population—are directly dependent on remittance from migrant workers'" (18).

18. Historians K. Scott Wong and Sucheng Chan document the efforts of early Chinese immigrants to seek treatment equal to that received by other groups in America on the basis of class similarities. See chapter 1 of *Claiming America: Constructing Chinese American Identities during the Exclusion Era*.

19. According to James Warren, by 1894 an average of about nine hundred Chinese women were entering the city's brothels per year ("*Ah Ku*" and "*Karayuki-san*," 74).

1. The 1.5 Generation

1. As Ella Shohat and Robert Stam note, "Neocolonial domination is enforced through deteriorating terms of trade and the 'austerity programs' by which the World Bank and the IMF, often with the self-serving complicity of Third World elites, impose rules that First World countries would themselves never tolerate" ("From the Imperial Family to the Transnational Imaginary," 147).

2. Another novel that deals with these problems is Bino Realuyo's *The Umbrella Country*, which I studied in *The Politics of the Visible in Asian North American Narratives*. Unlike Roley and Ong's works, Realuyo's is set in the Philippines. See chapter 9 of my book.

3. For a study of the way Filipino Americans are regarded as both "foreign and domestic," see Sarita See, Introduction to *The Decolonized Eye*.

4. In his study of Filipino American youth gangs, Bangele Alsaybar notes that "urban type" Filipino American gangs, like the Santanas, "grew out of the inner city; its homeboys lived initially in predominantly Latino neighborhoods, thus getting exposed to Latino culture. It is not surprising, therefore, that Sanatans has borrowed heavily from the Latino *Cholo* tradition" ("Deconstructing Deviance," 126).

5. My comparison of Asian and Chicano bodies is based on cultural perceptions of them. In *Racial Castration* David Eng analyzes the ways in which the "Asian American male is both materially and psychically feminized within the context of a larger U.S. cultural imaginary" (1). Hurtado, Gurin, and Peng note that first-generation Mexican immigrants "have to deal with stereotypes of the majority culture about them as manual labourers and about menial labor as 'Mexican work'" ("Social Identities," 264).

6. For a different reading of the novel that looks at impersonation, environmental blending, and the cultural geography of feng shui, see Hsuan Hsu, "Mimicry, Spatial Captation, and Feng Shui in Han Ong's *Fixer Chao*."

7. Preciosa's fascination with the films of this period is similar to that of

the Filipino American protagonist in Bienvenido Santos's *The Man Who (Thought He) Looked like Robert Taylor*. See my article that deals with the negative effects of Hollywood on the Filipino subject ("A Filipino Prufrock in an Alien Land").

2. Recuperating Wretched Lives

1. The *kisaeng* tradition of elite and educated prostitutes disappeared slowly during the colonial period, 1910–45, in Korea. With the annexation of Korea by Japan in 1905, a more Westernized and commercialized form of sexual work emerged (Lie, "The Transformation of Sexual Work in 20th-Century Korea," 312–13). This twentieth-century form of sexual work resembles the examples of prostitution Bell studies in her book. In colonial Singapore, prostitution had an ambiguous legal position, based "in part on the meaning given to sexuality in Victorian society" (Warren, "Ah Ku" and "Karayuki-san," 5).

2. In Canada, Remembrance Day occurs on November 11, and commemorates the sacrifice of veterans and civilians who died in World War I, World War II, and other wars. A red poppy is used as an emblem because poppies bloomed in many of the battlefields of Flanders in WWI.

3. Warren writes, "For an *ah ku* or *karayuki-san* to survive the first 5 years of prostitution was to do well. To last beyond 30 was to hit a streak of luck. To grow old in brothel prostitution and exit from it in Singapore was to cheat the system—like a gambler, who, once in a lifetime, breaks the bank" (*"Ah Ku" and "Karayuki-san,"* 358).

4. Warren notes that "euphemistic kinship terms were used to mask the intimidating, exploitative nature of the relations between the *ah ku* and *kwai po* whose property they were," 55. The prostitutes were referred to as "daughters" and the *kwai po* called "mother" (*"Ah Ku" and "Karayuki-san,"* 55).

3. "All of Us Are the Same"

1. *Mother Tongue* premiered at The Firehall Arts Centre in Vancouver in 1995 and was presented by Factory Theatre and Cahoots Theatre Projects in Toronto in May 2001.

2. On the issue of translation, Balibar says, "Not only should we therefore consider it a vital objective to preserve and improve our educational capacities to teach the skills necessary for translating between multiple languages as a 'daily' practice, but also we should conceive it as a basic instrument to create the transnational public space in a democratic sense, where ideas and projects can be debated by the citizens themselves across the linguistic and administrative borders" (5–6).

3. According to the prefatory materials, *Rice Boy* had its world premiere at the Yale Repertory Theatre in New Haven, Connecticut, in October 2000, directed by Liz Diamond. *Rice Boy*'s west coast premiere was at the Mark Taper Forum in Los Angeles, California, in April 2001, directed by Chay Yew. *Rice*

Boy had its Canadian premiere at the Canadian Stage Company in Toronto, Ontario, in March 2003, directed by Micheline Chevrier.

4. The fish seller shows his love for the servant girl by continuing to leave her a fish every time he calls on the family, 16.

4. Feminist Subversions

1. *Miss Orient(ed)* was first produced through the Carlos Bulosan Cultural Workshop (now called Carlos Bulosan Theatre). According to the program notes of December 2001, the Carlos Bulosan Cultural Workshop was founded in 1982 as a cultural wing of the North America–wide Coalition against the Marcos Dictatorship. It had produced about nine plays between 1984 and 1997, and also presented skits on issues affecting Filipino Canadians in Toronto. The Carlos Bulosan Theatre's mandate is to "reflect on social issues affecting the Filipino and broader community. CBT also seeks to encourage and develop writers, performers, and other artists within the community" *(Miss Orient(ed)* program notes, 2003). I want to thank Nadine Villasin for allowing me to read the unpublished script of *Miss Orient(ed)*.

2. For instance, the young characters in Bino Realuyo's *The Umbrella Country* simulate the Miss Universe beauty pageant in their games the year when the pageant was held in Manila (chapter 2). This was such a big event in the city that "the streets were cleared of beggars, [. . .] walls were built to hide the slum areas [. . .], men and women were hired to clean the streets in red-and-white uniforms and to flash welcoming smiles" (38).

3. *Fire*, Mehta's third feature film, based on an original screenplay, was written, directed, and produced by Mehta. *Fire* opened the Perspective Canada Program at the 1996 Toronto International Film Festival, where it tied with *Fly Away Home* for the Air Canada Peoples Choice Award. It was one of twenty-nine films selected from more than fourteen hundred entries, worldwide, for the prestigious New York Film Festival. At the Vancouver International Film Festival, *Fire* won the Federal Express Award for Best Canadian Film as chosen by the audience. At the Chicago International Film Festival, it won two Silver Hugo Awards for best direction and best actress. In Mannheim *Fire* won the Jury Award, and in Paris it was voted Favorite Foreign Film. *Earth*, based on Bapsi Sidhwa's critically acclaimed novel, *Cracking India*, is the second film in Mehta's trilogy of the elements, *Fire*, *Earth*, and *Water*. *Earth* was shot in New Delhi in January 1998. It had its world premiere as a special presentation at the 1998 Toronto Film Festival, where it was received with a standing ovation and critical acclaim. *Earth* won the Prix Premiere du Public at the Festival du film asiatique de Deauville in France in March 1999 and the Critics' Award at the Schermi d'Amore International Film Festival in Italy in April of the same year. See http://www.directorsnet.com/mehta/.

4. Australian camera assistant Jasmine Yuen-Carrucan recounts that when *Water* was supposed to begin filming in India, they "were greeted with the news

that 2,000 protesters had stormed the ghats, destroying the main film set, burning and throwing it into the holy river. Protesters burnt effigies of Deepa Mehta, and threats to her life began."

5. Mishra says, "The massive size of Indian cinema is obvious from the statistics: eight hundred films a year shown in more than thirteen thousand predominantly urban cinemas, viewed by an average of 11 million people each day, and exported to about a hundred countries" *Bollywood Cinema*, 1.

6. For example, in *My Big Fat Greek Wedding* Toronto was made to look like Chicago; in *Exit Wounds* it was made to look like Los Angeles. Particularly in the 1990s, the low Canadian dollar made cities such as Toronto and Vancouver attractive to the American film industry.

7. Egoyan's film *Exotica*, about a father's relationship with a young girl who works as a stripper, was set in a nightclub of the same name. For a study of the way it reflects English Canadian cinematic traditions, see my essay "Spectacular Pleasures."

8. This reference to Toronto's baseball team is a dubious one because the team has an uneven record, as most Jays fans know.

9. For example, the highly successful Hindi film *Kuch Kuch Hota Hai* (1998), directed by Karan Johar, is set partly in England (though filmed in Scotland), with dialogue in Hindi and English. One reviewer of the film notes that Farha Khan's choreography is great, though sometimes lifted directly from *Grease* (Minhas.net, "Review of *Kuch Kuch Hota Hai*").

10. Actress Lisa Ray, who plays Sunita, happens to be biracial. Her father is Indian, and her mother is Polish. See Viswanathan, "The Belle of Bombay," 34.

5. Shape-shifters and Disciplined Bodies

1. Many scholars have written on these novels. For example, see Rachel Lee, *The Americas of Asian American Literature*, chapter 1; David Li, *Imagining the Nation*, chapter 2; and Sau-ling Wong, *Reading Asian American Literature*, chapter 1.

2. In her paper "Carrying the Past into the Future," Miriam Raethel presents an excellent study of the way Lai writes a story for diasporized subjects like herself, and of the repetition of scenes between the two time frames.

3. Much has been written about the ways in which Asian writers exoticize themselves in the process of writing difference. For example, see Sau-ling Wong's critique of representations of Chinatown, "Ethnic Subject, Ethic Sign, and the Difficulty of Rehabilitative Representation."

4. Pilar Cuder-Dominguez notes that "Lai in particular seems to be influenced by Haraway's thought, specifically in the wealth of science fiction intertexts that surface throughout her novel, as well as in the way she has pushed forward the Frankenstein myth through the creation of a complex, innovative, Frankenstein creature in the clone Evie" ("The Politics of Gender and Genre in Asian Canadian Women's Speculative Fiction," 117).

5. In Greek mythology, Pallas and the river goddess, Styx, had four children, one of whom was Nike, the god of victory.

6. For Robyn Morris, the Sonias bring up the fear of racial otherness: "The identity paradox of the Sonias, Frankenstein's creature and the Replicants is such that though they are created by humans, their near white, but not ordinary white, visage indicates a transgression of strict social boundaries designed to maintain hierarchical divisions [...]. The figure of human-like doubles such as the Sonias is feared because of its unrecognisability; they have been made in the image of whiteness" ("What Does It Mean to Be Human?" 86).

7. For example, Karen Luscombe writes, "For Lai, feminist revolt comes out of sardonic scatological aggression. And the stench is overwhelming" ("Review of *Salt Fish Girl*").

8. Gita Rajan prefers the term "mystical realism" to *magic realism*. She says, "Other magic realists work with large canvases and bold brush strokes; they theatricalize the mundane by calling upon external powers, even supranatural forces, to seal gaps in the lived reality of their characters. Divakaruni, on the other hand, alters the genre such that her novel resembles an Indian miniature painting with fine, vivid, compact, and detailed brush strokes. She operates by drawing upon internal powers to gesture towards a deliberate mysticism, albeit a personalized, Orientalized mysticism," ("Chitra Divakaruni's *The Mistress of Spices*," 216).

9. In *The Politics of the Visible in Asian North American Narratives* I discuss the psychosocial effects of racial otherness on Asian North Americans. I look at the ways in which Asian bodies become always marked or visible, creating, paradoxically, subjects that are invisible and silent. See the introduction to that book, especially pp. 23–29.

6. Scripting Fertility

1. In addition to works by Asian North American writers, I am thinking of novels such as Chinua Achebe's *Things Fall Apart*, Jamaica Kincaid's *Annie John*, and Toni Morrison's early novels, including *The Bluest Eye* and *Sula*.

2. Attebery note that until the 1960s "gender was one of the elements most often transcribed unthinkingly into SF's hypothetical worlds. Even if an author was interested in revising the gender code, the conservatism of a primarily male audience—and the editors, publishers, and distributors who were trying to outguess that audience—kept gender exploration to a minimum" (*Decoding Gender in Science Fiction*, 5).

3. I am using *literalization* in the way that Margaret Homans does in her study of nineteenth-century women's writing. Using Lacan and Chodorow's insights, Homans argues that, unlike a son, a daughter does not have to give up the presymbolic communication that she had with her mother, and this retention has "profound implications for the differential valuations of literal and figurative, and for women writers' relations to them," (*Bearing the Word*, 13).

4. Traise Yamamoto has pointed out that Japanese American women are conflated with Japanese women and has argued that the "Western imagination has consistently infantilized and feminized Japan, constructing the Japanese woman as a metonym for Japanese national, racial, and cultural identity" (*Masking Selves, Making Subjects*, 5).

5. Oliver used data from the University of Texas Medical Center and the National Mental Health Association reports. See *The Colonization of Psychic Space*, p. 104.

6. For a more expansive discussion of Lacan's notion of the screen and Asian North American subjectivity, see the introduction to my book *The Politics of the Visible in Asian North American Narratives*, 10–11.

Coda

1. Miki notes that the term "Asian" operates "as an interface in its always shifting and shifty negotiations with the concept of Canadian" ("Altered States," 57). The term "'Asian' in 'Canadian' has always been a disturbance — a disarticulation that had to be managed" (57).

2. Wong explains denationalization in a number of ways: as the easing of cultural nationalist concerns; as the growing permeability between Asian and Asian American, and as the shift from a domestic to a diasporic perspective ("Denationalization," 429, 431).

3. The essays in Wai Chee Dimock and Lawrence Buell's volume *Shades of the Planet: American LIterature as World Literature* deal with the ways in which larger forces of the "planet" render the nation-based paradigm inadequate, as well as the problems with continuing to think of America as the center. See Dimock's introduction.

4. For a different reading of the novel, see Pirbhai, who argues that *The Ground beneath Her Feet* is "another chapter in the continuing saga of postcolonial India," a saga which comprises *Midnight's Children*, *The Satanic Verses*, and *The Moor's Last Sigh* ("The Paradox of Globalization as an 'Untotalizable Totality,'" 55).

5. For comments on the role of the desert, see Whetter, "Michael Ondaatje's 'International Bastards' and Their 'Best Selves.'" I have previously written on the way the novel critiques notions of nation; see Ty, "The Other Questioned."

6. Raj Rao contends that "gay fiction needs to be mapped differently, with sexuality rather than nationality, race, or gender as the determinants of identity, so that if a writer is gay it does not matter that he comes from the developed or developing world, or is white or black" ("Because Most People Marry Their Own Kind," 118). Rao's call for a remapping, though in terms of sexuality, fits with my argument that we ought to look at some novels through positionality rather than being confined by the national and racial identity of the author.

Works Cited

Abdulhadi, Rabab, Nadine Naber, and Evelyn Alsultany. Introduction to *Gender, Nation, and Belonging: Arab and Arab American Feminist Perspectives*. Special issue of *MIT Electronic Journal of Middle Eastern Studies* 5 (Spring 2005), June 7, 2008. http://web.mit.edu/cis/www/mitejmes.

Achebe, Chinua. *Things Fall Apart*. Portsmouth, N.H.: Heinemann, 1996 [1958].

Alsaybar, Bangele. "Deconstructing Deviance: Filipino American Youth Gangs, 'Party Culture,' and Ethnic Identity in Los Angeles." *Amerasia Journal* 25, no. 1 (1999): 116–38.

Al-Solaylee, Kamal. "Review of *Miss Orient(ed)*." *Eye*, May 29, 2003.

Ang, Ien. *On Not Speaking Chinese: Living between Asia and the West*. London: Routledge, 2001.

Aparita. "Review of *Rice Boy* by Sunil Kuruvilla." Mybindi.com, March 1, 2004. http://www.mybindi.com/arts-entertainment/whatson/riceboy.cfm.

Appadurai, Arun. "Disjuncture and Difference in the Global Cultural Economy." In *Global Culture: Nationalism, Globalization and Modernity*, ed. Mike Featherstone. London: Sage, 1990, 195–311.

———. *Modernity at Large: Cultural Dimensions of Globalization*. Minneapolis: University of Minnesota Press, 1996.

Appiah, Kwame Anthony. "Against National Culture." In *Text and Nation: Cross-Disciplinary Essays on Cultural and National Identities*, ed. Laura García-Moreno and Peter C. Pfeiffer. Columbia, S.C.: Camden House, 1996.

Aquino, Nina, and Nadine Villasin. *Miss Orient(ed)*. Script. Performed at the Factory Studio Theatre, Toronto, May 22–June 8, 2003.

Aquino, Nina Lee, and Nadine Villasin. *Miss Orient(ed)*. In *Love + Relasianships: A Collection of Contemporary Asian-Canadian Drama*, vol. 2, ed. Nina Lee Aquino, 93–128. Toronto: Playwrights Canada Press, 2009.

ASNIC (Asian Studies Network Information Center. "Singapore History." Excerpt from *Singapore 1994*. http://inic.utexas.edu/asnic/countries/singapore/Singapore-History.html (accessed August 18, 2007).

Attebery, Brian. *Decoding Gender in Science Fiction*. New York: Routledge, 2002.

Austen, Jane. *Pride and Prejudice*. London: Penguin Classics, 1972 [1813].

Bakhtin, M. M. *The Dialogic Imagination: Four Essays*. Ed. Michael Holquist. Trans. Caryl Emerson and Michael Holquist. Austin: University of Texas Press, 1981.

Bales, Kevin. "Because She Looks Like a Child." In *Global Woman: Nannies, Maids, and Sex Workers in the New Economy*, ed. Barbara Ehrenreich and Arlie Russell Hochschild, 207–29. New York: Metropolitan Owl Book, 2003.

Balibar, Etienne. "Strangers as Enemies: Further Reflections on the Aporias of Transnational Citizenship." Globalization Working Papers 06/4 (May 2006). http://globalization.mcmaster.ca/wps/balibar.pdf (accessed August 17, 2007).

Bannerji, Himani. "The Passion of Naming: Identity, Difference and Politics of Class." In *Thinking Through: Essays on Feminism, Marxism, and Anti-Racisim*. Toronto: Women's Press, 1995.

Barber, Pauline. "Agency in Philippine Women's Labour Migration and Provisional Diaspora." *Women's Studies International Forum* 23, no. 4 (July–August 2000): 399–411.

Bartky, Sandra Lee. "Foucault, Femininity, and the Modernization of Patriarchal Power." In *Feminism and Foucault: Reflections on Resistance*, ed. Irene Diamond and Lee Quinby, 61–86. Boston: Northeastern University Press, 1988.

Basch, Linda, Nina Glick Schiller, and Cristina Szanton-Blanc. *Nations Unbound: Transnational Projects, Postcolonial Predicaments, and Deterritorialized Nation-States*. New York: Gordon and Breach, 1994.

Beiser, Morton, and Feng Hou. "Ethnic Identity, Resettlement Stress and Depressive Affect among Southeast Asian Refugees in Canada." *Social Science and Medicine* 63, no. 1 (July 2006): 137–50.

Bell, Shannon. *Reading, Writing and Rewriting the Prostitute Body*. Bloomington: Indiana University Press, 1994.

Berson, Misha. *Between Worlds: Contemporary Asian-American Plays*. New York: Theatre Communications Group, 1990.

Bhabha, Homi. *The Location of Culture*. London: Routledge, 1994.

Bhutto, Benazir. "Pakistan's Foreign Policy: Challenges and Responses in the Post–Cold War Era." In *After the Cold War: Essays on the Emerging World Order*, ed. Keith Philip Lepor, 148–60. Austin: University of Texas Press, 1997.

Braidotti, Rosi. "Cyberteratologies: Female Monsters Negotiate the Other's Participation in Humanity's Far Future." In *Envisioning the Future: Science Fiction and the Next Millennium*, ed. Marleen S. Barr, 146–69. Middletown, Conn.: Wesleyan University Press, 2003.

Brecher, Jeremy, and Tim Costello. *Global Village or Global Pillage: Economic Reconstruction from the Bottom Up*, 2nd ed. Cambridge, Mass: South End Press, 1998.
Brown, Lesley, ed. *The New Shorter Oxford English Dictionary*, 2 vols. Oxford: Clarendon Press, 1993 [1933].
Bulfinch, Thomas. "Sir Gawain." Chapter 5 of *Bulfinch Mythology*. http://www.online-literature.com/bulfinch/mythology_chivalry/5/ (accessed March 21, 2005).
Bulosan, Carlos. *America Is in the Heart*. Seattle: University of Washington Press, 1973 [1943].
Bunyan, John. *Pilgrim's Progress*. Ed. W. R. Owens. New York: Oxford World's Classics, 2003.
Butler, Judith. *Bodies That Matter: On the Discursive Limits of "Sex."* New York: Routledge, 1993.
Byczynski, Julie. "A Word in a Foreign Language: On Not Translating in the Theatre." *Canadian Theatre Review* 102 (Spring 2000): 33–37.
Campomanes, Oscar. "Filipinos in the United States and Their Literature of Exile." In *Reading the Literatures of Asian America*, ed. Shirley Geok-lin Lim and Amy Ling, 49–78. Philadelphia: Temple University Press, 1992.
Chai, Arlene. *The Last Time I Saw Mother*. New York: Fawcett Columbine, 1995.
Chaucer, Geoffrey. "The Wife of Bath's Prologue and Tale." From *The Canterbury Tales*. In *The Norton Anthology of English Literature*, 6th ed., ed. M. H. Abrams, 1:117–44. New York: W. W. Norton, 1993.
Cheah, Pheng. *Inhuman Conditions: On Cosmopolitanism and Human Rights*. Cambridge, Mass.: Harvard University Press, 2006.
Chen, Ying. *Ingratitude*. Trans. Carol Volk. Toronto: Douglas and McIntyre, 1998.
Cheung, King-Kok, ed. *An Interethnic Companion to Asian American Literature*. New York: Cambridge University Press, 1997.
Chiu, Monica. *Filthy Fictions: Asian American Literature by Women*. Walnut Creek, Calif.: Altamira Press, 2004.
Cho, Lily. "The Turn to Diaspora." *Topia* 17 (Spring 2007): 11–30.
Chong, Kevin. *Baroque-a-nova*. Toronto: Penguin Books, 2001.
Chuh, Kandice. *Imagine Otherwise: On Asian Americanist Critique*. Durham, N.C.: Duke University Press, 2003.
Citizenshift. "Feminization of Migration (Pinay)." *Media for Social Change*, August 3, 2006. http://citizenshift.nfb.ca/node/6936&dossier_nid=1127 (accessed March 9, 2008).
Citizenship and Immigration Canada. "Working Temporarily in Canada: The Live-In Caregiver Program." Modified March 31, 2007. http://www.cic.gc.ca/ENGLISH/work/caregiver/index.asp (accessed March 8, 2008).
Clifford, James. *Routes: Travel and Translation in the Late Twentieth Century*. Cambridge, Mass.: Harvard University Press, 1997.
Cohen, Robin. *Global Diasporas: An Introduction*. Seattle: University of Washington Press, 1997.

CPO News. "March 22, 2003." *CPO News*, February 15, 2004. http://members.rogers.com/culturephilippinesofontario/f_news.html.
Crosby, Janice C. *Cauldron of Changes: Feminist Spirituality in Fantastic Fiction*. Jefferson, N.C.: McFarland, 2000.
Cuder-Domínguez, Pilar. "The Politics of Gender and Genre in Asian Canadian Women's Speculative Fiction: Hiromi Goto and Larissa Lai." In *Asian Canadian Writing beyond Autoethnography*, ed. Eleanor Ty and Christl Verduyn, 115–31. Waterloo, Ontario: Wilfrid Laurier University Press, 2008.
Davis, Lennard J. *Bending Over Backwards: Disability, Dismodernism and Other Difficult Positions*. New York: New York University Press, 2002.
Davis, Rocío. *Transcultural Reinventions: Asian American and Asian Canadian Short-Story Cycles*. Toronto: TSAR, 2001.
Day, Iyko. "Lost in Translation: Uncovering Asian Canada." *Pacific Canada: Beyond the 49th Parallel*. Special issue of *Amerasia Journal* 33, no. 2 (2007): 69–85.
De Beauvoir, Simone. *The Second Sex*. Trans. H. M. Parshley. New York: Vintage, 1989.
De Certeau. *The Practice of Everyday Life*. Trans. Steven Rendall. Berkeley: University of California Press, 1984.
"Deepa Mehta." DirectorsNet.com, August 9, 2004. http://www.directorsnet.com/mehta/.
Desai, Jigna. *Beyond Bollywood: The Cultural Politics of South Asian Diasporic Film*. New York: Routledge, 2004.
DiCenzo, Maria. "Editorial: Italian Canadian Theatre." *Canadian Theatre Review* 104 (Fall 2000). http://www.utpjournals.com/ctr/ctr104.html (accessed March 29, 2008).
Dimock, Wai Chee. "Introduction: Planet and America, Set and Subset." In *Shades of the Planet: American Literature as World Literature*, ed. Wai Chee Dimock and Lawrence Buell. Princeton, N.J.: Princeton University Press, 2007, 1–16.
Dimock, Wai Chee, and Lawrence Buell, eds. *Shades of the Planet: American Literature as World Literature*. Princeton, N.J.: Princeton University Press, 2007.
Dirlik, Arif. "The Global in the Local." In *Global/Local: Cultural Production and the Transnational Imaginary*, ed. Rob Wilson and Wimal Dissanayake, 21–45. Durham, N.C.: Duke University Press, 1996.
———. *Global Modernity: Modernity in the Age of Global Capitalism*. Boulder, Colo.: Paradigm, 2007.
———. *The Postcolonial Aura: Third World Criticism in the Age of Global Capitalism*. Boulder, Colo.: Westview, 1997.
Divakaruni, Chitra Banerjee. *The Mistress of Spices*. New York: Random Anchor, 1998.
Ehrenreich, Barbara, and Arlie Russell Hochschild. *Global Woman: Nannies, Maids, and Sex Workers in the New Economy*. New York: Metropolitan Owl Books, 2003.

Eng, David L. *Racial Castration: Managing Masculinity in Asian America*. Durham, N.C.: Duke University Press, 2001.
Eng, David L., and Alice Y. Hom, eds. *Q & A: Queer in Asian America*. Philadelphia: Temple University Press, 1998.
Enloe, Cynthia. *The Morning After: Sexual Politics at the End of the Cold War*. Berkeley: University of California Press, 1993.
Espiritu, Yen Le. *Asian American Panethnicity: Bridging Institutions and Identities*. Philadelphia: Temple University Press, 1982.
———. "Gender and Labor in Asian Immigrant Families." *The American Behavioral Scientist* 42, no. 4 (January 1999): 628–48.
Featherstone, Mike. "Localism, Globalism, and Cultural Identity." In *Global/Local: Cultural Production and the Transnational Imaginary*, ed. Rob Wilson and Wilmal Dissanayake, 46–77. Durham, N.C.: Duke University Press, 1996.
Finney, Gail. "Introduction: Unity in Difference?" In *Look Who's Laughing: Gender and Comedy*, Studies in Humor and Gender, vol. 1, ed. Gail Finney. Langhorne, Pa.: Gordon and Breach, 1994.
Foucault, Michel. *Discipline and Punish*. Trans. Alan Sheridan. New York: Vintage, 1979.
Fraser, Nancy, and Linda J. Nicholson. "Social Criticism without Philosophy: An Encounter between Feminism and Postmodernism." In *Feminism/Postmodernism*, ed. Linda J. Nicholson, 19–38. New York: Routledge, 1990.
Freeman, John. Review of *Fixer Chao* by Han Ong. *Pittsburgh Post-Gazette*, May 6, 2002. http://www.post-gazette.com/books/reviews/20010506review765.asp (accessed February 3, 2003).
Friedman, Susan Stanford. *Mappings: Feminism and the Cultural Geography of Encounter*. Princeton, N.J.: Princeton University Press, 1998.
Gawle, Rupa. "Bollywood Film with Hollywood Humour." Rediff.com, August 9, 2004. http://www.rediff.com/entertai/2002/nov/22bolly.htm.
Glick Schiller, Nina, Linda Basch, and Cristina Szanton Blanc. "From Immigrant to Transmigrant: Theorizing Transnational Migration." *Anthropological Quarterly* 68, no. 1 (January 1995): 48–63.
Goellnicht, Donald C. "'Forays into Acts of Transformation': Queering Chinese-Diasporic Fictions." In *Culture, Identity, Commodity: Diasporic Chinese Literatures in English*, ed. Tseen Khoo and Kam Louie, 153–82. Montreal and Kingston, Ontario: McGill–Queen's University Press, 2005.
———. "A Long Labour: The Protracted Birth of Asian Canadian Literature." *Essays on Canadian Writing* 72 (Winter 2000): 1–41.
———. "Tang Ao in America: Male Subject Positions in *China Men*." In *Reading the Literatures of Asian America*, ed. Shirley Geok-lin Lim and Amy Ling, 191–212. Philadelphia: Temple University Press, 1992.
Gopinath, Gayatri. "Nostalgia, Desire, Diaspora: South Asian Sexualities in Motion." *Positions* 5, no. 2 (1997): 467–89.
Goto, Hiromi. "Alien Texts, Alien Seductions: The Context of Colour Full

Writing." In *Literary Pluralities*, ed. Christl Verduyn, 263–69. Peterborough, Ontario: Broadview Press/Journal of Canadian Studies, 1998.

———. *Chorus of Mushrooms*. Edmonton, Alberta: NeWest Press, 1994.

———. *The Kappa Child*. Calgary, Alberta: Red Deer Press, 2001.

Grewal, Inderpal. *Transnational America: Feminisms, Diasporas, Neoliberalisms*. Durham, N.C.: Duke University Press, 2005.

Groen, Rick. "Fusion Fare That's Not Spicy Enough: *Bollywood/Hollywood*." *Toronto Globe and Mail*, October 25, 2002. http://www.globeandmail.com/servlet/ArticleNews/movie/MOVIEREVIEWS/20021025/RVBOLL (accessed August 9, 2004).

Gunew, Sneja. *Haunted Nations: The Colonial Dimensions of Multiculturalisms*. New York: Routledge, 2004.

Gunter, Bernhard G., and Rolph van der Hoeven. "The Social Dimension of Globalization: A Review of the Literature." Geneva: International Labour Organization, 2004. http://www.ilo.org/public/english/bureau/integration/download/publicat/4_3_283_wcsdg-wp-24.pdf (accessed March 28, 2006).

Hall, Stuart. "The Local and the Global: Globalization and Ethnicity." In *Dangerous Liaisons: Gender, Nation and Postcolonial Perspectives*, ed. Anne McClintock, Aamir Mufti, and Ella Shohat, 173–87. Minneapolis: University of Minnesota Press, 1997.

———. *Representation: Cultural Representations and Signifying Practices*. London: Sage, 1997.

Hattori, Tomo. "Model Minority Discourse and Asian American Jouis-Sense." *Differences: A Journal of Feminist Cultural Studies* 11, no. 2 (Summer 1999): 228–47.

Hayles, N. Katherine, and Nicholas Gessler. "The Slipstream of Mixed Reality: Unstable Ontologies and Semiotic Markers in *The Thirteenth Floor*, *Dark City*, and *Mulholland Drive*." *PMLA* 119, no. 3 (May 2004): 482–99.

Homans, Margaret. *Bearing the Word: Language and Female Experience in Nineteenth-Century Women's Writing*. Chicago: University of Chicago Press, 1986.

Hornaday, Ann. "Bollywood: Infectious Excess." *Washington Post*, October 3, 2003, C05.

Hsu, Hsuan L. "Mimicry, Spatial Captation, and Feng Shui in Han Ong's *Fixer Chao*." *MFS Modern Fiction Studies* 52, no. 3 (2006): 675–704.

Hurtado, Aida, Patricia Gurin, and Timothy Peng. "Social Identities—A Framework for Studying the Adaptations of Immigrants and Ethnics: The Adaptations of Mexicans in the United States." In *New American Destinies: A Reader in Contemporary Asian and Latino Immigration*, ed. Darrell Y. Hamamoto and Rodolfo D. Torres, 243–67. New York: Routledge, 1997.

Hutcheon, Linda. *A Poetics of Postmodernism: History, Theory, Fiction*. New York: Routledge, 1988.

Imbert, Patrick, ed. *Converging Disensus: Cultural Transformations and Corporate Cultures, Canada and the Americas*. Ottawa: University of Ottawa Research Chair with Gauvin Press, 2006.

Inter-Mares Management Services. "Inter-Mares Maid Agency." April 2001. http://www.lucky.com.sg/intermares/ (accessed March 11, 2008).
Ishiguro, Kazuo. *The Remains of the Day*. New York: Vintage, 1990 [1989].
Islanders BC: Filipino Canadian Community On-line. "Non-profit Society Launches 'Little Miss Forever Young Philippines' Beauty Pageant." February 15, 2004. http://islandersbc.50megs.com/incomm16.html.
Iyer, Pico. *The Global Soul: Jet Lag, Shopping Malls, and the Search for Home*. Toronto: Vintage Books, 2000.
Jameson, Fredric. *Postmodernism, or The Cultural Logic of Late Capitalism*. Durham, N.C.: Duke University Press, 1991.
James Tiptree Jr. Award Council. "The 2001 James Tiptree Jr. Award: Winner." http://www.tiptree.org/2001/winner.html (accessed February 23, 2005).
Jay, Paul. "Beyond Discipline? Globalization and the Future of English." *PMLA* 116, no. 1 (January 2001): 32–47.
Jin, Ha. *Waiting*. New York: Vintage International, 2000.
Kamboureli, Smaro. *Scandalous Bodies: Diasporic Literature in English Canada*. Toronto: Oxford University Press, 2000.
Kanaganayakam, Chelva, ed. *Moveable Margins: The Shifting Spaces of Canadian Literature*. Toronto: TSAR, 2005.
Kang, Laura Hyun Yi. *Compositional Subjects: Enfiguring Asian/American Women*. Durham, N.C.: Duke University Press, 2002.
Karamcheti, Indira. "Singapore on My Mind: Fiona Cheong, Lydia Kwa and Shirley Geok-lin Lim Compare Notes." Interview. *Women's Review of Books* 19, nos. 10–11 (July 2002): 24–25.
Kearns, Katherine. *Psychoanalysis, Historiography, and Feminist Theory: The Search for Critical Method*. Cambridge: Cambridge University Press, 1997.
Keller, Nora Okja. *Fox Girl*. New York: Penguin, 2002.
Kellner, Douglas. *Media Culture: Cultural Studies, Identity and Politics between the Modern and Postmodern*. London: Routledge, 1995.
Khoo, Tseen-Ling. *Banana Bending: Asian-Australian and Asian-Canadian Literatures*. Montreal and Kingston, Ontario: McGill–Queen's University Press, 2003.
Kim, Elaine. "Sex Tourism in Asia: A Reflection of Political and Economic Inequality." *Critical Perspectives of Third World America* 2, no. 1 (Fall 1984): 214–32.
Kincaid, Jamaica. *Annie John*. Vancouver: Douglas and McIntyre, 1997.
Kingston, Maxine Hong. *The Woman Warrior: Memoirs of a Girlhood among Ghosts*. New York: Vintage, 1977 [1975].
Kirkland, Bruce. "Bollywood High: Indian Exuberance Comes to Toronto." *Toronto Sun*, October 25, 2002. http://www.canoe.ca/JamMoviesReviewsB/bollywoodhollywood-sun.html (accessed August 9, 2004).
———. "Filmmaker Mehta Has a Love for Canada." *Toronto Sun*, October 20, 2002. http://www.canoe.ca/JamMoviesReviewsB/bollywoodhollywood-sun.html (accessed August 9, 2004).
Kogawa, Joy. *Obasan*. Toronto: Penguin, 1981.

Kong, Sook. "Sook C. Kong Interviews Hiromi Goto." *Herizons*, Fall 2004.
Koshy, Susan. "Morphing Race into Ethnicity: Asian Americans and Critical Transformations of Whiteness." *Boundary 2* 28, no. 1 (2001): 153–94.
Kristeva, Julia. *Powers of Horror: An Essay on Abjection*. Trans. Leon S. Roudiez. New York: Columbia University Press, 1982.
Kuruvilla, Sunil. *Rice Boy*. Toronto: Playwrights Canada Press, 2000.
Kwa, Lydia. *This Place Called Absence*. Winnipeg: Turnstone Press, 2000.
Lai, Eric, and Dennis Arguelles, eds. *The New Face of Asian Pacific America: Numbers, Diversity and Change in the 21st Century*. San Francisco: AsianWeek, 2003.
Lai, Larissa. "Future Asians: Migrant Speculations, Repressed History and Cybord Hope." *West Coast Line* 38, no. 2 (Fall 2004): 168–75.
———. "Political Animals and the Body of History." *Canadian Literature: Asian Canadian Writing* 163 (Winter 1999): 145–54.
———. *Salt Fish Girl*. Toronto: Thomas Allen, 2002.
———. *When Fox Is a Thousand*. Vancouver: Press Gang, 1995.
Lau, Evelyn. *Other Women*. Toronto: Vintage Canada, 1996.
Le, C. N. "Population Statistics and Demographics." In *Asian Nation: The Landscape of Asian America*. http://www.asian-nation.org/population.shtml (accessed August 23, 2006).
Lee, Erika. "Hemispheric Orientalism and the 1907 Pacific Coast Race Riots." In *Pacific Canada: Beyond the 49th Parallel*, guest ed. Henry Yu and Guy Beauregard. Special issue of *Amerasia Journal* 33, no. 2 (2007): 19–48.
Lee, Rachel. *The Americas of Asian American Literature: Gendered Fictions of Nation and Transnation*. Princeton, N.J.: Princeton University Press, 1999.
Lee, Robert G. *Orientals: Asian Americans in Popular Culture*. Philadelphia: Temple University Press, 1999.
Lee, Tara. "Mutant Bodies in Larissa Lai's *Salt Fish Girl*: Challenging the Alliance between Science and Capital." *West Coast Line* 38, no. 2 (Fall 2004): 94–109.
Lee, Young-Oak. "Nora Okja Keller and the Silenced Woman: An Interview." *Melus* 28, no. 4 (2003): 145–65. http://findarticles.com/p/articles/mi_m2278/is_4_28/ai_n6129667/pg_1 (accessed July 7, 2007).
Levitt, Peggy, and Mary Waters. *The Changing Face of Home: The Transnational Lives of the Second Generation*. New York: Russell Sage, 2002
Li, David Leiwei. *Imagining the Nation: Asian American Literature and Cultural Consent*. Stanford, Calif.: Stanford University Press, 1998.
Lie, John. "The Transformation of Sexual Work in 20th-Century Korea." *Gender and Society* 9, no. 3 (June 1995): 310–27.
Lieu, Nhi T. "Remembering 'the Nation' through Pageantry: Femininity and the Politics of Vietnamese Womanhood in the *Hoa Hau Ao Dai* Contest." *Frontiers: A Journal of Women's Studies* 21, nos. 1–2 (2000): 127–51.
Lim, Shirley Geok-lin. "Immigration and Diaspora." In *An Interethnic Companion to Asian American Literature*, ed. King-Kok Cheung, 289–311. New York: Cambridge University Press, 1997.

Lim, Shirley Geok-lin, and Amy Ling. *Reading the Literatures of Asian America*. Philadelphia: Temple University Press, 1992.

Lim, Shirley Geok-lin, John Blair Gamber, Stephen Hong Sohn, and Gina Valentino, eds. *Transnational Asian American Literature: Sites and Transits*. Philadelphia: Temple University Press, 2006.

Ling, Amy. *Between Worlds: Women Writers of Chinese Ancestry*. New York: Pergamon, 1990.

Ling, Jinqi. *Narrating Nationalisms: Ideology and Form in Asian American Literature*. New York: Oxford University Press, 1998.

Lo, Marie. "Passing Recognition: *Obasan* and the Borders of Asian American and Canadian Literary Criticism." *Comparative American Studies: An International Journal* 5, no. 3 (2007): 307–32.

Lowe, Lisa. "Heterogeneity, Hybridity, Multiplicity: Marking Asian American Differences." *Diaspora* 1, no. 1 (1991): 24–43.

———. *Immigrant Acts: On Asian American Cultural Politics*. Durham, N.C.: Duke University Press, 1996.

Luscombe, Karen. "Review of *Salt Fish Girl*." *Toronto Globe and Mail*, October 26, 2002.

Mackey, Eva. *The House of Difference: Cultural Politics and National Identity in Canada*. Toronto: University of Toronto Press, 2002.

Manderson, Lenore. "Colonial Desires: Sexuality, Race, and Gender in British Malaya." *Journal of the History of Sexuality* 7, no. 31 (1997): 372–88.

Manlove, Colin. *The Fantasy Literature of England*. Houndmills, Basingstoke, England: MacMillan, 1999.

McClintock, Anne. *Imperial Leather: Race, Gender and Sexuality in the Colonial Contest*. New York: Routledge, 1996.

Mercer, Kobena, and Isaac Julien. "Race, Sexual Politics and Black Masculinity: A Dossier." In *Male Order: Unwrapping Masculinity*, ed. Rowena Chapman and Jonathan Rutherford, 97–164. London: Lawrence and Wishart, 1988.

Merlin, Lara. "Review of 'The Mistress of Spices.'" *World Literature Today: A Literary Quarterly of the University of Oklahoma* 72, no. 1 (Winter 1998): 207.

Migration Policy Institute. "Legal Immigration to US Still Declining." *Immigration Facts* 9, October 2004. http://www.migrationpolicy.org/Factsheet_102904.pdf (accessed April 2, 2004).

Miki, Roy. "Altered States: Global Currents, the Spectral Nation, and the Production of 'Asian Canadian.'" *Journal of Canadian Studies* 35, no. 3 (Fall 2000): 43–72.

———. *Broken Entries: Race, Subjectivity, Writing*. Toronto: Mercury Press, 1998.

Minhas.net. "Review of *Kuch Kuch Hota Hai*." August 15, 2004. http://www.minhas.net/culture/indianfilms/duchkuchhotahai.

Miriam, Kathy. "Stopping the Traffic in Women: Power, Agency and Abolition in Feminist Debates over Sex-Trafficking." *Journal of Social Philosophy* 36, no. 1 (Spring 2005): 1–17.

Mishra, Vijay. *Bollywood Cinema: Temples of Desire*. New York: Routledge, 2002.

Miyoshi, Masao. "A Borderless World? From Colonialism to Transnationalism and the Decline of the Nation-State." *Critical Inquiry* 19, no. 4 (1993): 726–51.
Moon, Katharine H. S. *Sex among Allies: Military Prostitution in U.S.-Korea Relations.* New York: Columbia University Press, 1997.
Morris, Robyn. "'What Does It Mean to Be Human?': Racing Monsters, Clones and Replicants." *Foundation* 91 (Summer 2004): 81–96.
Morrison, Toni. *The Bluest Eye.* New York: Plume, 2000.
———. *Sula.* Toronto: Vintage, 2004.
Muppidi, Himadeep. *The Politics of the Global.* Borderlines, vol. 23. Minneapolis: University of Minnesota Press, 2004.
Myers, Linda. "US Underestimates Jobs Lost to Outsourcing." *Cornell Chronicle*, October 21, 2004. http://www.news.cornell.edu/chronicle/04/10.21.04/outsourcing_jobs.html (accessed March 11, 2008).
Naficy, Hamid. *An Accented Cinema: Exilic and Diasporic Filmmaking.* Princeton, N.J.: Princeton University Press, 2001.
Nguyen, Viet Thanh. *Race and Resistance: Literature and Politics in Asian America.* New York: Oxford University Press, 2002.
Okada, John. *No-No Boy.* Seattle: University of Washington Press, 1976.
Okihiro, Gary Y. "Is Yellow Black or White?" In *Asian Americans: Experiences and Perspectives*, ed. Timothy P. Fong and Larry H. Shinagawa, 63–78. Upper Saddle River, N.J.: Prentice-Hall, 2000.
———. "When and Where I Enter." In *Asian American Studies: A Reader*, ed. Jean Yu-Wen, Shen Wu, and Min Song, 3–20. New Brunswick, N.J.: Rutgers University Press, 2000.
Oliver, Kelly. *The Colonization of Psychic Space: A Psychoanalytic Social Theory of Oppression.* Minneapolis: University of Minnesota Press, 2004.
———. *Witnessing: Beyond Recognition.* Minneapolis: University of Minnesota Press, 2001.
Omi, Michael, and Howard Winant. "On the Theoretical Status of the Concept of Race." In *Asian American Studies: A Reader*, ed. Jean Yu-Wen Shen Wu and Min Song, 199–208. New Brunswick, N.J.: Rutgers University Press, 2000.
Ondaatje, Michael. *Divisadero.* Toronto: McClelland and Stewart, 2007.
———. *The English Patient.* Toronto: Vintage Books Canada, 1993.
Ong, Aihwa. *Flexible Citizenship: The Cultural Logics of Transnationality.* Durham, N.C.: Duke University Press, 1999.
———. "The Gender and Labor Politics of Postmodernity." In *The Politics of Culture in the Shadow of Capital*, ed. Lisa Lowe and David Lloyd, 61–97. Durham, N.C.: Duke University Press, 1997.
Ong, Han. *Fixer Chao.* New York: Farrar, Straus, Giroux, 2001.
Ozeki, Ruth. *All Over Creation.* Toronto: Penguin Paperbacks, 2003.
———. *My Year of Meats.* Toronto: Penguin Paperbacks, 1999.
Palumbo-Liu, David. *Asian/American Historical Crossings of a Racial Frontier.* Stanford, Calif.: Stanford University Press, 1999.

Parreñas, Rhacel Salazar. *Servants of Globalization: Women, Migration and Domestic Work*. Stanford, Calif.: Stanford University Press, 2001.
Pearson, Wendy. "Saturating the Present with the Past: Hiromi Goto's *The Kappa Child*." *Strange Horizons*, January 6, 2003. http://www.strangehorizons.com/2003/20030106/kappa_child.shtml (accessed February 23, 2005).
Pirbhai, Mariam. "The Paradox of Globalization as an 'Untotalizable Totality' in Salman Rushdie's *The Ground beneath Her Feet*." *International Fiction Review* 28, nos. 1–2 (2001): 54–66.
Planet Bollywood. "*Bollywood/Hollywood*: Film Review." *Planet Bollywood*, August 9, 2004. http://planetbollywood.com/Film/BollywoodHollywood/.
Polan, Dana. "Globalism's Localisms." In *Global/ Local: Cultural Production and the Transnational Imaginary*, ed. Rob Wilson and Wimal Dissanayake, 255–83. Durham, N.C.: Duke University Press, 1996.
Pratt, Mary Louise. *Imperial Eyes: Travel Writing and Transculturation*. New York: Routledge, 1992.
Quan, Betty. *Mother Tongue*. Winnipeg: Scirocco Drama, 1999 [1996].
Rabie, Lisa Limor. "*Rice Boy* Explores Search for Identity." *Yale Daily News*, October 27, 2000. www.yaledailynews.com (accessed March 1, 2004).
Raethel, Miriam. "Carrying the Past into the Future." Paper presented at Beyond Ethnicity: Writing Race and Ethnicity in Canada, Wilfrid Laurier University, Waterloo, Ontario, April 28–30, 2005.
Rajan, Gita. "Chitra Divakaruni's *The Mistress of Spices*: Deploying Mystical Realism." *Meridians: Feminism, Race, Transnationalism* 2, no. 2 (2002): 215–36.
Rajan, Gita, and Shailja Sharma, eds. *New Cosmopolitanisms: South Asians in the US*. Stanford, Calif.: Stanford University Press, 2006.
Rao, R. Raj. "Because Most People Marry Their Own Kind: A Reading of Shyam Selvadura's *Funny Boy*." *ARIEL: A Review of International English Literature* 28, no. 1 (January 1997): 117–28.
Realuyo, Bino. *The Umbrella Country*. New York: Ballantine, 1999.
Reed, Susan. "Re-telling of 'Sir Gawain and Dame Ragnell.'" Sisters of the Silver Branch. March 21, 2005. http://www.silver-branch.org/ssbcreations/GawainLL.html.
Rich, Adrienne. "Compulsory Heterosexuality and Lesbian Existence." *Signs: Journal of Women in Culture and Society* 5 (Summer 1980): 631–60.
———. *On Lies, Secrets, and Silences: Selected Prose, 1966–1978*. New York: W. W. Norton, 1979.
Rodowick, D. N. "Introduction: Mobile Citizens, Media States." *PMLA* 117, no. 1 (January 2002): 13–23.
Roediger, David. "Whiteness and Ethnicity in the History of 'White Ethnics' in the United States." In *Race Critical Theories*, ed. Philomena Essed and David Theo Goldberg, 325–43. Malden, Mass.: Basil Blackwell, 2002.
Roley, Brian Ascalon. *American Son*. New York: W. W. Norton, 2001.
Ross, Andrew, ed. *No Sweat: Fashion, Free Trade, and the Rights of Garment Workers*. London: Verso, 1997.

Rushdie, Salman. *The Ground beneath Her Feet*. Toronto: Vintage Canada, 2000.

———. *Imaginary Homelands: Essays and Criticism, 1981–1991*. London: Granta Books, 1991.

Russo, Mary. *The Female Grotesque: Risk, Excess and Modernity*. New York: Routledge, 1994.

Safran, William. "Diasporas in Modern Societies: Myths of Homeland and Return." *Diaspora* 1 (Spring 1991): 83–99.

San Juan, Epifanio Jr. *Articulations of Power in Ethnic and Racial Studies in the United States*. Atlantic Highlands, N.J.: Humanities Press, 1992.

———. *The Philippine Temptation: Dialectics of U.S. Literary Relations*. Philadelphia: Temple University Press, 1996.

See, Sarita. *The Decolonized Eye: Filipino American Art and Performance*. Minneapolis: University of Minnesota Press, 2009.

Selvadurai, Shyam. *Funny Boy*. Toronto: McClelland and Stewart, 1994.

Shaw, Martin. *Theory of the Global State: Globality as Unfinished Revolution*. Cambridge: Cambridge University Press, 2000.

———. "War and Globality: The Role and Character of War in the Global Transition." In *The New Agenda for Peace Research*, ed. Ho-won Jeong, 61–80. Aldershot, Hampshire, England: Ashgate Publishing, 1999. http://www.sussex.ac.uk/Users/hafa3/warglobality.htm (accessed December 7, 2005).

Shohat, Ella, and Robert Stam. "From the Imperial Family to the Transnational Imaginary: Media Spectatorship in the Age of Globalization." In *Global/Local: Cultural Production and the Transnational Imaginary*, ed. Rob Wilson and Wimal Dissanayake, 145–70. Durham, N.C.: Duke University Press, 1996.

———. *Unthinking Eurocentrism: Multiculturalism and the Media*. London and New York: Routledge, 1994.

Sone, Monica Itoi. *Nisei Daughter*. Seattle: University of Washington Press, 1979.

Spiegel Online International. "Merkel Takes On Fat Cats." *Spiegel Online International*, December 11, 2007. http://www.spiegel.de/international/germany/0,1518,522480,00.html (accessed March 11, 2007).

Spivak, Gayatri Chakraborty. *A Critique of Postcolonial Reason*. London and New York: Routledge, 1999.

Srikanth, Rajini. *The World Next Door: South Asian American Literature and the Idea of America*. Philadelphia: Temple University Press, 2004.

Stallybrass, Peter, and Allon White. *The Politics and Poetics of Transgression*. Ithaca, N.Y.: Cornell University Press, 1986.

Statistics Canada. "100 Years of Immigration to Canada." http://www12.statcan.ca/english/census01/products/analytic/multimedia.cfm26January 2004 (accessed April 3, 2006).

———. "Study: Canada's Visible Minority Population in 2017." *The Daily*, March 22, 2005. http://www.statcan.ca/Daily/English/050322/d050322b.htm (accessed April 3, 2006).

Steger, Manfred. *Globalization: A Very Short Introduction.* Oxford: Oxford University Press, 2003.
Stewart, Susan. *On Longing: Narratives of the Miniature, the Gigantic, the Souvenir, the Collection.* Durham, N.C.: Duke University Press, 1993.
Stout, Janis. *The Journey Narrative in American Literature: Patterns and Departures.* Westport, Conn.: Greenwood, 1983.
Sumi, Glenn. "Tongue Lashing." *Now Magazine* 20, no. 37 (May 17–23, 2001). http://www.nowtoronto.com/issues/2001-05-17/stage_theatrereviews5.html (accessed March 3, 2004).
Takaki, Ronald. *Strangers from a Different Shore: A History of Asian Americans.* Boston: Little, Brown, 1989.
Teles, Steven. "Public Opinion and Interest Groups in the Making of U.S.-China Policy." In *After the Cold War: Domestic Factors and U.S.-China Relations*, ed. Robert S. Ross, 40–69. Armonk, N.Y.: East Gate, 1998.
Transnational Institute: A Worldwide Fellowship of Committed Scholar Activists (TNI). "Sex Crimes and Prostitution/Outposts of Empire: The Case against Foreign Military Bases." March 2007. http://www.tni.org/detail_page .phtml?&act_id=16374&menu=11e (accessed July 6, 2007).
Ty, Eleanor. "Complicating Racial Binaries: Asian Canadians and African Canadians as Visible Minorities." In *AfroAsian Encounters: Culture, History, Politics*, ed. Heike Raphael-Hernandez and Shannon Steen, 50–67. New York: New York University Press, 2006.
———. "A Filipino Prufrock in an Alien Land: Bienvenido Santo's *The Man Who (Thought He) Looked like Robert Taylor*." Asian American Literature and Culture, Part II, ed. Karen Chow. Special issue of *Lit: Literature Interpretation Theory* 12, no. 3 (2001): 267–83.
———. "The Other Questioned: Exoticism and Displacement in Michael Ondaatje's *The English Patient*." *International Fiction Review* 27, nos. 1–2 (2000): 10–19.
———. *The Politics of the Visible in Asian North American Narratives.* Toronto: University of Toronto Press, 2004.
———. "Spectacular Pleasures: Labyrinthine Mirrors in Atom Egoyan's *Exotica*." In *Pop Can: Popular Culture in Canada*, ed. Lynne Van Luven and Priscilla L. Walton, 4–12. Scarborough, Ontario: Prentice-Hall, 1999.
Ty, Eleanor, and Christl Verduyn, eds. *Asian Canadian Writing beyond Autoethnography.* Waterloo, Ontario: Wilfrid Laurier University Press, 2008.
Viswanathan, Padma. "The Belle of Bombay: Lisa Ray, Star of the Film *Bollywood/Hollywood*." Photographs by Gabor Jurina. *Elm Street*, November 2002, 30–32, 34, 36, 38, 40.
Warren, James Francis. *"Ah Ku" and "Karayuki-san": Prostitution in Singapore, 1870–1940.* Singapore: Oxford University Press, 1993.
Waugh, Thomas. "Queer Bollywood, or 'I'm the Player, You're the Naive One': Patterns of Sexual Subversion in Recent Indian Popular Cinema." In *Keyframes: Popular Cinema and Cultural Studies*, ed. Matthew Tinkcom and Amy Villarejo, 280–97. London and New York: Routledge: 2001.

Weich, Dave, and Ruth Ozeki. "Ruth Ozeki, Bearing Witness: Exclusive to Powell's Author Interviews." Powell's Books Author Interviews, March 18, 2003. http://www.powells.com/interviews/ozeki.html (accessed August 8, 2005).
Weinbaum, Alys Eve, and Brent Hayes Edwards. "On Critical Globality." *ARIEL: A Review of International English Literature* 31, no. 1 (January–April 2000): 255–74.
Wendell, Susan. "Toward a Feminist Theory of Disability." In *The Disability Studies Reader*, ed. Lennard J. Davis, 260–78. New York: Routledge, 1997.
Whetter, Darryl. "Michael Ondaatje's 'International Bastards' and Their 'Best Selves': An Analysis of *The English Patient* as Travel Literature." *English Studies in Canada* 23, no. 4 (December 1997): 443–58.
Wikipedia. "List of Canadians of Asian Ancestry." *Wikipedia: The Free Encyclopedia*, June 28, 2008. http://en.wikipedia.org/wiki/List_of_Canadians_of_Asian_ancestry (accessed July 2, 2008).
———. "Overseas Filipino." *Wikipedia: The Free Encyclopedia*, March 8, 2008. http://en.wikipedia.org/wiki/Overseas_Filipino (accessed March 9, 2008).
Wilson, Rob, and Wimal Dissanayake, eds. *Global/Local: Cultural Production and the Transnational Imaginary*. Durham, N.C.: Duke University Press, 1996.
Wimmer, Andreas, and Nina Glick Schiller. "Methodological Nationalism and Beyond: Nation-State Building, Migration, and the Social Sciences." *Global Networks* 2, no. 4 (2002): 301–34.
Wolf, Diane L. "Family Secrets: Transnational Struggles among Children of Filipino Immigrants." *Sociological Perspectives* 40, no. 3 (1997): 457–82.
Wolf, Naomi. *The Beauty Myth*. Toronto: Vintage Books, 1990.
Wolmark, Jenny. *Aliens and Others: Science Fiction, Feminism, and Postmodernism*. Iowa City: University of Iowa Press, 1994.
Wong, K. Scott, and Sucheng Chan. *Claiming America: Constructing Chinese American Identities during the Exclusion Era*. Philadelphia: Temple University Press, 1998.
Wong, Sau-Ling Cynthia. "Denationalization Reconsidered: Asian American Cultural Criticism at a Theoretical Crossroads." In *Asian Americans: Experiences and Perspectives*, ed. Timothy P. Fong and Larry H. Shinagawa, 428–37. Upper Saddle River, N.J.: Prentice-Hall, 2000.
———."Ethnic Subject, Ethic Sign, and the Difficulty of Rehabilitative Representation: Chinatown in Some Works of Chinese American Fiction." *Yearbook of English Studies: Ethnicity and Representation in American Literature* 24 (1994): 251–62.
———. "Ethnicizing Gender: An Exploration of Sexuality as Sign in Chinese Immigrant Literature." In *Reading the Literatures of Asian America*, ed. Shirley Geok-lin Lim and Amy Ling, 111–29. Philadelphia: Temple University Press, 1992.
———. *Reading Asian American Literature: From Necessity to Extravagance*. Princeton, N.J.: Princeton University Press, 1993.

Xie, Shaobo. "Is the World Decentered? A Postcolonial Perspective on Globalization." In *Global Fissures: Postcolonial Fusions*, ed. Joseph Clara and Janet Wilson, 53–75. Amsterdam: Rodophi, 2006.

Yamamoto, Traise. *Masking Selves, Making Subjects: Japanese American Women, Identity, and the Body*. Berkeley: University of California Press, 1999.

Yamashita, Karen Tei. *Tropic of Orange*. Minneapolis: Coffee House Press, 1997.

Yergin, Daniel. "The Age of 'Globality.'" *Newsweek*, May 18, 1998. http://www.newsweek.com/id/92486 (accessed March 6, 2008).

Yu, Henry, and Guy Beauregard, guest eds. *Pacific Canada: Beyond the 49th Parallel*. Special commemorative issue of *Amerasia Journal* 33, no. 2 (2007).

Yuen-Carrucan, Jasmine. "The Politics of Deepa Mehta's *Water*." *Bright Lights Film Journal* 28 (April 2000). http://www.brightlightsfilm.com/28/water.html (accessed August 9, 2004).

Filmography

Bend It like Beckham. Gurinder Chadha, director. Twentieth-Century Fox, 2002.

Bollywood/Hollywood. Deepa Mehta, director. Different Tree Same Wood, 2002.

Earth. Deepa Mehta, director. Zeitgeist Films, 1999.

Eat Drink Man Woman (Yin shi nan nu). Ang Lee, director. 1994.

Fire. Deepa Mehta, director. Kaleidoscope Entertainment, 1996.

The Ice Storm. Ang Lee, director. Touchstone, 1997.

Kuch Kuch Hota Hai. Karan Johar, director. Dharma Productions, 1998.

The Mistress of Spices. Paul Mayeda Berges, director. Balle Pictures, 2006.

Pretty Woman. Garry Marshall, director. Touchstone, 1990.

Sense and Sensibility. Ang Lee, director. Columbia, 1995.

Smoke. Wayne Wang, director. Miramax, 1995.

Index

Abdulhabi, Rabab, xx
abjection, 12–14, 37, 40, 60, 71, 98, 125; abject others, 13
African American, 13, 16, 34–35
aging, 90, 104–6
Allen, Woody, 78
Alsaybar, Bangele, 145n4
Al-Solaylee, Kamal, 64
Alsultany, Evelyn, xx
America: American dream, 3–5, 19, 64–65, 109; American son, 12; culture, 16, 75, 104; democracy, 14; music, 135
Andersen, Hans Christian, 90
Ang, Ien, xxiv, xxx
Angel Island, 144n10
Appadurai, Arjun, xxix, 91
Appiah, Kwame Anthony, 136–37
Aquino, Nina, xxxv, 63–76
Asian American, xv, xvii, xix, xxi, 46, 109, 125, 127, 141–42; authors, xiv–xv, 94; employment, 55; identification, xxx, 138; literature, xviii, xx, xxxii, 89, 129–30, 132; narratives, xxix; population, xxiii
Asian British, 133, 141–42
Asian Canadian, xv, xvii, xix, xxi, 109, 141–42, 150n1; authors, xiv–xv, 136; demographics, xxiii; employment, 55; identification, xxx, 129–30, 138; literature, xviii, xxxii, 89; narratives, xxix, 77
Asian global, 130, 132–33, 140, 142
Asian North American, xvi, xvii, xx, 132, 141–42; and displacement, xxvi–xxvii; globalization, xxx; narratives, xxix, 89, 109; Studies, xxxi; subjectivity, xix; as travelers, xxviii
assimilation, 70, 109; desire for, 58–59, 134
Attebery, Brian, 149n2
Austen, Jane, 83–84, 141

Bakhtin, M. M., 69–70, 90; Bakhtinian carnival, 83
Bales, Kevin, 24

Balibar, Etienne, 45, 146n2
Bannerji, Himani, xviii
Barber, Pauline, 74
Bartky, Sandra Lee, 72, 91, 106, 115–16
Basch, Linda, 6, 25–26
beauty, 105, 115–16; myth, 104, 106; pageant, 64–69, 73, 75
Beiser, Morton, 55
Bell, Shannon, 21–22
Bend It Like Beckham (Chadha), 77
Berson, Misha, 44
Bhabha, Homi, xxix, 71, 129
Bhutto, Benazir, xiii
Bildungsroman (novel of development), 19, 110, 130
Bollywood, 63, 76–77, 81, 86
Bollywood/Hollywood (Mehta), 76–86
borders: national, xiii, xiv; borderless, 19
boundaries, ix, xii, 134; between dominant and minority culture, 44; weakening of, xiv
Braidotti, Rosi, 99, 111
Brecher, Jeremy, 104
Bulfinch, Thomas, 105
Bulosan, Carlos, xxxii, 89
Butler, Judith, xxx, 43, 82
Byczynski, Julie, 46

Campomanes, Oscar, xxvi
capitalism, ix, 97; critiques of global, xiv–xv, xxxvi, 4, 11
Carey, Mariah, 64, 69
Chai, Arlene, 130–31, 137
Chan, Sucheng, 145n18
Chaucer, Geoffrey, 105
Cheah, Pheng, xxviii–xxix
Chen, Ying, 130, 140
Cheung, King-Kok, xix, xx
Chin, Frank, xxxii
China, 28, 30, 44, 91, memories of, 47–48
Chinese, xvii; Canadian, 45–53, 85; traditions, 47, 49; women, 29, 95

Chiu, Monica, 98–99, 122
Cho, Lily, xvi, xxi, 144n13
Chong, Kevin, 140
Choy, Wayson, 89
Chuh, Kandice, xix, xxiv
Clifford, James, xxvi, xxvii, xxix, xxxiii, 127
cloning, 90, 94, 97
Cohen, Robin, xxv–xxvi, xxxvi
cold war, xii–xiii
comedy, 63, 69, 79
cosmopolitanism, xxxvii; cosmopolitans, 133, 136–37, 141–42
Costello, Tim, 104
Crosby, Janice, 90
Cuder-Dominguez, 148n4

Davis, Lennard, 43–44, 47
Davis, Rocío, 130
Day, Iyko, xxi
de Beauvoir, Simone, 43, 104
de Certeau, Michel, xxx, 62
denationalization, 130, 150n2
Desai, Jigna, 79, 85
diaspora, xvi, xviii, xxi, 30, 100, 127, 130, 133, 144n13; diasporic culture, 49, 75
Dimock, Wai Chee, 130–31, 150n3
Dirlik, Arif, xii, xiv, xxv, xxxii, 4, 95, 101
disability, xxxiv, 43–62, 90
dislocation. *See* displacement
displacement, xxvi–xxvii, xxxiii, 18–19, 44–45, 53, 127
Dissanayake, Wimal, xxxii
Divakaruni, Chitra, xxxvi, 89–91, 100–107
domestic worker, x–xi, xxvi, 73–74
dystopia, xxxvi, 98

Earth (Mehta), 76, 80, 139, 147n3
Eat Drink Man Woman (Lee), 137
Eaton, Edith Maude: and Winnifred, xix
Edwards, Brent, xiii

Egoyan, Atom, 79–80
Ehrenreich, Barbara, xxvi, 21
Eng, David, 9–10, 58, 71, 132, 145n5; *Q & A*, xx
Enloe, Cynthia, 23
environment, xiii, xxxvi
Espiritu, Yen Le, 55, 129
ethnoscape, 91
exclusion law, xvi
Exit Wounds (Bartkowiak), 148n7
Exotica (Egoyan), 148n7

Factory Theatre, 52, 71
fantasy, xxxvi, 90, 107, 117–18, 127–28
father figure, 12, 59, 109
Featherstone, Mike, 63
femininity, 106
feminism: feminist elements, 63; feminist studies, xxxi
Filipinos, 68; Filipina bodies, xxxv, 17–18; Filipino Canadians, 63–76; overseas, 143n4; women, 73; youths, 3–19, 145n4
Finney, Gail, 69–70
Fire (Mehta), 76, 80, 86, 147n3
food: imagery, 115; production issues, 120–21, 126
Foucault, Michel, 64, 91
Fraser, Nancy, 93
Freeman, John, 13
Friedman, Susan Stanford, 131–32, 141
Fung, Richard, xix

Gamber, John, xviii
Gawle, Rupa, 77
Gere, Richard, 77
Gessler, Nicholas, 112
Glick Schiller, Nina, 6, 24–26
globality, ix–xiii, 62, 109, 135, 138, 140; critical, xiii, xv, xxx; global identity, 86; literature, xxxvii, 131
globalization, ix, xi–xv, xviii, 90, 109, 130–33, 144n7; critiques, 15, 109; effects, xxv, xxviii, xxxvii, 4–6, 16, 102, 104; first phase, 24–25; and local, xxxi, 78–79; servants of, xi; and women, xxvi, 21
Goellnicht, Donald, xviii, xxi, 9, 27, 30, 95
Gopinath, Gayatri, 32, 138–39
Gordimer, Nadine, 130
Goto, Hiromi, xxxvi, 89, 108–20, 127–28
Grewal, Inderpal, xxxiii, 130
Groen, Rick, 76, 78
grotesque, 116
Gunter, Bernhard, xv

Hagedorn, Jessica, xxxii, 89
Hall, Stuart, 79, 125, 140
Hattori, Tomo, 123–24
Hayles, Katherine, 112
hemispheric, xx
heteroglossia, 70
history: omissions, 20–24, 73, 94–95, 101
Hochschild, Arlie, xxvi, 21
Hollywood: films, 80–81, 116; influence of, 4–5, 17, 64, 77; parody of, 63
Hom, Alice, xx
Homans, Margaret, 149n3
Hornaday, Ann, 76
Hou, Feng, 55
Hsu, Hsuan, 15, 145n6
Hutcheon, Linda, 77
hybridity, xxix, 125, 134; hybrid identity, 69, 85, 91, 114, 117

Ice Storm (Lee), 131, 140
illness, 38; depression, 28, 54, 117; sexually transmitted diseases, 28–29, 31, 40
Imbert, Patrick, xxiv–xxv, xxxvi
immigration, xi; children of, 5, 49; compared to European immigrants, xxii; employment, 55; sending countries, xvii

imperialism, xiii
India, 44, 139; Indian British, 133; Indian Canadian, 53–62, 76–86; memories of, 61; rituals, 55–56; women, 56
Irigaray, Luce, 51
Ishiguro, Kazuo, 130, 131, 140
Iyer, Pico, xvi

Jameson, Fredric, 93, 99
Japan, 28
Japanese American, 150n4
Japanese Canadian identity, 114
Japanese North American, xxxvi; literature, 108–28
Jay, Paul, 130, 138
Jen, Gish, 89
Jin, Ha, 131
Julien, Isaac, 10, 11

Kamboureli, Smaro, xxvii
Kamel, Rachel, 121
Kang, Laura Hyun Yi, 95–96, 109
Kearns, Katherine, 20
Keller, Nora Okja, xxx, xxxiii, 20–23, 33–40, 109
Kim, Elaine, xviii, 21
Kingston, Maxine Hong, xxxii, 89, 94, 130
Kirkland, Bruce, 81
Kitchener (Ontario), 53
Kogawa, Joy, xix, xxxii, 89, 108, 130
Korea: camptown, xxxiv, 33–34; Korean War, xxxiii, 33, 35; women, xxxiv, 33–40
Koshy, Susan, xxii, xxiv
Kostash, Myrna, 144n14
Kottayam (India), 53–54
Kristeva, Julia, xxxi, 13–14, 98
Kuch, Kuch Hoa Hai (Johar), 148n9
Kuruvilla, Sunil, xxx, xxxiv, 44–45, 53–62
Kwa, Lydia, xxx, xxxiii, 20–33, 109

labor: flexibilization of, xi, 95–97; international division of, xii; migrant, xi
Lai, Larissa, xx, xxxvi, 89–100, 107, 109
Latinos, 13, 16
Lau, Evelyn, 140
Lee, Ang, xxxvii, 131, 140
Lee, Chang-rae, 89
Lee, Erika, xx
Lee, Rachel, xxxii, 132
Lee, Robert, 10
Lee, Tara, 97
legend: Arthurian, 105
Levitt, Peggy, 48
Li, David, xxxii, 14, 132, 141
Lieu, Nhi T., 64
Lim, Shirley, xvii–xviii, 130, 132, 137
Ling, Amy, xviii, xxvi, 132, 137
Ling, Jinqi, 129, 132
Little, Judy, 69–70
Little House on the Prairie (Wilder), 111–13
Lo, Marie, xxi
Lowe, Lisa, xix, xxi, 125, 129
Luscombe, Karen, 149n7

Mackey, Eva, xxiv
magic realism, xxxvi, 100, 110, 149n8
Manlove, Colin, 90
Marcos, Imelda, 64, 73
masculinity, 4, 8–11; Asian males, 9–10, 58; war, 23, 40
Massey, Douglas, xxii
McClintock, Anne, 63
Mehta, Deepa, xxxv–xxxvi, 63, 76–86, 137, 147–48n4
memory, 91–95, 98
Mennonite, 55, 57
Mercer, Kobena, 10, 11
Merlin, Lara, 102
Miki, Roy, xxvii, 112–13, 129, 150n1
minority: model, xxiii, xxxvi, 113, 122–24, 128
Miriam, Kathy, 40

Mishra, Vijay, 77, 84, 148n5
Mississauga (Ontario), x, 67, 68, 143n2
Miss Orient(ed) (Aquino and Villasin), xxxv, 63–76, 147n1; photographs, 65, 66
Mistress of Spices, The (Berges), 101
Miyoshi, Masao, xiv, xxv–xxvi
mobility, xi, xii, xvi, xvii, xxiv, xxvii–xxix, xxxiv, 102, 127; and motion, xv, 144n9
Moodley, Kogila, xxiii–xxiv
Moon, Katharine, 23, 34–37
Mootoo, Shani, xix
Morris, Robyn, 149n6
mother: motherhood, 90; mothering, 38
Mother Tongue (Quan), 44–53, 146n1
Moulin Rouge (Luhrmann), 77
Mukherjee, Bharati, xx
Mullard, C., xxiv
multiculturalism, xi; Canada's official, xxiii;
Muppidi, Himadeep, xvii
music: musical comedy, 63
My Big Fat Greek Wedding (Zwick), 148n6
Myers, Linda, xiii
myths, xxxvi, 90, 104, 128; fox girl, 39; Jingwei (bird), 52–53; kappa (water sprite), 119–20; Orpheus, 133; Pallas, 149n5

Naber, Nadine, xx
Naficy, Hamid, 80
nation: nation building, 39–40
Native American, 102–3
Nguyen, Viet, xxviii
Nicholson, Linda, 93
nostalgia, 67

Oakland, California, 90, 100, 102, 107
Okada, John, 108
Okihiro, Gary, xxiii
Oliver, Kelly, xxxi, 21, 27, 50–51, 116–17

Ondaatje, Michael, xxxvii, 130, 131, 136–37, 140
Ong, Aihwa, xii, 95, 97; flexible citizenship, xxvi
Ong, Han, xxxiii, 4, 12–19
"Oriental," 64, 75, 109, 113; Orientalism, 99
otherness, 7, 10–11, 14, 34, 37, 44, 110; alien, 111; monstrous, 99; racial, 149n6, 9; women, 22, 116–17
Ozeki, Ruth, xx, xxxvi, 108–10, 113, 120–28

Pacino, Al, 80
Palumbo-Liu, 124
parody, 63, 70, 72
Parreñas, Rhacel, xi, 4, 6–7, 74, 145n17
Pearson, Wendy, 112
performative, 82–83
Philippines, 40, 64–68, 138
Pilgrim's Progress (Bunyan), 92
Pirbhai, Mariam, 134–35, 150n4
Polan, Dana, 3
pop music, 131, 134
postmodernism, xviii, 93, 99, 133
poststructuralism, xviii
Pratt, Mary Louise, xxxiv
Pretty Woman (Marshall), 77–78, 83–84
prostitutes, xxxiii, 20–40, 146n1; *ah ku*, 23, 25, 26, 28–33, 146n3, 4; *karayuki-san*, 23, 146n3, 4; male, 12, 16; *tap tang*, 30
psychoanalysis, xviii

Quan, Betty, xxxiv, 44–53, 62
queer sexuality, 30–32; 85–86; desire, 90

Rabie, Lisa, 53
race: classification, xxii, 144n14; identity, 43; racialized bodies, xi, 8; racism, xix, 5

Raethel, Miriam, 148n2
Rai, Aishwarya, 104
Rajan, Gita, xxvii, 100, 149n8
Rao, Raj, 150n6
Ray, Lisa, 148n10
Realuyo, Bino, 145n2, 147n2
recognition, 50
Reed, Susan, 105
Rice Boy (Kuruvilla), 44–45, 53–62, 146n3; photograph, 54
Rich, Adrienne, 40, 109, 139
Roberts, Julia, 77, 83
Rodowick, D. N., 133
Roediger, David, xxii, 144n14
Roley, Brian Ascalon, xxxiii, 3–12
Ross, Andrew, 97
Roy, Arundhati, 130
Rushdie, Salman, xxxvii, 67, 130, 133–36, 150n4
Russo, Mary, 116

Safran, William, xxi
Salonga, Lea, 73
San Francisco, 65
San Juan, Epifanio Jr., 3
Santos, Bienvenido, 146n7
Schiller, Nina Glick. *See* Glick Schiller, Nina
science fiction, 93, 110–11, 117–18, 149n2
See, Sarita, 145n3
Selvadurai, Shyam, 130, 131, 137–38
Sense and Sensibility (Lee), 131, 140
sex workers, xxxiii, 20–40
Shakespeare, William, 80, 84
Sharma, Shailja, xxvii
Shaw, Martin, x, xii
Shohat, Ella, 77–78, 145n1
simulacrum, 93
Singapore, 23–28
Sinhalese, 139–40
Smoke (Wang), 140
Sohn, Stephen, xviii
Sone, Monica Itoi, 108
Sook, Kong, 113

South Asian, xvii; diasporic community, xxxv–xxxvi, 63, 76–86, 90, 100–107
South Asian American literature, xx
Spivak, Gayatri, 82
Sri Lanka, 138–40
Stallybrass, Peter, 76
Stam, Robert, 77–78, 145n1
Sterling, Bruce, 112
Stewart, Susan, 66–67
subjectivity: collective, xviii; intersubjectivity, 50
Sumi, Glenn, 52
Sumida, Stephen, xviii
Szanton Blanc, Cristina, 6, 25–26

tactics, xxxi, xxxvi, 62
Takaki, Ronald, 9
Tamils, 138–40
Tan, Amy, 89, 94
Teles, Steven, xiii
Third World, xiv, xxiv; labor, 95, 138
Toronto, 63, 65, 67, 69, 71, 77, 78–79
transcultural, 130, 142
transmigrants, 6–7, 12, 17, 19, 26, 74
transnationalism, xviii; corporations, xiv, 121–22; emotional, 5, 48, 69; labor, 95, 109; transnational, xii, xx, 25, 44–45, 54, 101, 130–31, 133–34, 138, 142
trauma, 50–51
travel, xxvii–xxviii, xxxiii; travelers, xxviii
Ty, Eleanor: *Asian Canadian Writing*, xviii; *Politics of the Visible*, 102, 149n9

unfastened, xxi, xxvi

Valentino, Gina, xviii
Vancouver, xx, 65, 67, 90
Van der Hoeven, Rolph, xv
Verduyn, Christl, xviii

Villasin, Nadine, xxxv, 63–76
violence, 9–12, 40
visible minority, xvii, xxii–xxiii

Walcott, Derek, 130
Warren, James Francis, 23, 28–29, 145n19, 146n3, 4
Water (Mehta), 76, 147n3, 4
Waters, Mary, 48
Waugh, Thomas, 85
Weinbaum, Alys, xiii
Wendell, Susan, 60
White, Allon, 76
whiteness, xxii
Wilson, Rob, xxxi–xxxii
Wimmer, Andreas, 24–25, 26

witnessing, 50–51
Wolf, Diane L., 5, 69
Wolf, Naomi, 104
Wolmark, Jenny, 93
Wong, Jade Snow, 94
Wong, K. Scott, 145n18
Wong, Sau-ling, xv, xviii, xx, xxxii, 9, 94, 130, 148n3, 150n2

Xie, Shaobo, xv

Yamamoto, Traise, 150n4
Yamashita, Karen Tei, 89
Yergin, Daniel, ix–x,
Yu, Henry, xxi, 144n11
Yuen-Carrucan, Jasmine, 147n4

Eleanor Ty is professor of English and film studies at Wilfrid Laurier University in Waterloo, Ontario. She has published widely on Asian North American literature and film and on eighteenth-century British literature.

www.ingramcontent.com/pod-product-compliance
Lightning Source LLC
Chambersburg PA
CBHW032128160426
43197CB00008B/554